# Angeltown

# Angeltown
## Joseph Callahan

**Baker Street Press**

To all my teachers and students.

Copyright © 2024 by Joseph Callahan
All rights reserved
ISBN: 9798330200894

Printed in the United States of America

# Contents

Chapter 1: Angeltown
Chapter 2: The Creation of Jane
Chapter 3: Martin
Chapter 4: The Czar Teaches Jane
Chapter 5: Czar World
Chapter 6: Benz family gets pregnant
Chapter 7: The Rally New
Chapter 8: Teachers
Chapter 9: Benz move away from society
Chapter 10: Home Life
Chapter 11: Jane's New Assignment
Chapter 12: Work Study
Chapter 13: Doctor Benz
Chapter 14: Detectives Find
Chapter 15: Chava the Valiant
Chapter 16: Trackers and Drones
Chapter 17: Chava the Red
Chapter 18: Split

# Chapter 1
# Angeltown

June 19th, 2035: The dissolution of giants *UniversalEducation* and *All Schools Management* led to a third of all education stock losing ninety percent of its value. There was nothing to worry about, the experts said, for *there was still enough education for everyone who deserved it.*
Citizens' News

    In his time in the military in the 2040s, Martin worked the border between the Southwest United States and North Mexico. He had various skills including breaking and entering, assault, destroying property by hand, explosives, and demolition, silent killing, loud killing, all sorts of killing. Martin could even subdue his prey in various ways without killing, if asked to.

    He stood five-foot-six, muscular, and worked out constantly as if the muscles could make up for him being shorter than most men in the military. He had little hair on his body, never did have much. His skin turned tanning-bed brown due to *life-enhancing chemicals* (steroids) he ingested and outdoor activities involving his work. Martin would never admit that some of that pigment came from gypsies. At thirty-two, he expected more out of life, but considering he came from a family of grifters and travelers, he did well for himself.

He wasn't part of the regular patrol; they had stations every two hundred miles along the fortified border. His job was to intercept Coyotes and Barracudas trying to bring illegal crossers over. And Martin had a dozen informers that each had dozens of informers and so on, a whole network across the South. The State Auto-Defense Forces also called upon him when chatter on the Governet indicated there might be an illegal crossing, and by 2045, five years after North Mexican independence, all crossings were illegal.

Martin was stationed in Angeltown, and that meant hours of driving to and from the border or days on the road in stations and hours waiting for action. Crossing overland was suicide due to the searing heat, the wolves looking for meat, and the man-made traps disabling or killing crossers; only the most fool-hardy tried a land crossing. Mexican loyalist and a few other unfortunates had no other option but to escape overland or be killed by the North Mexican Army, a collection of drug lords, business interests, and former officers from the military. Most crossers, however, tried to enter through bribery or by boat from the Gulf of North Mexico or the Pacific Ocean.

Martin's squadron received a reliable report that illegals would be trying to cross into the U.S. at Steven Spielberg National Beach and Recreation Area, so they drove to the coast north of Saint Monique to investigate. Martin wasn't much for the open sea, in fact, he would get seasick in a bathtub. So he took the squadron to the coastal landing point and let another commander take the boat.

Weeds and desert scrub enveloped the coast up to the clearing at a boat landing. Martin's team waited for the arrivals at the edge of the road where the beach started, and three forcemen waited in a boat slightly north of the inlet. After a few minutes, they heard a motor coming up the coast, then the gurgling of the engine in the water after it shut off. Once again, the informant had earned his pieces.

Martin's team waited in silence for nearly ten minutes until they could hear the boat landing in the opening in front of them. Moments after the North Mexicans landed, Martin rolled a flare onto the tiny beach at the feet of the unauthorized entrants. The rest of the forcemen turned their flashlights on them. He saw a familiar sight: a Barracuda, the captain of the small boat, a man, a woman who was probably his wife, three kids, maybe aged three, eight and ten years old. Six people in all.

"Manos arriba!" shouted Martin in his border-guard Spanish. They all raised their hands, including the barracuda. The forcemen moved forward into position and Martin shot the boat captain between the eyes, making the other entrants jump in the sizzling heat like grease off a steak. The parents covered their children's eyes. His men didn't bat an eye. *You would think death would be a deterrent to barracudas coming up the coast with cargo, but they keep coming*, thought Martin. "Hanson!" he shouted, "Make sure this corpse is sent south as an example." *Maybe they will catch on this time.* Hanson and another forceman unrolled a stretcher, placed the barracuda on it, and walked to their support van. They drove off toward the nearest airfield to dump the body over the border for would-be entrants to see.

Martin turned to the other forcemen. "Let's get these folks in the truck for distribution." Then he signaled the boat the all clear by waving a flashlight in their direction. The boat motored off. Martin and his squad walked back to the van with the illegal entrants in tow. They were placed in the back with Duke Johnson and Robert Lee Johnson, no relation, although Robert Lee swears he's related to a general from something called The Confederacy.

Martin went into the driver's seat with another senior officer riding shotgun. Two other men sat behind them with the five passengers in the cabin sitting on the benches on either side of the truck bed with Johnson and Johnson. Martin drove off and took a left down a hidden roadway covered with tall grasses and headed north toward the main access road that traveled east.

They drove for twenty-five minutes to a warehouse where the children would be auctioned off. Since The Sterilization, wealthy parents were paying top dollar for kids even ten-years-old. The three-year-old would fetch the highest price. The three children were escorted to the entrance of the warehouse where they would be put into their holding cell. A commodities assessor greeted them and started to work out an initial bid on the merchandise and a child psychologist talked to the children in an attempt to keep them well behaved and thus fetch a higher price at auction at the end of the week.

As the children were taken away, the mother shouted "No lleva mis niños, no!" as she tried in vain to escape the grasp of a man one hundred and fifty pounds heavier than her. The forcemen sedated the mother. They sent her in another vehicle to where they recruited maids for the Insiders. *She's young enough*, thought Martin.

"Que va a pasar con mi familia?!" yelled the father, jumping forward.

Martin held him back. "You're family's going to work, a trabajar. We're giving them a new life, an oportunidad bien…bien." The illegal tried to get past Martin who clamped onto his throat, and lifted him off the ground as a warning. Then Martin spoke slowly and deliberately while holding him aloft, "It's an oportunidad to gain your freedom. Me entiendes, señor?" The migrant froze in terror and started losing oxygen. Once his wife was out of sight, Martin released him.

Perhaps he would be a gardener or work construction. However, Martin had another idea. He was moonlighting as a recruiter for something they called *The Middle Eastern Hunt,* a game show where trackers would chase down Middle Eastern looking men. Martin walked to the van, gathered his tablet, and went back to the father.

"Como se llama?" Martin asked.

The father caught his breath. "Hector," he answered.

"Okay Hector, want to earn some money, dinero?" Martin rubbed his thumb against his first two fingers. "Dinero?"

Then he turned on his tablet and hit the video conference button. He clicked *kgriffin* from the menu. Kyle Griffin's tablet beeped three times before he picked up.

"Martin, it's late, what the hell?" whined Kyle.

"Kyle, I found another player for your television show." He turned the tablet toward Hector who sobbed. "Cuantos años, señor?" He scanned the tablet up and down Hector's body for Kyle to inspect.

Hector trembled. "Triente años." Martin turned the tablet back toward himself. "He's thirty years old. He has a family, and if you could promise him a reunion with his wife, at least, he'll play along."

"Send me a picture," said Kyle half asleep.

"And we have the same deal, right Kyle?" asked Martin. "Yea, same deal." Kyle hung up.

Martin looked at Hector, "It's your lucky day. Estas de suerte, Hector. Mi jefe tiene trabajo para ti. We have some work for you." Hector looked uncomfortable at the suggestion. "Venga," said Martin.

Martin opened the passenger seat. "Get in. We have a long trip ahead." Hector got in the car and Martin shut the door.

At 6:30 am, Theo met his mother at the door of their home as he left for school.

"Do you have to leave so early, Thelonious Adisa Babar?" asked his mother.

Theo kissed his mother on the cheek. "I told Francis I would meet him early to help him with some homework," he said.

Dad had already gone to work, and mom would be leaving soon. He left their small, comfortable home and ambled like an ostrich, bobbing his head and afro up and down, toward the school library that opened at 7 a.m. That would give him and Francis about forty minutes to study for their math test.

Thelonious Babar, Theo, was born in January of 2036. He was thin and lanky with a milk chocolate complexion. His mother, Elizabeth Petros, was a Greek American and his immigrant father, Antoine Babar, was a refugee from Tunisia.

The Babar family were poor but comfortable and hardly noticed their economic state unless a crisis arose like an unplanned medical bill. Their car mostly stayed in the driveway except for special occasions or emergencies. They had each other and had the necessities of life.

On Friday nights, their friend Larry, a neighbor from down the street who worked with his dad, would come over with a Japanese horror movie.

"Hey Larry," said Theo, "What you got for us this time?"

"I thought I would change it up a bit and we could watch *The Bad Seed,* a classic from when cinema mattered."

"What is *The Bad Seed* about?"

"Well, my fine people," Larry said to Theo and his parents with an air of British pomposity. "*The Bad Seed* is a scary film full of surprises about a bad, evil little girl and all of the trouble she causes."

"Sounds good. Perhaps we can stay up late and watch my favorite, *Kwaidan* afterwards." He look to his parents.

His parents nodded in agreement. They were just glad to have a distraction from the tragedy of daily life.

Larry winked at his parents. "I think your son likes *Kwaidan* because he's attracted to the tattoos, aren't you, Theo?"

Theo smiled and played it off. "Well, the body art is fantastic."

The 2035 English Only Laws banned Spanish and other languages from public and private usage. Using Spanish was a criminal offense and all place names and signs in Spanish would be changed to English over time. Thus, Los Angeles became Angeltown. The government couldn't, however, fix everyone's names, yet. So those foreign words were left to die out.

Theo blended in well with the Mexican Americans and liked Spanish. If he wasn't considered *Mexican* at school, others would think he was Middle Eastern. That was fine in his neighborhood, but at school, he could get hassled by whites and other non-Arabs.

Most of the Latinos came from North Mexico or were born in Angeltown, and despite the English only laws, still spoke Spanish at home. Theo was an American from Angeltown who spoke English better than most people in California and most of his friends.

He had his share of insecurities, but his friend Francis was a living identity crisis. Francis described himself as "a dumpy white kid" from the ghetto. That made Theo sad, but also made him laugh.

"Come on Francis, you have potential," Theo would say, trying to convince himself and Francis at the same time. "Let's make sure you keep your C rating, okay?" They dug into the math, with Francis again questioning the purpose of learning algebra when he *would never be a scientist.*

"How about learning enough so the scientists can't take advantage of you," Theo said. Francis smiled even though he didn't quite understand what Theo meant.

Theo studied and read a lot of history, and that got him into trouble with his teachers; by 2035, teaching history that happened before 2008 was prohibited in Angeltown. "Mr. Smits, what happened in 2001 that led to the Mideast wars?" Theo asked.

He was quickly shot down. "The Mideast Wars are fabrications of the radical left who want to overthrow the government." The teacher looked at his seating chart, "and that will be enough from you Babar!" Theo knew what that meant, and after that, he stopped asking questions of his teachers. He stuck to asking questions of his mom and dad who remembered time before history.

Theo found historical material in underground bookstores and the hidden sections in the Central Library in Angeltown with the help from the keepers of the books. He didn't live far from the library, only a thirty-minute walk from his house. There, he found old history books like *L.A. Confidential,* a true crime history of Los Angeles. In these books, Theo learned about the dangerous past of L.A., now Angeltown. Mentioning Los Angeles was prohibited, and the novels were historical documents, Raymond Chandler and Joan Didion being the most profound archivers of the history of Los Angeles.

Though many people called Theo the "coolest kid in school," all he felt was ordinary. For his strange appearance and unique background, he saw himself as just a regular kid with typical teenage angst and desires: what girls to like if you even like girls, how to talk to them, what classes to take, who to spend time with, what to eat, if to eat, what to wear, even who to sit next to in class. The one social advantage he had was he really liked people. He had friends in every formal and informal club at school, from nerds to jocks to speech club to drama, every club except the Patrioteers who were too bigoted and nationalistic for Theo to want to befriend.

"Hey Bob," Theo said to his classmate as they headed to lunch.

"Hey Theo," said Bob, looking down at his shoes.

"Still having trouble with the algebra?"

"Yeah," he said. "The teacher always stands over me and pokes his finger on my paper when he talks."

Theo put his arm on Bob's shoulders, "Here's what you do. Volunteer when you know an answer. Most teachers will leave you alone for the rest of the class if you volunteer once."

"Thanks," Bob said, still looking at his shoes.

"Hey Bob, I'll be at the library on Saturday if you want to study some math."

"Thanks."

Theo's trick for making friends was that he listened. He had learned to listen from his mom who learned studying communication and working as a counselor at Angeltown College. One day Theo talked to her about going to high school, the Belmont High Nanomed Academy, about making friends and being accepted. His mother told him, "All you have to do is be quiet and listen, and people will accept you or not." Theo practiced listening every day. Sometimes he had difficulty paying attention when he didn't really like someone, but he understood it was still a good habit.

---

On Saturday morning, Theo walked to the Central Library.

His trips took up half his day with the rest of his time spent walking to friends' homes. He walked through his neighborhood of boarded up buildings and visible debris of torn down houses—ranch style, A-frames, all styles. The area showed signs of decay similar to other poor areas of Angeltown.

On one trip, he met a girl from his school that he recognized, Chava Chavez. She was an athletic and slim girl, half-Jewish and half-Mexican, nothing special, he thought, except she retained a curiosity about the world and asked lots of questions. And, she had purple hair. Girls could get away with purple hair as long as they dressed neat and clean and not provocatively. Chava also ran on the school track team, like Jesse Owens who ran against the terrible Nazis in the book "The Jesse Owens Story." *Being able to run like that is cool.*

Because of the danger of being sent to truancy prison, Theo saw no other way but to tutor his friends so they wouldn't be expelled from school. He taught them how to respond to teachers in class, how to navigate software programs, and how to answer standardized test questions to stay above a C rating in school.

"Hey, how's it going in school, still keeping those Cs?" Theo asked Chava. After asking, Theo thought that the question was kind of an insult.

But Chava didn't take it that way. "I'm fine, except history, I can't get into that sh…stuff, you know?"

"Sure, I know what you mean. It's pretty terrible. But I can show you how to write the essays and pass, and they seldom change the questions. They want you to basically mimic the prompts but use your own language. I got into trouble once actually answering a question with an original thought. I didn't do that again," Theo explained.

Chava laughed.

She met Theo at the library the next Saturday. Theo showed

her how to write the essays and how or to get along with teachers in class.

"The trick is not to stand out by asking too many questions or showing initiative, said Theo. "Just answer the questions asked and don't ask any."

"But what if I have questions?"

"Okay, I'll make a deal with you. If you have a question, you can ask me, and we can look for the answers together."

"Deal." She nodded.

"And keep your eyes on your paper, book, or tablet. If you catch the teacher's eye, they might call on you," he added. "Most of all, look busy, even if you are bored."

The next time he saw Chava, Theo gave her one of his favorite books on Angeltown history, *Ask the Dust* by John Fante. "It's about a time he called *The Depression*, when people lived really poor but had dreams of love and success, well, not success so much as survival," Theo said. "Kind of like today."

Chava nodded, "Thanks." She liked that Theo included her, even if the book sounded kind of sad.

Inside the front cover, Theo had slipped his family's one cell phone number with a note, *Call any time*.

Theo used to enjoy the quiet of the library. No more. Now, advertising covered the place. There were even two large billboards outside, one facing West 5th Street that was ten by twenty-five feet and the other facing South Grand Avenue measuring a massive twelve by forty-eight feet. The larger billboard advertised the Governet. The message was:

## The Internet is Dead; Long Live the Governet!

with a picture of an ax coming down on an old computer that represented the Internet and a new, shiny computer growing out of a purple poppy that represented the Governet.

The smaller billboard recruited for the Truancy Squad:

> We Need You to Control Yourselves
> Join the Truancy Squad!

The text was centered and featured pictures of young men and women dressed in military camouflage with a big "Truancy Squad" logo over their chests, shotguns over their shoulders and on the right, a male and female squad member arresting a dangerous looking young man of indeterminate background. He could have been Muslim or Mexican or some other *dangerous* race. He wasn't white. As if the billboard weren't disturbing enough, the man being arrested looked a lot like Theo, except shorter. No matter that the population of the state was majority non-white, wealthy whites ran Angeltown like his dad said was done in South Africa and Angola for years.

Advertising drones would also buzz around the library and central Angeltown with banners streaming behind them with messages like "Control your own drone for the Truancy Squad", "Czar World: Family Fun!" and "Nanomed: Drugs for Complaints You didn't Know you Had." Theo didn't see many advertising drones in his impoverished neighborhood, only police drones with their weaponry and stun capabilities.

The inside of the library was also replete with ads, and the one that made Theo laugh and cringe was an ad for the "Cock Asian Supremacy" restaurant chain. *What were they thinking?*

Theo wasn't athletic, but he stood taller than his friends, so they always invited him to play basketball at night. The city was too hot to play at other times. Besides, he always had interesting stories to share about history and news about Belmont High, and people liked to have him around.

One player razzed Theo. "Hey Mr. Triple AAA, too bad you can't score on the court like in school."

"Or with the girls, am I right?" said another.

"Score in basketball, no, with the girls?" Theo said, "no comment."

They laughed at his response.

*I've got more important things to think about than relationships*, he thought.

He went to play with Francis, who wasn't tall, but could dribble and could pass. He liked Francis on his team because Theo always got open shots when Francis got him the ball, though he usually missed.

Theo never missed an opportunity to agitate for his causes, so he started talking about the truancy squad and treatment of people in their neighborhood. The State Auto-Defense Force, SADF, never came around to courts in Angel Heights; they thought that local kids would kill each other playing ball, and the powers in Rampart and Saint Bernard were fine with that. But the courts were a time to play ball and get together, not shoot each other. Besides, only the police could afford to have guns any more after the SADF confiscated them from the poor neighborhoods.

Theo asked the players while passing the ball, "How are your brothers and sisters doing in their classes?" and they started to share their stories.

One local kid from North Mexico told the group that his sister missed school when she fell and broke her arm, and the Truancy Squad knocked down their door and took her off to prison for missing class.

Another kid stopped dribbling and said, "I was taking my brother to visit our dad in the hospital and the Truancy Squad came and took him away for failing some pinche tests."

This occurred all around Angeltown, kids being sent to truancy prison because they were missing school, failing tests, and not meeting arbitrary education standards set by the Insiders.

On the way home, Francis confided in Theo what he didn't feel comfortable sharing with the group. "My brother Andy was in a wheelchair, really sick you know, and he couldn't do the assigned homework. They took him away, Theo, and we're not allowed to visit." He held back his tears. "You should have seen him try to pick up the pen or press on the tablet to do his homework. His hands are shriveled up so badly, he can't even open his fingers," explained teary eyed Francis. "They didn't care; they put Andy in prison."

"That's inhumane. We've got to have a rally, Francis, for people like your brother and all the brothers and sisters arrested sent away for missing class and failing their tests." Theo looked up in thought. "Let's make a handout and get started."

Francis sniffed in some mucus and wiped it on his t-shirt. "I know where we can get a flyer copied. We'll make it simple and leave no trace back to us." They designed a third-of-a-page handout, easy to fold and easy to hide. It would contain no personal information, just a time and date for the walkout the following spring before final testing for the year:

*No truth, no truancy, no testing!*
*Student walk out, 8 AM, May 14, 2053. Meet at the Central Library.*

Theo copied them at one of the last organized hold-outs of socialism in Angeltown, the Emma Goldman Underground Copy Center (EGUCC) in downtown that one of his school-mate's uncles worked at. The copy center was hidden in the basement of an abandoned "Uptown Dresses" store. If you wanted to get in, you had to have the combination to open the metal gate into the atrium. Theo's friend Javier gave the code to him. And once inside, you had to hit a buzzer, dot dot dot, dash dash dash, dot dot dot.

Then, you held up an official business card to the camera that was given to you with the password printed on it in a one of a kind EGUCC font. It read: "The most unpardonable sin in society is independence of thought." That Goldman quote would confuse most of the SADF if you were caught with the card; they wouldn't get the sarcasm.

The door opened with a buzzing sound. Theo went inside and down a narrow wooden staircase into the dark and windowless basement that housed the copy center. They used an old Midstar 37 that had dozens of parts replaced over the years.

"Theo!" said Uncle Caesar. Caesar was all business. "Javier said you had something to copy. You have the paper?"

Theo gave him the two reams of paper he had commandeered from the Central Library using his bag and help from a friend.

The copies were free if you brought your own paper and you were willing to spread other posters they printed around Angeltown. They would otherwise cost fifty cents a copy, still a bargain in the 2050s.

"We need all of this copied, three notes per page," said Theo in a serious voice. "And you can cut them for us, right?"

"Sure. And you have to put up a few of these fliers," said Caesar, who gave him a stack of posters for an outdoor concert at Beautiful View Park. The SADF would arrest you if you called it Buena Vista Park.

*Join us for a celebration of local music and life, Saturday at Beautiful View Park. Paine's Pallbearers are headlining an acoustic set.*

Theo looked at the flyer. *Cool, Paine's Pall Bearers! Great lyrics*, he thought. He sang to himself and tapped his foot.

*Be friendly, they beat you*

*Be nice, they beat you*
*Surrender, they beat you*
*Run, they beat you*
*You can't change, the color of your skin!*

Theo and Francis used word of mouth and handed the flyers directly to students after getting their commitment join the rally. Each student would pass two fliers on and get them to pass two on and so forth. Theo did the math and shared the results with Francis. "If we share flyers with ten people and they share it with two people each, we will be out of flyers after six exchanges."

"Let's make sure they don't share the information with any members of the Patrioteers Club or with any adults," said Francis.

Theo nodded. He knew that if they got caught, Truancy Prison, with its solitary confinement and deprivations, would be the least of their problems. So they gave flyers only to trusted allies and let them use their judgement.

Theo used his time tutoring to test the water, and if it seemed safe, he gave the students a sales pitch about the walkout. "Hey Chin, a few students and I are going to have a rally about the tests and Truancy Prison. Why don't you join us? It could be fun; you can even make a speech if you want." Theo reached out with a flyer.

"No thank you," Chin said, refusing the handout. "Why don't you just announce this online?"

"And have the Governet track us?" He held the notice up for Chin to take. "They can't track paper back to you. And hey," he nudged his classmate, "I know that some of the kids from our math class will be there, like Nancy." Chin's face turned red, and he took a flyer. Theo gave him three more and said, "Pass it on, but don't tell any adult. You promise?"

Chin raised his right hand. "Promise."

Chin's cousin, Wei, spent over a month in prison and the guards released him once they realized he hadn't missed class, that it had been a computer error that lead to Wei's arrest.

He shared his story with Chin and Theo "They don't give you hardly any food, a pile of gruel every morning and a potato at night, without even salt on it. Some of the guards on the night shift would play loud music with lots of guitars and screaming. They would run down the halls and bang on the metal bars of the cells to the rhythm of the songs to keep us awake. If you complained, they put in the hall and forced you to stand on one leg with your arms out for maybe thirty minutes. Some of us got to work, the lucky ones."

Truants who worked in prison had long hours making signs in English to replace Spanish named locations, sewing jackets for the State Auto-Defense Forces, packaging household goods to be shipped to Saint Bernard where the Insiders lived, and other tasks. They worked twelve to sixteen hours a day and were paid one piece per hour. They were fortunate to get that.

These stories were shared by other students not long after the truancy prison system opened. No one shared the stories with administration or teachers anymore because they were complicit and got bonuses if they sent enough kids to prison. Theo got eleven trustworthy allies to become recruiters as he walked them home. These students were desperate, and the rally sold itself even if the risk was prison.

Theo's parents worked late, mom at the college and dad in the Angeltown Sanitation Division, what was left of the department, and didn't get back until around 8 PM. That gave him plenty of time after school to spend with his friends, go to the library if he wanted, and work on his homework and housework. Theo often had friends over to review their school assignments, and though he hated math, the repetition and practice made him a decent student.

"Theo," Mrs. Charles said, "again you surprised me by outscoring Sally here, who has always been so good at math." Theo knew the trick to scoring well on tests, after putting in the hard work, was to stay relaxed and breathe.

Theo really excelled in writing; he always could write what the teacher wanted. He knew telling teachers what they wanted to hear was best. But he didn't have to pander like some. He used his wits:

*The object of school is to make sure that the students succeed in what the leaders want them to be good at,* Theo once wrote in an essay on school and leadership. The teacher didn't realize that Theo meant his essay as a criticism. And the teacher loved him for his writing. *Irony is dead.*

One Saturday while sitting underneath the staircase between the 2nd and 3rd floor, his favorite spot in the library, Chava, the girl with the purple hair, came by. She didn't care about AAAs. Her goal was to not be expelled.

"Hey Theo, reading another crime history?" she asked as she sat down across from him.

He looked up. "Oh, yeah, I'm reading scary stories by this author named King. It's interesting, and rare. He also has one story about prison break that is impossible to find. So of course, I want to read it." He stopped himself. "How's the rating?" he asked, meaning her student rating.

"A solid C, thanks to you."

Theo smiled. "Well, as you say, you did the hard work. Any assignment you want to show me?"

"Well," she said, "my teacher gave us this essay to write on 'what makes a good education.' I think they want a specific answer, but I don't know what."

"You're right. Hold on." He pulled a round carbon composite disk out of his pocket that measured two centimeters in diameter and two millimeters thick. Theo put it onto his tablet. He clicked a couple of buttons then hit copy. He picked up the disk and gave it to Chava. She looked at him quizzically. "It's a copy of my answer to that same question I had last year," he said. "The teachers reuse the questions because it isn't worth the effort for them to do anything original and be questioned by the Czar's Office of Education. Last year, Mrs. Greene asked students to write about their future dreams, and no one has seen her since."

"Oh, no!" She cringed and spoke more softly. "So, that wasn't an approved topic?"

Theo shook his head. "No."

Chava placed the disc in her front shirt pocket and buttoned it, as if hiding some secret code. "Thanks. How do you know all this?"

"I pay attention," he said, tapping his forehead twice with his index finger. "Just remember to change the wording, put in a couple of new ideas, and you will maintain that C you are striving for," Theo said, half jesting.

Chava smiled. "Gotta get home. My mom is waiting for dinner," she explained.

"How is your mom doing?"

"Well, you know." Chava didn't want to think about her mom's cancer.

"Hey, it's good you can be there for her." Theo wasn't sure the right time was right, but he gave Chava a flyer to the walkout. "We're having a rally, no big deal if you can't go, but..." He grinned. "Keep it between us students, or it could be big trouble...okay?"

Chava gave him a quick hug. "Sure." She folded the flyer

and put it in her pocket with the disk containing the essay. "Thanks again!" She waved goodbye and started off.

---

Four forcemen of Truancy Squad 8 stood outside a single-wide trailer in a Venice, CA mobile-home park. They were assigned to apprehend a fifteen-year-old girl who had missed classes all week without a call or a notice to her school. She was a danger to society and a bad example to all the law-abiding citizens of Angeltown.

The squad leader pounded on the door. "On the orders of the Office of the Czar of Education, we demand you open the door and let us in."

No one answered. He looked at the warrant while the other forcemen drew their automatic weapons. "We are here to arrest a Whitney Lopez on the charge of "Failure to learn in the first degree." We demand you come out with your hands up!"

Still no answer. The commander stood back and drew his Razer XD pistol with five fifty-caliber armor piercing rounds, enough to penetrate doors and sides of buildings. "I will give you to the count of ten to turn yourself in. Ten, nine, eight…" He counted as the forcemen clicked off their guns' safeties and prepared to fire. "… three, two, one." They commenced firing. By the time they were done, over 80 rounds had struck and penetrated the side of the trailer, centered around the doors and the windows. "Rex, Wilson, get inside and look around," the commander ordered.

They ran inside the trailer and searched.

An old man with a scrunched-up apple-doll face came out of his trailer next door. "Sir!" he yelled to the commander. "Them folks left a week ago. I don't think they be coming back. Too bad, I really like them, and the wife made a mean mole sauce."

The commander stepped forward to address him. "Do you know where they may have gone?"

He scratched his protruding chin. "I don't know. I woke one mornin' and they weren't there. I figur' they went back to North Mexico, but they didn't tell me nothin'. It was like they were running from something."

Rex and Wilson came out of the trailer. "There's no one here, Commander," said Rex.

"I reckin' not," the commander said.

#

# Chapter 2
# The Creation of Jane

*New formulas for school funding will continue to include student test scores and time on task using the computer software. Funding will also be determined by the number of students expelled from schools, with the truancy prison system giving a stipend to each school for every student expelled and sent to one of their prisons.* Office of the Czar of Education memorandum issued January 15, 2051

    Five-year-old Jane Caitlin Winston couldn't wait to start school in the fall. She had to get away, especially her mother who wouldn't let her do anything for fear of losing the only child she could bear.

    Jane grew up in Glendale, CA in a middle-class home with parents who saw life as a series of lost opportunities and had an excuse for every financial and personal set back. They were social climbers with no rungs who came from upper middle-class backgrounds but were now one recalled loan away from destitution. Only the house that Jane's mother had inherited from her abusive father kept their upper-class facade functioning.

    Jane's mother was tall and slight with spindly limbs like a naked dogwood tree. Her short black hair and her pale skin gave her a ghostly appearance, frightening her family and most everyone she encountered. If Jane's father could be described as a piece of clothing, it would be plain white underwear, boring and essential for covering up the sinful parts.

For Jane's fifth birthday present, Mallory vetted childhood friends for her daughter. She needed to make certain that Jane only befriended the right kind of people. The candidates came from Jane's upcoming kindergarten class, so they were the pick of the litter.

Families wanted their children to befriend Jane because the Winstons were the right kind of family and knew the Czar of Education, so they said. They calculated that their children being friends with Jane could elevate their social status.

The prospective childhood friends waited on a faux marble bench in the atrium of Jane's house. Then Jane's mother would take them to her unlit study with drawn curtains that blocked out the sun. Mallory sat on a high wingback, paisley-patterned chair in browns and grays and the children sat across from her on armchairs with the same pattern.

Jimmy, the first candidate, was a mousy five-year-old you could topple with a feather, and he could barely see Mallory's face as she spoke from the shadows. "Jimmy." He jumped. "Why do you want to spend time with our precious Jane?"

His voice quivered. "I don't know."

"Really!" Jane's mother said. "You don't know why you want to spend time with Jane? That's ridiculous! You don't have one reason? You think she's pretty, don't you? Everyone does."

The boy was terrified into silence.

"Well?" He began to cry. "You can go, Jimmy." She waved him away. "Go back to your parents. Clearly, you aren't good enough for our Jane."

Mallory wasn't only tough on the boys. Sally, an intelligent girl wearing a simple sun dress, faced similar interrogation. "Sally, why do you want to be friends with Jane?"

Sally sat up, straight and proper. "Well, I think Jane's nice."

"Jane *is* nice. Are you nice Sally?"

"I try to be, Mrs. Winston."

Mallory plucked at her fingertips and looked down at Sally from her pointed nose. "Try?" Then Mallory changed direction. "You're jealous of Jane, aren't you? You aren't nearly as pretty as she is, so you only want to take advantage of a pretty friend, right?"

Sally, like the other candidates, was speechless. "It's okay Sally," Mallory said. "Clearly, you can't bring status to Jane. Just look at you, you are…" Mallory looked for the word, "plain."

But unlike the other candidates, Sally Irvington got up and walked away, having too much dignity to put up with the process. "I don't want to be friends with Jane anymore," she muttered as she left. Jane overheard her from outside the door Sally exited. *Well, I don't want to be your friend either!*

None of the candidates passed Mallory's examination, and none of them came to play at Jane's house. And since none of the candidates were worthy, Jane was not allowed to visit them at their homes either.

"Mom, when can I go to school?" Jane asked soon after her fifth birthday.

Her mother answered as she was dressing Jane in her white dress with red polka-dots, white tights, and black shoes. "Soon Jane, in a few weeks."

"Mom, can I wear my white chiffon dress to school?" asked Jane.

"We'll see how you feel at the time. I think you will have to wear your black dress with your white shirt. That's the school uniform," her mother said.

*I don't have to obey a stinky dress code*, thought Jane. *The teachers will see how cute I am and let me wear what I want.* But Jane could not tell mom that, so instead she asked, "Will they like me mom?"

"They will love you as much as we do," Mallory said.

Jane knew this was a lie. *If she loved me so much, why does she cry every night and never read to me anymore?*

Mallory was terrified about what would happen to Jane in school. *If I let Jane go to school, she will get infected and die, or worse, Jane will take on the sin of the other children and become evil! I can't let her go! God will punish her for her parents' sin.*

Contrary to Mallory's fears, doctors noted how healthy Jane was. "When I tested her blood, she has a complete set of antibodies against all sorts of diseases and a remarkable number of white blood cells. Her oxygen level is 100 percent and her production of ATP, the essential energy molecule, is off the chart.

Mallory looked puzzled. "I don't know how she could be so healthy. I have anemia and my husband has an abnormal lung and only medication keeps him alive."

"Well, whatever you are doing, keep it up," said the doctor.

---

Jane was relieved when school started, and meeting other children led to lots of questions about her family. "Mom, why don't I have any brothers and sisters?" Jane asked the day her teacher read a book called "Brother Owl and Baby Pig" to her class.

"We only wanted one child, a special child, and that's you," her mother said as she gave Jane a hug.

Jane hugged her mom because that's what her mom wanted. But Jane knew that she was lying again. She overheard her parents as they rode back from the hospital. Jane was in the back seat of the car, and her parents talked as if she wasn't there.

"Mallory, the important thing is that you are okay. It doesn't matter that you can't have another child," her dad pleaded with her mom. "I don't care if we have another—"

"Well I do!" shouted Mallory. Her mother was driving, and Jane was too afraid and confused to reach out to her. Jane wasn't sure she wanted to. She never did.

---

"Jane, I have a new dress to give you," her father said. He opened a box they received from the Governet online shopping site and lifted out a beautiful light pink, tulle dress.

Jane pouted, "I wanted a white dress!"

"But all your dresses are white, and your mother and I thought this pink dress would look nice on you."

"I hate pink!" Jane flopped herself on the bed, hiding her face.

"But you like the earrings we got you, right?" Chuck beseeched.

Jane sat up, hiding her fake tears and put on a fake smile. She nodded, teary eyed. "Yes."

"I hope so. Those were the ones you liked from the picture we showed you, the earrings with the diamonds."

*Those are fakes.* Even though Jane knew they weren't real diamonds, she gave her dad a real hug. It might have been the last time she did something to make someone else happy without expecting something in return.

---

Charles Winston and Mallory Waterford met at Eden Community College in Glendale in an evangelical prayer group that convened after their religious instruction. They decided to marry and have a large family to please the Lord and their church ordained it. By marrying, they would cleanse their sins of lust and make love to God who would give them children.

"Charles Winston and Mallory Waterford, we forgive you for your sins," said Minister Hath. "You will marry today, under this roof, before God, so if you ever bear children from your sinful fornication, Mallory Waterford," he pointed his scepter at her, "they will be born under the sanctity of the church!"

Charles and Mallory continued to copulate, now with the goal of having children under the institution of marriage. It was for the glory of God, no longer a sin. However, it was the miracle of science and black market fertility drugs smuggled through North Mexico that brought on Mallory's tumultuous and life-threatening pregnancy.

Jane was born, and Mallory would never be the same. The pain was unbearable and The Manpower Church that helped them get illegal drugs for fertilization deemed pain killers and cesarian births a sin. They had already sinned out of wedlock, and Charles and Mallory spent the rest of their foreshortened lives trying to purify themselves in the eyes of the church by raising Jane in a God-fearing household.

---

Jane made it through kindergarten by obsessively drawing, reading, and planning her life after she left home. First grade was harder because Jane had to interact more with other students. She learned, from her parents and experience, that the only worthwhile interaction was with those that could help her with her work or give her some of their treats at lunch. Otherwise, there was no value to it.

"Jane, what ya reading?" asked Jimmy.

"Who are you?"

"I'm Jimmy."

"And why should I care?" She looked at him for a while. "Give me your chocolate milk, and you can talk to me."

"I already drank it."

"Then go away and bring me one tomorrow."

Jimmy sucked in his lips and looked up. "Okay."

Jane got her chocolate milk and Jimmy was allowed to sit with her for five minutes during lunch.

Jane got through the first grade trading her time for treats, favors, and on the rare occasion, because someone could give status to Jane. However, Sally Irvington never even tried, and Jane cultivated a hatred of her. Jane didn't understand that Sally was popular because she was nice to people. That concept eluded her. However, Jane did think, *I'm so much prettier. Why do people bother with her?*

On the last day of first grade, Jane waited on a bench outside her school for Mallory to pick her up. All the other kids had gone home. It was over one hundred degrees in May, and it would have been hotter except for the dark clouds overhead, a rarity in Angeltown. Jane was wearing her favorite white dress with the crinoline petticoat to celebrate the last day of the school year. Her teacher *liked it very much,* but the other children laughed at her and called her a *fancy Nancy.*

Rain started to pour down, the first time since Jane had started school nearly two years earlier. The bench had no cover. She ran to the school, but it was locked. With nowhere to hide, Jane was drenched, and the hot sulfur-filled rain ruined her pretty dress and curly, dark brown hair. "Mommy! Mommy!" yelled Jane as she cried. "Mommy, mommyyyyy!" Jane slumped down against the door of the school, legs forward, shoulders collapsed, head tilted, bouncing up and down with her chest filled tears.

Minutes later, Mallory picked up Jane. Jane stopped crying as soon as she saw the car. Her mother lifted her up gingerly, trying not to get Jane all over her, as if she were picking up a bag of manure wrapped in a fancy ball gown.

"Look at you, you're a mess," said Mallory. *Jane is my penance, Jesus is watching, I must take care of this curse of a child.* Mallory put Jane in the front and buckled her in.

Jane didn't complain or say anything. She sat there without a word, stared forward and they never talked about the incident. Jane was a good girl, and she was rewarded for her silence by being left alone the rest of the day.

---

In third grade, the Czar's new education plan stated that there would be no more art in schools, for art was *a waste of valuable time.* There were no more sports for elementary school children, and music was out of the question, for any age. "Not only is music a waste of time, it glorifies the flesh and causes emotional disturbances, distracting us from what is good for the nation."

Jane's wish was they got rid of recess too. She didn't do well outside of class in the playground, but in class, she dominated the group activities with her cleverness and powerful personality.

Often when Jane was playing with blocks or various manipulatives in the classroom, she would tell the other students what to do. "No stupid, you put this block here and this one under it." Jane pointed at the back of the box the blocks came in. "See, it says so in the instructions." The other kids sat back in silence as Jane manipulated the blocks the way she wanted and then stopped, satisfied. "Now, see how easy it is to calculate the area and volume of an object if you do it right?"

At recess, Jane always sat alone, usually with her legs dangling off a swing. The other kids played around her, avoiding contact. One day, Jane stomped back into the school instead of playing outside. The teacher, Mr. Lucci, was sitting at his desk.

"Teacher, can I do more math?"

Mr. Lucci frowned. "Just this once, but tomorrow you will need to spend the whole time outside with the other kids." Jane sat at her desk, angry and determined.

---

After school, Jane went to talk to the principal about having more time in class to work on math and science, things she really liked. Jane waited for the receptionist to be gone for the day before entering the office. She walked to enter and stopped when she heard the terrible teacher telling on her. She stood just outside the door and listened.

"You have concerns about one of your students, Mr. Lucci?"

"Yes." He fidgeted, rubbing his hands together. "Principal Behr, Jane Winston is smart enough, but she doesn't play with the other children. She is terribly upset when the lessons end and complains and sometimes cries. When the school day is over, she refuses to leave."

*I'll get that rotten Mr. Lucci!*

Jane went home that Friday and spoke to her mom. "Mom, my teacher says you don't love me, that you never loved me."

Mallory pulled out her phone. "I'll call and tell that principal right now!"

On Monday, Jane had a new teacher.

---

In the fifth grade, Jane started to stay after class and help her new teacher put away the books. It was either that or go home. Besides, she could tell that her teacher, Mrs. Abernathy, was a valuable person to know.

"You don't have to do that Jane," her teacher said.

"But I want to help." After that, Jane became the teacher's

special helper, putting away supplies, straightening chairs, cleaning the tablet screens, doing whatever the teacher needed. At home, her parents didn't let her do anything. She hated them.

Mrs. Abernathy had a lesson on patriotism in school, and Jane excelled. She knew love of country came first, then love of parents, which Jane never understood since parents didn't always love you, and then love of the Czar. By extension, that meant love of obedient teachers such as she had.

From her parents Jane learned to get close to those that can help you, like her parents did with the Insiders whose children they taught. "You must stroke their egos, tell them that their kids are brilliant, even if they aren't. And if you have to exaggerate a little and tell parents of prospective students that you know the Education Czar personally, then you do. Besides, I know people who know people who know the Czar," her father said. They were the good kind of teachers, but not always good parents.

That night, a dinner of chicken and string beans was served. *Always chicken*. Jane hated the chicken, and no matter how many times she told mom, she still served chicken. *See, she doesn't love me* thought Jane when she saw the chicken. Jane did eat all her string beans, however.

"Jane, won't you eat your chicken?" her mom asked. Jane glared at her, folded her arms tightly, and pursed her lips in silence. "I'll cut it up for you, sweetie," begged Mallory.

After a while, dad would intervene in their feud, grab the chicken leg or breast and say, "It's okay, I can take it for lunch."

In order to be as invisible as possible at home, Jane mastered the craft of being sneaky and silent.

"Why do you let her get away with it!" her mother yelled from their bedroom as Jane listened from an air vent.

"She is a little girl. She'll grow out of it," said her dad, trying desperately to console his increasingly inconsolable wife. But mom's tone had changed, no longer sad, mom was angry. It frightened Jane.

"I should never have had that child," Mallory said through gritted teeth. "Why did you coerce me take those drugs so I could become pregnant? If God wanted us to be sterile, His will be done."

Jane ran away to her room, slammed the door, and didn't come out until the next morning to go to school.

Her mother continued to yell. "How could I let you and the church convince me to try to have another baby!"

"How was I to know the drug therapy wouldn't work again?" asked Jane's father.

"I could have bled to death. Do you care?" Chuck failed to answer. "I'm done! No more!" Mallory collapsed and folded her skeletal legs into the chair so her husband couldn't embrace her.

---

Jane's reading lessons that year consisted of a series of books that taught reading comprehension and all the morals for young students featuring stories about Skipper the Dog. There were animals called 'cows' in the books that made a bellowing sounds, and they were good to befriend. The cats and rats were sneaky liars that worked together to bring down the dogs and sheep. Every dog aspired to be a sheep and every sheep was a good sheep.

> *One day Skipper was in the backyard at home, and he noticed the gate to the outside was left open. Skipper always wondered what was beyond, but other than walking the straight and narrow path each day with the man to the designated places, he knew nothing of the world. Skipper*

*heard of stories about dogs who got lost and never returned from the outside. But Skipper could not resist. He was, after all, a dog.*

*He stuck his head out of the gate and started wandering across a field. As he wandered, Skipper sniffed and sniffed the ground, something that the man had tried to stop him from doing. Everything, from the manure to the flowers, smelled wonderful. It was intoxicating.*

*Eventually, Skipper found himself surrounded by trees. What strange place was this? All the newness frightened him, and he wished that he could be with the sheep once again. He could hear the scurrying of the rats as they scratched about the ground. He could hear the mewing songs of the cats all around. It was like the man had warned him; wandering without aim could be dangerous and was thus forbidden. All actions and things had a purpose, and Skipper knew that now, knew it more than ever. It was Skipper's destiny to become a sheep one day, whether on earth or in heaven.*

*Just then, Skipper heard the shouts of the man, "Come on Skipper, come on, get up, it's time for your walk." He felt the man's hand shake his belly and wake him. Skipper was so relieved that it had only been a bad dream. He was comfortable where everything was familiar, safe, safe on his bed, safe on the floor of the cage were the man had left him in when he was gone. And Skipper was ready for the walk through all the familiar places, vowing never to wander again.*

---

The Winstons arrived at the $100 million Reverend Manpower Christ Revival Church on Saturday morning. The church had a large central spire and four smaller spires that formed a square, all decorated with stained glass. The Manpower service was the last remaining face-to-face sermon in Angeltown of over ten people, for too much of the city had been abandoned. Around three hundred congregants showed up that day, and as recently as 2045 they had nearly 1000 in attendance. The church was funded by well-timed purchases of Governet stock and a few wealthy benefactors who, by giving money to build the church, purchased absolution for any past, present, or future transgressions.

Chuck and Mallory Winston sat in the center of the nave and Jane was sent to play with the other children in a room near the front of the church. Mallory was happy that Jane would spend time with other children, but Chuck was concerned, not for Jane, but for the others. By ten years of age, Jane had become abusive and manipulative of other children using her superficial charm and relentlessness to bully them.

Minister Hath was no longer on Earth, having ascended, and thus Reverend Manpower, Junior addressed the flock with arms raised, palms upward to the sky.

*Welcome beloved children of God.* He looked up into the tall central spire. *God wants to be exalted in your heart today.* He looked down and smiled at the people in attendance. *Let us talk about Isaiah, the prophet of Israel.*

> *Isaiah saw God, and God saw Isaiah. God sent to Isaiah a Seraphim…an angel that was the face of God.* He pointed at the flock in the nave. *You, you, and you! When was the last time you got on your face before God and said, 'God, I can't even look at you'? When have you last gotten on your knees before God and said, 'God, you are so beyond me'?*

*We are all sinners, and only by God's grace do we not go down to the eternal flame. You...and I...are of unclean lips. You have sinned and have fallen short of the glory of God. Everyone, you must realize that you are sinners. Death is the price of sin.*

He paused and took a deep breath and came back louder and with increased energy. *We will be slaughtered for our misdeeds! Here were sheep, bulls, and goats that were killed, and then came the lamb of God, Jesus Christ. Here I am lord, send me! You either turn or you burn!*

He paused once more and observed the gazing, gawking, and fidgeting of the congregation. Reverend Manpower dispatched his final message piece by piece like unraveling a fine silk carpet.

*We live in challenging times. We have teachers who won't turn toward God. They don't surrender to the way of the Czar, and they try to find the individualistic path. They have met God's wrath. Soon, we will need teachers no longer, for God is making our women barren.*

Mallory clutched her wedding ring and started pulling the shaft up and down her finger.

*Teachers will no longer have children to corrupt. As a matter of fact, the Czar told me personally that within three years, the last elementary schools will be closed permanently, and if we don't go forth and multiply, the human race will be no more than dust within 100 years.*

He pointed to the sky.

*Yes, God is punishing us for our wickedness by laying waste to this land with fire, dust, and damning wombs to shrivel and lay fallow. Thus, my children, The Reverend Manpower Church can no longer remain in Angeltown.*

The congregation gasped in unison.

*We must move to The Center, where wombs can still give life. We can't stand against this sin alone and we must unite with the Insiders against the final judgement. Like the desert sands in Israel encroaching on the Holy Lands, we cannot resist this judgement. We can only be righteous and pray that the Insiders and the Czar will deliverer us from evil.*

People murmured to each other about the meaning of this last part of the sermon. "Are they leaving us?" "What are we to do?" "God really has forsaken us."

*God's will be done*, thought Mallory.

Chuck's mouth was agape and his mind blank.

Then the choir started their spirituals to mollify the crowd. They sang 'God Unto Thee,' 'Holy is thy Lord' and ended with a rousing sing-along of 'Jesus Saved you, what have you saved for Him?' The service concluded with a few words for those who had passed on and blessings to suffering humans and pets. After announcements, people stood to go.

Chuck addressed his wife. "Mallory, I better get Jane." He rushed to the front of the church and to the right into the wood-paneled room that had a small stage, tables and chairs, books, toys, crayons, paper, and games. Jane was on the stage reading about Skipper the Dog and gesticulating as she spoke. The childcare attendant and most of the children were watching her, with few exceptions. Jimmy was moping at one table and drawing wild circles with various crayons on a sketch pad and Sally sat across from him combing the hair of a doll.

Chuck approached his daughter. "Jane, it's time to go."

She scrunched up her face and glared at him.

"But go ahead and finish that book. Besides, I like to hear you read."

Jane smiled and in two more pages finished the book, then she turned the book to show the other children the drawings on the last page. She put down the book, skipped over to her dad, and grabbed his hand. "Thank you, daddy."

---

It was another night and another battle for control. "Jane, why don't you ever eat what we give you!" Mallory shouted. "Pick up your clothes!" "Stop making so much noise!" "Don't slam the door!" "Look at me when I talk to you!" Shouting had become the typical way mom communicated with Jane.

Finally, Jane looked her in the eyes. "You can't blame me because you can't have any more babies!" Jane scowled. Then she leaned forward into her mother's stunned face and said, "You're a rat, rat, rat, rat." She crooned, "Rat, rat, rat" over and over in a melodic tone and danced around the dinner table as her dress flounced up and down. Mallory went after her, fully intending to slap her daughter.

Chuck grabbed his wife tightly by the arm, and she was too weak to resist. There was a knock at the door. A man appeared wearing a blue pinstriped suit with automatic cooling ventilation technology for the ever-hotter climate. He worked for Penrose and Thicket and they were hired to promote the new and improved State Auto-defense Force.

"Good evening," said the man at the door. He presented his credentials on his phone's screen. "I represent Penrose and Thicket and we have been informed by your daughter's teacher, Mrs. Abernathy, that Jane would be ideal for our new advertising campaign."

Jane's parents stared, jaws dropping. "You want to know what?" asked Jane's father, incredulously.

From behind him came Jane's exasperated voice, "They want me to be in an ad, dad."

Still confused, dad said, "Well, come in."

Earl Penrose looked at Jane. "Your teacher speaks very highly of you, young lady."

Mallory looked emaciated, her eyes and head shifted left, then right, then left again. She interrupted, "She's too young. She can't. She's…she's all we have."

*Mom is having another fit*, thought Jane. She knew she had to jump in. Jane stepped forward and gracefully interceded. Her mother was frozen in disbelief. "Hello Mr.?" He showed Jane his tablet phone. Jane read it aloud, "Mr. Penrose. Are you—"

He interjected, "No, that's my father, I just work for him."

"And you like it? Working for him?" asked Jane as she escorted him to a seat.

"I like meeting all sorts of interesting people," he said.

"So do I," agreed Jane.

Her mother tried to step in. "We don't feel that—"

Jane stopped her with a chilling glance, and said sotto voce, "Mother, don't."

Chuck grabbed Mallory by the arm and walked her into the bedroom. She had little force to resist. As he escorted his wife away, Jane overheard Chuck say, "I can handle this; why don't you rest?" Her father came back into the dining room. He sat down next to Jane and she took her father's hand.

Chuck explained, "Excuse my wife, Mr. Penrose. She's under a lot of stress at work. I'm sure a man in your position can understand the stress of an important job." He paused, then continued. "What can we do for you?"

"Right to the point then," he said. "Mrs. Abernathy, Jane's

teacher," he smiled at Jane, "thinks that Jane would be perfect for our new campaign for the State Auto-defense Force. Mr. Abernathy is my boss and the husband of Jane's teacher. He is relying on me to inspect Jane."

He gestured to the girl with an open hand. Jane flashed a smile at him.

"Come here Jane and stand in front of me," said Mr. Penrose.

Jane jumped into position, still smiling.

Mr. Penrose put his right hand on her cheek. "Keep smiling please, and show me your teeth."

Jane obeyed.

"Good, good." He made a mark on a tablet with a stylus. "Now, open your mouth."

Jane opened her mouth and Penrose squeezed her jaw to get her mouth to open wider. He bent to look up at her teeth, then down.

"Good, no cavities." He made another mark and cupped her cheeks with both hands. "Rounded cheeks, small for her age of ten, looks younger."

He looked at the father who waited eagerly, not concerned by the way Mr. Penrose man-handled his daughter.

"Excellent." Penrose addressed the father. "The part is for a girl younger than Jane, but she will pass as an eight year old, and being ten and so...precocious, will make your daughter easier to direct. And Jane has the right look."

Penrose looked down at her feet.

"Good, small, size four shoes?"

Jane nodded.

"Well Jane, that's all for now. Here's my card." He handed it to her father. "Send over Jane's school and medical reports, standard procedure." He clutched his tablet with both hands. "Oh, and you will have to supply a blood sample. I am sure a doctor can procure one and have them send it to our office." He pointed. "The address is on the card."

"Certainly," said Jane's father.

"I will return with the contract and we can get started with the filming. We will do the screen tests next weekend, film the commercial even. It's a small," he looked at Jane, "but crucial role."

Mr. Penrose and Jane's father shook hands.

After meeting Jane, Penrose knew she was the girl for their campaign. Jane was what doctors call prototypically attractive: black hair, green eyes, and good skin. And the Winstons were the ideal, hard-working, spiritual and upright family, perfectly suited to represent Angeltown in their recruitment for the State Auto-defense Force (SADF). Penrose couldn't have been more certain of his company's choice.

Jane was going to be the face of the new SADF, the face of those who would suffer if the force hadn't formed. Her face would be on moving and stationary billboards, on the television and on virtual reality and Governet commercials and advertising. Her mother might have been worried, but Jane didn't care. *I'm going to be famous, have friends and be liked.*

#

# Chapter 3
# Martin Emerges

*Why burn the books when you can better manage the population by controlling the content of the books that you tell people are facts.*
The Czar of Education

For over a year, Martin supplied players for Griffin's game show, *The Middle Eastern Hunt*, and Griffin paid him in pieces or hard to find valuables. To celebrate their anniversary, Griffin gifted his best recruiter a cedar handled, four-inch collapsible hunting knife with "Martin" engraved on one side. "Thanks Kyle, that's very thoughtful. I am sure this will come in handy." The knife would be handy in ways Martin never expected.

His job had long, tedious hours and its own set of rules. One was, *don't misuse the merchandise* as they euphemistically called rape and murder of refugees. He suspected that one of his men was breaking that rule. After one trip up the coast, Martin phoned the Labor Distribution Center for Women to check on Rosa V., the detainee they found wondering alone after her boat sank and the bodies of her son and husband were found dead, floating in the high tide. "So, no Rosa was dropped off in the last twenty-four hours…thank you."

Duke Johnson entered the border patrol office where the team operated. "Hey Duke, how did that drop off of Rosa V. go?"

asked Martin.

Duke hesitated and then put his tablet down on a desk. "Oh, fine. It was so routine that I forgot all about it."

"So, no trouble?"

"No, why would there be any trouble?" asked Duke.

Martin kept pushing to see how far he would go in the lie. "The recruitment center found her a placement?"

"I don't know. I'm sure they will, I mean, why not?"

"Why not indeed," Martin said.

Martin waited until the next trip to trap Duke, to catch him in the act instead of accusing him on the spot without direct evidence. Martin was acting off the books in case he was wrong, but he wasn't.

Illegal traffic was down now that life on both sides of the border was unlivable, so it took a couple of weeks for the next crossing. On that trip, it was only three illegals, two men and one woman at the Cool View tunnel. It was a three hour drive from Rampart, and they collided with two pollution clouds along the way. But San Diego was no longer habitable and the trip paid well. Besides, Martin might get another bonus payment from Griffin.

Since the men and women go to different distribution sites miles apart, it was natural that the forcemen separate. Martin ordered Duke to take the woman and he stayed behind to talk to the men. As soon as Johnson left, he sent the other forcemen to take the illegal male entrants to the job center. Then Martin took a cruiser and turned on his tablet. He hit the *track* application. The computer spoke, "Headed north on state route twenty-three." *Johnson was going the wrong way. Time to catch up.* Martin accelerated and drove east on Eastwood Highway, a once teeming road that lead from the border through Theater View, Table Rock to Saint Bernard, and turned north on twenty-three.

After about ten minutes, his tablet spoke again. "Exiting

right on Summit Meadow Road, two minutes ahead." He was catching up. Martin made sure to go fast, but he didn't want to get too close. He saw lights up ahead veering to the left. He turned off his head lights having learned to see in the moonlight from the long nights of stakeouts, this night a crescent moon, and that was good enough for Martin to follow the lights of Duke's car ahead of him.

Martin turned off the volume on the tablet. The car ahead of him veered right and the road was now gravel and sand. Suddenly, he saw the car stop up ahead. The car lights went dark. Martin waited to see what Johnson would do. He saw Duke get out and go to the passenger side. Duke opened the door and pulled out the woman. Martin heard her screams. This time, Martin could do something about the violence.

He drove up behind the parked car after Johnson was inside the cabin. His approach wouldn't be heard over the woman's screaming, and Martin quickly skulked up to the front door while pulling out his engraved knife. He rammed the wooden door with his full force. The door exploded, splinters flying, letting Martin through. Duke was on top of the woman, attempting to take off her clothes, hitting her.

Martin briefly saw a flash of his father swinging at his mother. "Bastard!" He yelled, lunging at Johnson and quickly stabbed him once under the armpit, paralyzing his right arm and starting a river of blood.

Duke was on the ground, writhing and cursing. "What the hell!"

The woman gathered herself and ran from the men into the next room. Duke was now screeching. Martin leaned over him and rubbed the bloody knife onto Duke's cheek. "What did you do with the other women, Duke?" asked Martin.

Martin could hear the woman sobbing on the bed in the next room. "Come on Duke." Duke couldn't answer. He was trying to keep the blood from leaving his body by squeezing his left arm under his right armpit. Agony leaked out of him like air out of tire. Martin took a pillow off the sofa, roughly lifted up Duke's right arm, stuffed the pillow underneath and put Duke's left over it. Martin sneered. "You're lucky I held back. You could have lost your whole arm"

"Why'd you do it Duke? Why? Men like you deserve to die, preying on the weak." Duke now sobbed in pain, not guilt. "I'll tell you what. I won't kill you if you confess for me, huh?" A calm overcame Martin. "Don't move, or you know what's coming," he said, waving his knife in Duke's face. Martin walked to the entrance of the cabin and looked back at Duke. He's not going anywhere, he thought.

He came back from the car with a Nanomed kit and his tablet. "Let's take a look at you, Duke. Looks like someone stabbed you pretty bad. Tsk tsk, you must have done something to really piss him off." He opened the plastic box that contained medicines. First Martin took out a needle that read "Darpovan" on it. All he knew was that when he stuck a suspect with it, they didn't wake up for at least two hours.

He put it aside, then grabbed the Nanomed enzymes used to seal wounds. He filled the palm of his right hand with the gel and took out a large wad of gauze in his left hand. In a series of smooth motions he took out the cushion, ripped opened Duke's shirt to expose his armpit, put the wad of enzymes on the wound then covered it with gauze.

All the while, Duke was wheezing, "You bastard!" with all his remaining breath.

Martin took out some medical tape and wrapped it under Duke's arm and over his shoulder tightly three times. After, he took out the needle and stuck the anesthesia into Johnson's neck. Ten seconds later, Duke faded out. Martin lifted him up and put him on the couch.

"Oye, señora!" Martin yelled to the woman. Nothing. Martin went into the other room and saw her curled up on the corner of the bed hugging the bedsheets to her. "Ven" he said, "vamanos." Her eyes darted around, looking for danger. "Oh," said Martin, "El hombre malo no va a molestar nadie, el vaya al dormir."

"The bad man's asleep?" she asked.

"Yes." As they walked out to the car, the woman glanced over to see Duke passed out on the couch. Martin called it in. "Man down at my location." They tracked his signal.

"Martin, can't you take him?" they asked.

"Well, it might kill him if I do. Send a chopper with a medic and some way to heal a...stab wound and get him stable. I did what I could." He hung up, and as he did, Martin heard, "damn!", over the phone.

The woman shook, looked back at the cabin then at Martin, and having nowhere else to go, entered the car. Martin gave her some water and a food bar and she stared at it, not knowing whether it was poisoned or not. Martin grabbed the bar, tore it in two, and quickly ate half, giving the rest back to the woman.

"I'm Martin," he said as he started the car. He sat a moment to think. "Shit," he exclaimed as he turned off the car. He took the medical kit from behind him, got out and walked back to the cabin. He put a healthy dose of healing gel on a large adhesive bandage. Then he pulled out his monogrammed knife, rolled Johnson's body to face the couch and stabbed him quickly in the spine, not too deep, enough to paralyze him. Then he applied the gel and pad. "Okay you bastard, you won't kill again," he said to the unconscious body. The blood stopped flowing from his back wound, Martin detected a pulse. "He'll be okay," he said, "I hope."

Martin dropped Carla off at the work center, put in a good word for her and hoped she found a family to be with. It was five in the morning by the time he got back to Rampart.

As soon as Martin exited the elevator to the second floor, three officers grabbed and cuffed him. "Martin! What the hell were you doing out there?" yelled Martin's commander, Colonel London, head of criminal recovery and operations at Rampart III. The commander continued, "You know you paralyzed Johnson. You didn't have to do that."

Martin started to speak, and was cut off. "No 'buts'. We were investigating Johnson, and now you screwed it up! We'll never get a conviction." He paused. "Well!? Talk!"

Martin answered. "You weren't going to get a conviction. An officer killing illegals? Even if there was evidence, no judge would prosecute." This time, the now handcuffed Martin cut off his commander. "Besides, now he'll never kill again. It's a win-win." Martin let out a chuckle.

London ended the conversation. "We'll see how funny it is when you are in The Pits. Take him out of here!" They dragged him back onto the elevator. Martin had a wry smile on his face as he descended. He knew as a former SADF officer what he would face in prison. He also knew that with the preponderance of evidence against him, he had been found guilty already without a trial just as other offenders were incarcerated without a legal proceeding. Trials were only for high-end white collar crimes.

Martin was brought to Pit #1, a huge city-block-sized rectangular hole dug in the ground for the central headquarters of a bank that failed in the 2050 crash. He was condemned for assaulting a fellow SADF officer, something most prisoners only dreamed about. As he saw it, his crime was justified, and he knew the other prisoners felt their crimes were justified as well.

The Pit Investment Conglomerate, PitCo, had a rich Nanomed contract that paid the state to test drugs on the prisoners, so the institution made a small, but reliable profit. The Pits were here to stay. But they never tested drugs on Martin. Law enforcement had other plans for him.

Prisoners were lifted inside a metal cage into The Pit by a crane. As they floated in their cage, an alarm sounded and a voice came over the loudspeakers; *in-coming, prisoner A293, do not approach the box, or you will be shot. You WILL be shot.*

The walls to The Pit were fifty-feet high with ten-inch razor sharp spikes embedded on the sides starting at ten feet on up. There was no way out, but your food and water needs were met. You could drink a total of four times a day from one of four water stations, and if you had drunk your share, the fountain in the corners of The Pit wouldn't operate when you pushed the button.

Sometimes a bigger, more intimidating prisoner would physically force a smaller, weaker prisoner to push the button for water so the bruiser could get an extra dose. When that happened, cameras would signal any one of ten robotic rifles located at the top of the wall to shoot him. Still, the larger prisoners would try, and despite the dismal success rate, some did succeed. If a physical fight started, the robotic security would shoot anyone who started the altercation and anyone who fought back. This security protocol saved on personnel costs and hassle for everyone. Auditory threats and insults between prisoners were ignored, for if they weren't, none of the foul-mouthed barking dogs in the pits would last for more than one day without being shot. No, it was the prisoners that bite and damaged the medical test subjects that PitCo was concerned with.

At the edge of The Pit, prisoners urinated or defecated into a trough that sucked down their waste. PitCo couldn't afford all the water, so prisoners were cleaned every seven days. The Prison Corporation of America (PCA) would play Governet TV on a special channel programmed for prisoners. A detective show called *Pops America* was popular. Public service announcements would play about how crime doesn't pay. "Being kind is better than being cruel" it stated, and also presented "the ten rules for a moral life." It wasn't a complete waste of programming; the detainees found these announcements hilarious.

Martin had little patience for others' foibles and lies and was known for stabbing suspects who talked too much because *listening to them wasn't part of his job.* In Pit #1, he never attacked anyone unprovoked, and he had developed a method for dealing with the bullies and the hardened psychopaths. Depending on the opportunity, his first technique was to provoke one into attacking him. One such unusually violent man, even for Pit #1, was Hawk Rogers. Hawk made Martin look like a tiny boy in comparison, but Martin knew that if he wanted to survive, he would have to deal with him.

Martin quickly learned to use the security features, like the robotic rifles, to his advantage. One day he called Hawk over to a drinking station after clearing out the other residents. Martin asked, "Hawk, you want a drink?"

"What?!" said Hawk incredulously. "You're that damn forceman!"

Martin asked again, glancing down at the fountain, "I just want to get on your good side, Hawk. You want a drink?"

Hawk looked Martin over, and finally said, "Sure."

"Then go piss yourself," said Martin.

On reflex, Hawk raised his right fist to clock Martin. And before the strike hit, Hawk was shot in the right leg. He collapsed as the bullet hit his femur. Hawk screamed out revenge. "I'll get you for this, Martin!" Hawk bled for a while, and he was taken out on a stretcher by four attendants. He was still alive, and he was in too much pain to plot revenge for the time being.

Martin stood and said loudly to those watching, "I was defending myself, you saw it." Inside, he was laughing, of course. Martin soon became the enforcer, cornering bullies out of visual range of the automatic rifles and laying down the law. "You insist on bullying the others in here, and you will have to deal with me." He often gave them this speech with his hand wrapped around their neck or balls. Martin wasn't the biggest man, but he had the grip of a bear trap. They got the point. But he never picked on the weaker, more helpless residents. And for that, he was given full respect and honors of the others. Within in a year, Martin was out of Pit #1. He had been recruited into the new off the books SADF tracking squad.

Lieutenant Gomez had started a new unit to apprehend the most hardened scumbags, and he thought of Martin. Military-trained men like Martin were exactly what Gomez was looking for.

"I like the way you administered justice in Pit #1. You have a real knack for handling yourself." Martin remained silent. Gomez continued, "I also like the way you handled Sergeant Johnson. You could have let him go, or you could have killed him as he might have deserved. But you solved it so he could live and not harm others. That's real rehabilitation." Martin let out a rare smile.

After a pause, Gomez changed subjects. "I know you were recruiting for that producer Griffin. We can overlook that if you come work for me." Gomez showed Martin his monogrammed knife that was taken when he was arrested. "Let's hope you won't have to use this." He slid it across the table.

Martin picked it up. "Thanks. What will I have to do?"

"All you will have to do is track down the most elusive and

dangerous criminals and fugitives in Angeltown and environs. That's all," Gomez said. "You will get a salary, access to the tools of the trade, and a bonus for each successful mission, depending on the degree of difficulty of course."

Martin played coy. "Suppose I don't capture a fugitive, what then?"

Gomez glanced at him. "You'll do it. I have read your record. You enjoy it, and you're good at it."

"Still, Colonel London did put me in the pits. My history won't be a problem for you?"

"No, this squad if off the official books. And if you don't succeed, we'll fire you and put you under house arrest in the luxury suites we have upstairs to live out your sentence. It's not the Wilshire, but it's not The Pits."

Martin reached out his hand to shake. Gomez looked across the table and placed a tablet in front of him, ignoring Martin's outstretched arm.

Martin looked him in the eye then to the tablet. "I understand," he said. He pocketed his knife and then he signed the tablet after glancing at the agreement and seeing the pay. "I am happy to join your team. Who else you got?"

"So far, it's only you."

---

Brothers Sonny and Donny Williams, criminal freelancers available for hire when not plotting their own crimes, were well known for their knife-wielding prowess. They weren't afraid to kill forcemen and agents of the state when they deemed it necessary, and they also gave mercy to those whom they thought were innocent.

Donny, the older and bigger brother at 180 pounds and 28 years of age, and Sonny, the faster and hot-headed younger brother at 24 and 160 pounds, were talking over their plans for the night from their simple one bedroom squat they took over from disappeared owners. Donny's phone rang. "Hold on Sonny." He answered. "Donny here…how did you get this number…yes, sir, I see…and you want what…are you trying to get us killed…so that's how it is…no, sir, no complaint…just I, uh we, wouldn't want to disappoint you…I see." He hung up, looked at his phone and started to read the text he just received.

"What is it Donny?"

"Apparently, someone has a job for us, just us, and…you won't believe it. Just look at your phone. They sent us both the details."

The job involved entering a drone depot with only knives and a code for a combination lock the man on the phone said he got off a former guard, whom those in charge may or may not have influenced with threats to him and his lover. "This code opens a door to a drone depot where we are to procure an assault drone and wait for further instructions," said Donny.

"You're fucking kidding me. That's suicide. Who are these guys?"

"Read the whole text, Sonny. Remember the married couple who were going around breaking and entering and abusing members of the tax-paying public as they were evacuating the redundant zones of the city."

"Yea." Sonny knit his brow.

"These people say they were the ones who had them capped when they failed to terminate certain citizens that the state asked them to kill. Look at the photo of the bodies that were sent."

"You mean the bodies no one found?"

Donny nodded. "Yes. You want to die, Sonny, or do you want to take our last job and then retire?"

"How do you know it was them?" asked Sonny.

"They mentioned two shots, one in each temple of the dead couple using military-issued pistols. And who other than the Truancy Squad, SADF, and other law enforcement can afford guns anymore?"

"Let's just leave Angeltown. I hear Franks By the Bay has some great opportunities for cutthroats like us."

"Read the last line of the text, Sonny…read it aloud."

"If you try to make a break for FBB, we will cut your balls off and make you feed them to each other." Sonny shivered at the idea.

"Now read the payment plan, the paragraph above."

Sonny's lips moved as he read and you could hear audible traces of the words…100,000 credits…full lifetime immunity…if the target is taken down. "What the hell Donny?" Sonny rubbed his hands through his shaggy hair.

"I think our plans have changed," the older brother said.

---

"Time to get the cycle out, Sonny," Donny said, referring to their 2035 JC-90 turbo two-seater, three-cylinder motorcycle.

"I'm glad the family we borrowed this from had the stealth mode installed," said Sonny.

"They don't make them like this anymore, brother. Time to get our drone."

Donny drove and Sonny sat in the back flipping his knife open and closed as they drove west toward the Port of Angeltown. Traffic was a rare sight at the port with a worldwide population collapse, but there were goods that people with pieces still purchased from Asia and South America that couldn't be made in U.S. prisons and in North Mexican factories. The drone depot rested south of the port in a former airplane hangar near what was left of Long Beach. It sat next to the dried up Angeltown River where kids used to skate but now was so filled with debris that it was like skating in a landfill.

According to the man on the call willing enough to risk the lives of the Williams Brothers, they were looking for a WASP drone, model number 3000 or later. They would never get a model 5000. Those drones were all in service in active war zones in Wyoming, the North Mexican border, and South Africa where white supremacist had taken over U.S. factories.

Donny got out his special set of sharpened throwing knives that he bought when he had dreams of being in the circus and put them in the slots of his Marine vest. Sonny had two blades he made from bayonets that he wielded along his arms on springs ready to snap forward in case of trouble. They also carried their favorite butterfly knives.

They arrived and put their motorcycle out of sight of the security cameras and looked around. The brothers put on their light-reflecting, flexible silicon-carbon masks to avoid cameras getting a good photo of their faces and moved toward the fence. Donny put a gloved finger to his lips signaling Sonny to remain silent. *The man better be right and the gate is open, or we're done.* He checked it and inched it open.

A long parking lot lay between them and the side door where they had access with the code they were given. They scurried across the edge of the lot against the sides of the building to avoid the cameras until they were at the door.

This is suicide! thought Sonny.

This code better work, thought Donny. He looked at the slip of paper where he had it written down and punched it into the keypad.

The door clicked open.

We're dead, we're dead, we're dead, thought Sonny.

"All right, hands up!" shouted a security officer with a light and a gun trained on them. He aimed his weapon at Donny. "I told you—"

Before he finished his second sentence, Donny's knife hit him dead center in the throat.

Once more Donny put his index finger to his lips to remind Sonny to remain silent. He looked at the guard splayed on the ground. *You were saying?* Donny thought about taking the knife but left it. Too messy.

Donny held up four fingers to Sonny then closed one. That meant three guards remained. Once inside the door they slid down the beveled tin walls and kept their eyes open for more guards. Donny again pantomimed to his brother, he pointed forward, then to the right, then to the left.

Sonny remembered the pattern on the map and followed right behind his brother. The further they progressed the darker it got, like a cave. Donny came across an intersection, looked to the left and turned right. An armed guard came out of the wall and aimed at Donny. Sonny, who was within arms-length of his brother, slid the handle of his knife onto his left hand and sliced the guards head half off. Donny's eyes bulged and his heart rate increased. Death still surprised him.

They moved a little further and got to the door that led into the storage area. The brothers looked around, worried about encountering the other two guards who could have been waiting for them behind the steel barrier. The brothers had entered a room unannounced before and got into position. Sonny went to the right of the door and Donny took out two knives and crouched down ready to throw. Sonny reached across and opened the portal and ducked back behind the frame. Donny immediately threw his weapons. Sonny didn't hear anyone fall or gun shots coming back at them.

Donny stood and walked into the vast storage room, 120,000 square feet of emptiness. Sonny looked around the corner. Donny had hit two wooden support beams twelve feet apart at eye level. If they had been guards, they would each have a blade in their brains.

Sonny tapped Donny on the shoulder and shrugged. Donny shook his head, collected his knives, and pulled his brother to the side, away from the open door.

Donny's new burner phone vibrated in his vest. *Who the fuck is this now!* He looked at his phone and the display read, 'Pick up Donny.' Only Sonny has this number.

He took a deep breath, looked again and the screen read, 'Last warning, Donny.' He answered and listened for a moment, then put it on speaker for his brother. "Say that again for Sonny to hear."

"Gentlemen," the male voice said. "We are so sorry. The drone depot has moved to a more secure location. We just learned about it."

"And the other two guards?" asked Sonny.

"Don't worry about them. They were relocated too. I assume the remaining guards didn't give you any trouble."

"Trouble?" said Donny. "You might not know this, but I don't like to kill unless I have to. What a waste!"

"If it makes you feel any better Donny, the guards had no dependents, so the only loss is to their employer."

"You mean the people we were hired to steal from," Donny said.

"One in the same."

Sonny raised his hand for his turn to talk.

"Yes, what is it Sonny?" asked the voice on the phone.

*How did he know?* "Where is this new secure location we have to steal from now?"

"That would be a suicide mission, Sonny. They built a new sub-basement at Rampart and they are being stored there. Change of plans fellas. I deposited 40,000 pieces into your account to purchase a WASP 3000 for us. I just sent you the details. Your profit is the difference between the sale price and the 40,000."

Donny gritted his teeth and flapped his arms up and down. *Mississippi Hell! Why you lying, cheating, son of a bitch, squirrel-brained—*

"Take it or leave it, Donny."

# Chapter 4
# The Czar of Education Teaches Jane

*There are facts and there is the truth. Only teachers who know the truth will be tolerated, and those who peddle facts will be dismissed.*
The Czar of Education

On Friday, the Winstons ate a dinner of pork chops and apple sauce, Jane's favorite. Jane knew it must have been dad's idea.

Dad lifted a glass of milk for a toast. "Here's to Jane and her new acting career!"

"Thank you, Daddy." She noticed the dejected look on Mallory's face. "Don't worry Mom, it's just play-acting." Jane was happy to have a role in this important campaign for the SADF. Knowing mom was upset was a bonus and made her smile. "And I'll have my own make-up artist to make me pretty and get to be on camera, and lots of people will see it."

Mallory's eyes darted back and forth, unable to look at Jane directly. She finally focused on Jane's plate. "I'm…at least you…finish your supper dear, you need your strength."

Jane scrunched up her face and resisted the urge to stick out her tongue at Mallory. *Why don't you finish your supper, mom!*

Mr. Penrose arrived after the meal with the contract that had already been signed by Mr. Penrose, Senior and a representative from the Governet. He sat at the Winston's rare pinewood, oval dining table with Jane, Chuck, and sitting farthest from Mr. Penrose, Mrs. Winston.

"Let's look at the highlights of the contract," said Mr. Penrose. They went through the main parts of the contract that concerned Jane and her family, the Governet role, her role and so forth. Penrose let Mr. Winston hold the tablet and read through the contract while he opened a manila folder he carried that had one piece of paper in it with one line and handed it to Jane. "Here is your spoken part."

Jane read it and gave it back to Mr. Penrose.

"You sure you don't want to keep it, practice it a few times for tomorrow?"

She placed her arms onto her lap and smiled. "I'm sure."

Chuck spoke up. "I don't want to be indelicate, but what is my daughter's compensation?"

Penrose took the tablet back from Mr. Winston. "There is a one-time payment," he went to the bottom of the screen and open a new tab in the contract. He pointed. "Here"

Jane's saw the amount and nodded.

Chuck's heart started pounding rapidly at the amount offered Jane, almost a full year of his own salary. He swallowed and scanned through the compensation tab. "What about residuals? This is going to play everywhere, so you will be using Jane's likeness all over."

"We feel this one-time payment will be sufficient. We're not even sure how much this will play or how many people will see the commercial or advertisements. Besides, there will certainly be more opportunities in the future for young Jane."

"And you're certain of that?" asked Mr. Winston.

Jane took her dad's hand and grinned. "Of course."

Penrose nodded. "Certainly." He took a deep breath and addressed the father. "If you could look this over, initial on the bottom of each page, including the separate section on compensation…you too Jane."

Mallory stood and came over to where her husband and daughter were reading and leaving their initials.

Mr. Penrose stood and raised a hand to stop her. "Mrs. Winston, we only need one parent to sign. You won't be needed."

Mrs. Winston sat back down in her seat and stared blankly at the wall.

---

The next morning, the Governet picked up Chuck and Jane in a limousine and drove them to a studio in central Angeltown for the filming of the commercial and the photo session. Jane wore a mid-length white sundress sparsely covered in pale bluebells. Chuck put on a suit and a happy face for the event.

Mallory had a headache, took a sedative, and went back to bed. She didn't even wish Jane good luck or wave them off. Mallory couldn't believe what was happening to her life and didn't want to support her family's dissolution by going to watch Jane.

In the back of the limousine where Jane and Chuck sat, there was a complimentary food bar with exotic sweets and snacks, some that were illegal to import. But the Governet had no difficulty accessing food banned to the public. There was soda from Mexico and Russia, water from the last lakes in the Middle East, and jerky from animals that were extinct, including koala bear and American opossum.

Jane, who usually didn't ask permission, looked to her dad. "Can I have a sweet?"

"I assume they put it there for us. Go ahead."

Jane took a chocolate whose label read: *From one of the last cocoa plants in West Africa.*

Chuck took an individually wrapped hard yellowish candy made from Mongolian bees' honey, according to the label. Chuck had no idea where Mongolia was. *Gee, those people make good bees. It has to be a sin to eat something this good.* The grin on his face remained the entire forty-minute journey to the studio.

They arrived at a former downtown grocery store warehouse, a Governet communications center that had merged with the Czar of Education and the official leadership of Angeltown and surrounding area. One of four garage doors opened, each large enough to fit an eighteen wheel truck, and the limousine entered the environmentally conditioned parking and storage area. The rooms beyond the garage consisted of large and small sound stages, recording studios, and a radio station. There were also editing bays for Governet-Casts, video production, virtual reality, and holocasts featuring the latest hologram celebrities such as Diamond Joe Forceman, Mary Lamb and soon, Skipper the Dog.

They parked in a spot labeled *Special Guest* and were escorted up a short flight of stairs into a frigid hallway.

"Good luck Jane! I'm cheering for you," Dad said. Then he got on his phone to look at his students' test scores.

The escort took Jane down the hall and pointed into the first room with an open door. "Here you are young lady," said her guide.

Jane entered a dressing room painted emerald green and saw a petite, twenty-year-old woman with dyed blonde hair waiting for her. "Jane," said the makeup artist. "I'm Sonya. I am here to help you get ready today. That includes helping you select the right clothes and putting on your makeup." The room had one door, one mirror curved at the top with lights around it, one closet, one overhead light, and one makeup tray. Sonya walked to her left to the wardrobe and opened the accordion doors from the middle. It was full of white dresses and a few pink, purple, green, and yellow ones. "Take your pick, Jane."

Her eyes opened wide. "Really?"

"Yes, on orders from the director."

She gawked at the selection in the closet. None of the dresses were terrible, even the pink ones, but one stood out as the most appropriate: a plain, white, below the knee chiffon dress with long sleeves and lace at the cuffs. "How about this one?"

"Good choice. Why don't we put that back in the closet, then put on the make-up, and then put on the dress?"

"Okay," Jane said.

"I need you to take off your clothes and put on this smock, and we can get started."

Jane changed into the smock and grinned from Mississippi to the Moon.

"Ready?"

Jane giggled and then caught herself. She cleared her throat. "Yes."

Sonya started tossing the back of Jane's hair up and down. She gave it a bouncy curl, applied a little eyeliner, more mascara to make her fiery green eyes stand out and skipped the blush; they wanted her to have rounded checks, so contours were out. She had been blessed with full eyebrows that didn't need darkening with a pencil. Then Jane put on her dress and was now a thing of beauty, a fluffy white cake with piping, exquisite and innocent.

"Ready?" asked Sonya.

"Yes!"

Sonya walked Jane to the small sound studio.

The director looked at Jane. "Sonya, you outdid yourself, again!"

"It was simple, Zeus. Jane was the model actress, patient and cooperative."

Zeus looked at Jane. "Is that right, sweetheart?" He pivoted away and changed tone. "All right, places everyone." He waved Jane over who stood staring at the set. "That includes you honey." He pointed at an X on the floor. "Right here."

Jane walked over and stood on the X. She pointed at the green wall. "Mr. Zeus, what's that for?"

He smiled. "That's sweet, honey. It's just Zeus. That is a green screen. I put it there, and then I can put in effects later where the green is." He whispered to her as if it was a secret. "It's really old technology, from before *I* was born. But it works wonders."

That is old, thought Jane, careful not to say it out loud. "So it helps you make the advertisement?"

"It's a commercial honey, I film commercials. Ads are for billboards." Zeus pursed his lips. "Quiet on the set!" He bent to Jane's height. "Do you want to practice or do a take."

"Where do I face?" said Jane.

"Good question." He stood and tapped his bearded chin with his index finger. "Let's try it three times, once facing each camera." He point for Jane to see. "I'm sure we can edit it together later." He paused. "Look at that camera here and recite your line when you are ready."

Jane took a deep breath and remembered the time she was left outside and Mom didn't pick her up. She had never been more afraid in her life. She recited her line.

"Wow." I better not say more and spook the little princess, Zeus thought. "Left camera, once more."

Jane repeated the line with the same effect, to the left and then the right.

"One more, just like that, forward."

She did it once more.

"Cut. We got it." He walked over to Jane. "You really seemed afraid! Whatever you got, keep it up." He looked around. "Sonya, take Jane to the photo session. We're done here."

Jane reached out and shook Zeus's hand. "Thank you, Sir."

A red-headed woman took the photos for the print ads and promotions. Jane enjoyed being photographed by the nice lady. Then on the way home, they had the limousine stop for ice cream and pizza to celebrate. Jane was now a child actress.

The commercials for the State Auto-Defense Force consisted of montages of explosions, shootings, and general chaos projected behind Jane's cute and trusting face looking terrified in the foreground in a medium shot. After fifteen or thirty seconds of mayhem, depending on the length of the commercial, Jane spoke her one line in an innocent, helpless voice: "Please protect me." Then an SADF logo crashed onto the screen with a forceful male voiceover, "Protect the innocent, join the State Auto-Defense Force!" The SADF contact information appeared on the bottom of the screen for a few of seconds, then the commercial faded to black.

They watched the news after dinner one night, as was the custom. However, this night was special; they would be showing Jane's ad at the first commercial break. First, there was a new bulletin from the Czar of Education. The logo of the Czar appeared: the Eagle with lightning bolts and sheaves of wheat in its talons. You never saw the face of the Czar for *We must avoid a cult of personality.* He made an announcement: "In the coming months, and in accordance with Czar Law 51, we will begin closing areas of Angeltown that are no longer productive and are too costly to maintain. Watch this channel for announcements of areas that we will soon be closing."

They went to commercial, and Jane saw her ad for the first time on TV with her Mom and Dad.

"Way to go Jane!" Dad said. He gave her a hug.
"It's a little violent," said Mom as she pulled on the ends of her fingertips. "What are you so afraid of?"

---

After people saw her face in TV commercials, on billboards, on banner ads flown by drones and the same ads online, Jane became a celebrity in Angeltown and the Sovereignty of Southern California. Parents would point at Jane in stores and tell their children, "Look, there's that pretty girl from the television ad."

People would also see Jane out with her dad in restaurants and ask for her autograph. "Of course, who should I sign it to?" Jane knew it was okay because they wouldn't let deplorables into nice restaurants like ones she went to with her family.

The general public loved Jane, especially parents, but not everyone was nice to her at school. A few of the students would mock her by saying "Please protect me" when Jane walked by. Some of the boys tried to lift up her dress to get a peak, and she slapped them away. Jane warned the worst of them, "I'm going to tell the principal and get you expelled!" She did just that and the boy wasn't seen at school again. Afterwards, the other boys stopped teasing Jane.

"Daddy, why do kids make fun of me about being in the ads?"

"They're jealous, Jane, and that's what they do. It's about their insecurity, not you."

"Thanks, dad. Were you ever famous or real popular?"

"No. Only when they wanted help with their studies or

engineering projects. Then I was somehow the most popular guy in school."

"So, you were useful."

He nodded. "That's a nice way to look at it, Jane."

"Did you ever engineer things?"

"No. They needed math teachers, and I wanted to work with your mother. So, I took a job at the Insiders' School for the Gifted instead, where I still teach today."

"Oh. Teaching is also useful."

Chuck smiled and hugged Jane.

Jane spoke at celebratory dinners for the SADF, the anniversary of Rampart Station's founding, and for the Czar's birthday, though no one knew when it was, and people celebrated his birthday five times a year. Jane even wrote some of the words for the celebration herself, with help from dad, and wore her pretty white crinoline dress with a sash and a bow in front.

> *Thank you all for coming tonight. I am sure, like me, you all feel safer knowing that the good men, and women, of the State Auto-Defense Force, Angeltown Division, are protecting us day and night from those who would take away our freedoms. So let's give a hearty cheer of thanks to the new class of recruits for our State Auto-Defense Forces.*

The crowd cheered and clapped, and Jane felt a rush of energy coming from the audience. *I want to feel this way forever!* The recruits ran onto the stage, and Jane rushed off.

The Governet ran the five television stations: The Game Show Channel, The Threat Level Channel, The Soap Opera Channel, The Enterprise Channel, as well as The News Channel. And because of Jane's increasing visibility and charming personality, the News Channel invited her to be interviewed for a segment they called *People Who Make Angeltown Worth Loving*. At the age of eleven, almost twelve as Jane was quick to point out, she was the youngest guest ever on the News at Noon show. Jane wore one of her pretty Governet supplied white dresses, similar to the one she wore in the commercial, and the producers of the news show fully endorsed the choice.

"Hello, Jane. Very nice to meet you," said Farrah Monroe, a dyed blonde, athletic former dancer who had to take up reading the news to make ends meet. They sat close to each other facing the cameras in two cream-colored round-back chairs with yellow cushions. "How did you get your role in the State Auto-Defense Force campaign?"

"It's very nice to meet you too. My dad and I watch you all the time. We really like the way you present the news, and personally," Jane batted her eye lashes and looked up, feigning shyness. "I love your nails. They match your outfits so well."

Farrah smiled. "Why thank you Jane; it's nice to know someone noticed." She chuckled. "So, tell us how you got selected for this campaign."

"I was having dinner with my family," she looked directly into the camera and waved, "Hi mom, hi Dad, love you." A chorus of "aw's" played over the audio track. Like a professional, Jane counted to three for the sound to subside, then continued. "And Mr. Penrose came over and said I was the girl they wanted."

"Amazing," said Farrah. "I hear it was your teacher that first noticed your talent."

"Yes, Mrs. Abernathy. She's the greatest."

"She is one of the few good teachers then." The audio played the laugh track. "What do you do to serve the community as a spokesperson for the men and women who protect and serve us in the State Auto-defense Force?"

"Other than being in the campaign, I speak at events about

the importance of having a strong security force and encourage people to join the academy. And sometimes I visit children who have charred lung and emphysema at care centers."

"That's so nice you can visit those awful patients." There was a moment of silence, then Farrah spoke again. "What are your future plans, Jane?"

"More acting, of course." Her voice rose. "And I want to visit with the Insiders and help the Czar of Education make our schools number one again!"

Farrah patted Jane on the hand. "That's very noble of you." Mrs. Monroe looked directly into the camera. "Now, in honor of our guest, we will hear from one of our many sponsors, the State Auto-defense Force. Like a good citizen, the SADF is there."

The show went to commercial. Farrah shook Jane's hand. "Thank you Jane. You're quite the young lady." Jane basked in her role of spokesmodel for the last time.

The limousine dropped Jane at home and dad was waiting for her. "You were great honey, just like we practiced it." He gave Jane a hug. They rushed inside away from the heat.

"I think she really liked the story about the nails. Good one, dad!"

"And that idea about saying hi to your mother and me? That was great."

"Thanks daddy. Did you get the pizza?"

"You bet!"

---

Jane turned twelve, and she could no longer fit in the dresses that the Governet had given her to wear to SADF events on the *Protection of the Family and Children*. She not only filled out, but she grew her final four inches and was now five-foot-four.

After the change in her body, Jane, who had never been

told about what it meant to become a woman, went to her dad. She had one hand on her stomach and one hand between her legs. "Daddy, I don't feel well."

He furrowed his brow. "What is it honey, you have a tummy ache?"

"Yes, but it hurts further down, and I know I didn't cut myself, but it's like I did and I'm bleeding from inside."

Chuck recoiled, shouting out, "Mallory, Mallory! Come deal with your daughter!" Jane wanted to cry at her dad's response, but was too shocked and disappointed. *Dad was always the one who loved me. Now he's disappointed at me for being sick.*

Mallory took one look at Jane and scolded her. "You take off those filthy clothes and get into the shower, right away." Jane paused and stared. Mallory flung out her stick of an arm and pointed to the bathroom. "Go!"

Jane refused to cry as she stomped away. She took off her clothes and got the water running at the temperature she liked. Jane stood alone as the water washed over her, washing away the blood for fifteen minutes before Mallory cracked open the door and flung in a package of light pads that hit the translucent door to the shower and fell to the floor. "That's all I have. I don't need them anymore," said Mallory, who had lost her menses due to her anorexia. Mallory paused but didn't look into the bathroom. "Read the instructions on the package and, I don't know, look it up on the Governet if you need help." Mallory sighed and clung to the wall for balance. "I laid out new clothes for you on the bed." She shut the door and left it to Jane to adapt to her new body on her own.

Jane's brief career as a child actress was over, and the promise that she would get more acting jobs came to nothing. Her short stature and petite features that got her the SADF job prevented her from more mature roles.

Jane had forgotten all about the money that she had been

paid, until her dad sat her down to talk. "Jane, I want to tell you that we had to take some of your earnings from the commercial and help pay for your mother's treatments."

Jane's jaw tightened and she clinched her fists.

"You want your mother to get better, don't you sweetheart?"

No, she thought, maybe, as long as she leaves me alone. Jane's body relaxed, and she teared up at the loss, all her work and the last chance to use the money and leave home. Her dad misinterpreted.

"Don't be sad, Jane." He reached out to grab her hand and she pulled away. "Jane, it will be okay. Your mother is doing much better now. She's been seeing a specialist who is helping her stabilize."

Jane covered her face. *I'm not going to cry.*

Now she had to go back to public school. "Dad! I'm not going back to school. Only losers go to public school!"

"Jane," said dad, "the Czar of Education went to public school. They'll be lucky to have you."

Jane grinned. "Thanks Dad."

Jane walked around school like a twelve-year-old empress in her pinafore dress that fit her new curves and wore simple black bar shoes. "Jane, you look so nice today," said her English teacher, Mr. Yorke, who offered her a treat, "would you like some chocolate?"

"It is so great to see you, Jane," said another teacher. Other teachers gave Jane similar greetings.

However, some teachers feared that if Jane felt she was mistreated, the SADF would come after them. They walked quickly by her and averted their eyes. In the atmosphere where certain teachers were blamed for every problem in society from pollution to The Sterilization, fear was a normal reaction. The fact that Jane's commercials and the advertisements were seen on almost every bus, billboard, and TV show increased their trepidation.

Jane made sure to visit the principal at lunch and after school as often as she could. "Jane, I am so glad you have come to The Belmont Nanomed Middle School," said Principle Sklar, a balding middle-aged man with a swimmers build and a master's degree in business management. He was also the principal of the high school to save on administrative costs and exert *continuity of control* between the two schools. "We can use someone with your talent." He chuckled. "And it won't hurt recruitment to have a well-known celebrity in attendance." Jane nodded. "Please, come to my office anytime you need anything, Ms. Winston." He learned toward Jane as if sharing a secret. "Let me tell you, my friend the Czar is a big fan of yours." Jane beamed with pride.

As she exited the principal's office, Jane bumped into Theo Babar who ambled down the hall on his way to meet Francis for lunch. Though he was the same age as Jane, he stood eight inches taller. Theo excused himself, "Pardon me, I didn't see you," *down there*. Jane gave him a sideways glance and realized this gangly clown wasn't worth her time.

Principal Sklar's job was secure as long as Jane was in attendance. She was good for business. So the principal got her private tutors that met with Jane in the school after classes that her parents couldn't afford, and she gave Principal Sklar information about the other students. "Information is power," he told Jane.

On every visit to the principal, she offered news about what was going on with the students who either didn't notice her meetings with the principal or were too afraid to speak out about their suspicions. "Sir, did you realize that some of the students are meeting secretly outside of class?"

He shook his head and replied, "No, I did not know that. Thank you Jane. I'll take that list."

Jane slid a data disk with a list of students' names and their deeds and misdeeds on it over to the principal. She straightened her dress and leaned forward, eager to curry favor. "And some of them made fun of your nose," Jane told the principal, feigning shock at this revelation.

"Thank you Jane, anything else?" he asked. Jane smiled and caught his eye; she was happy to be making a valuable contribution.

Penny Carver visited Principal Sklar one afternoon with a dower look on her face.

"What's wrong, Penny?" he asked.

"Principal Sklar, I need to tell you about something that I…and others are concerned about. It's Jane Winston. She seems to be spying on us, and I…we…want to let you know."

The principal swiveled his chair away, screwed up his face, and then took a deep breath before turning back. "Penny?"

"Yes, sir."

"You say Jane is spying? How do you know?"

"Well, she's always writing down things that we say."

"Has she ever called you names, fought with you, stolen from you, or harmed you in any way, other than being a writer?"

"Well —"

"She hasn't, has she?"

Penny froze. "No."

"Who else have you told about this?"

"No one, I thought it would be good to come to you first."

"What did you say your student rating was?"

"I didn't, sir."

He tapped on his computer and typed in her name. "Penny

Carver, *B* rating, it was an *A* last year, and it could easily become a *C* this year, or lower. It could become an *A* again, that's up to you."

Her eyes opened wide.

He glared at her while he talked. "Did you know, Penny, that as a principal in Angeltown, I can have a student expelled for any reason, or no reason whatsoever? So I would be careful who you falsely accuse."

Penny glanced around, looking for a way out.

"Do you remember Mark Rogers, star of the football team?" He quickly waved it off. "No, of course you wouldn't. He was quarterback of our championship team, he talked back to me, and falsely accused me of all sorts of behavior. I had him dragged out during practice and expelled, permanently. So, if I can get championship winning quarterback expelled, I can certainly do it to anyone else."

She clutched her books close to her.

"And don't think about telling any of the teachers. I can have them fired just as easily. And your parents? Well, your expulsion would be my only recourse."

She froze.

He clasped his hands together. "Have you heard the rumors about truancy prison? They're all true." He looked back to his computer. "Thank you for coming to me. That will be all."

Others questioned the principle about Jane, but none had hard evidence and were written off as paranoid and threatened with expulsion. No one wanted to go to truancy prison, so the complaints stopped and students made sure to watch for Jane like they would watch for the teachers or staff.

Over the next two years, Jane continued to be well-known throughout the school by making the announcements on Fridays, singing and dancing at the talent show, and speaking at assemblies.

Theo found the best thing about the assemblies is he could

sit in the back behind the other students and work on this math homework. No one bothered him. Most of the time he listened to Paine's Pall Bearers, or other local bands he liked, on his school tablet with his wireless earphones. So despite what the administration called *important gatherings for school and community unity,* Theo didn't notice the proceedings, not even Jane's speeches, parts she took from speeches by the Czar.

> *Freedom is earned, like we earn our dinner and our air. When civil society merges its desires with those of the corporate state, the economy will once more be in balance. The needs of the individual must be sublimated to the needs of the corporate state so that all actions benefit the whole.*

---

The office of the Czar of Education posted a memorandum on the Governet about the failure of our economy. They concluded that the economy was failing because of teachers. Not all the teachers, but the old guard, the ones who couldn't adjust to the new mandates and clung to their unions. These teachers are *too lazy, maladjusted, supported socialist ideas, were too lenient on kids, were moochers, were overpaid, lived beyond their means* and *the reason our children don't learn. They must be stopped!*

One night Jane and her dad watched news about a rash of killings of teachers who violated the Moral Turpitude Laws of 2046. Jane knew that those teachers, the unionized teachers, deserved what they got; that's what everyone on TV, and her dad, said. "If some teachers didn't do anything wrong, they wouldn't be in trouble," he said. Jane nodded in agreement.

Her parents were the best kind of teachers and got to teach the Insiders' children. "One day you can teach for the Insiders as well. They already love you. Just be patient," her dad said. Jane read that *Of the forty-five teachers who were shot, all had criminal records, the most common offence being 'failure to teach within the scope of the curriculum.'* The other teachers were safe because they followed the rules.

Footage of a dirty, half-shaven man with an ill-fitting jacket and loose pants appeared on the screen coming down the steps of the Rampart Courthouse. "This former teacher was caught reading a book called, 'The Bridges of Madison County' in his class. It is a dangerous book about co-mingling and wasting time engaging in the non-productive act of 'sight-seeing.'"

They carted the unkempt man to a van and threw him in the back. Then they showed his mug shots on the screen. The Czar continued, "Of course the villainous rogue, the scoundrel teacher, said that he 'used the book to teach children about old customs, art and architecture.'"

Then the news reader spoke. "Let's talk to SADF Forceman Buggles who was involved in the apprehension of this dangerous teacher."

The shot opened on Buggles, a stout, barrel-chested male with a wispy beard and thinning hair. "These filthy, useless, literature-pushing villains forcing teens to read garbage from the time before history. It's dangerous!" Jane and her dad nodded in agreement.

"Thank you Officer Buggles." The News Channel cut away from the scene outside the courthouse and went to a commercial for Cock Asian Supremacy Restaurant, 'a Cock above.'

Jane continued to report to the principal and used her influence to get what she wanted: her favorite teachers, the best seat in the lunchroom, access to the faculty bathroom, and other perks. Students either made sure they were on her good side or like Theo, ignored her altogether. They didn't want to end up expelled, caught missing classes, then sent to Truancy Prison like other students.

When Jane reached the 9th grade, she ran for president of the Patrioteers Club, a club that represented the whole student body at Belmont Nanomed High School and was a model of student government for all of Angeltown.

To be a Patrioteer, you needed a triple A rating. And if you wanted to run for president, you needed three recommendations from teachers, the principal, or other administration. "Jane, I would be happy to write you a letter of recommendation for the presidency, and don't worry," said Principal Sklar, "I can get those other two letters for you as well."

"Thank you, sir."

Most people thought it was an honor to join the Education Czar's vanguard, The Patrioteers. Not surprisingly, Theo Babar ignored all entreaties to join what he called the *Nazi Youth of Angeltown*. He knew he could say that to almost anyone, and they wouldn't know what 'Nazi' was. They might think it synonymous with *patriotic*. Besides, Theo was too busy tutoring and coming up with plans for a rally to protest the student rating system and Truancy Prison to join any club.

All the presidential candidates had to make a speech and present their case to other members of the Patrioteers. Jane had a head start in the elections; everyone thought her family knew the Czar. She didn't disabuse people of that; in fact, she helped spread the rumor. She came to believe it herself over time. And with the help of the principal and support from her dad, she was guaranteed a victory.

"Dad," Jane said. "How do you get people to like you?"

"Are you worried about your speech, Jane?" he asked.

"No, but how do I get them on my side?"

"People don't have to like you. As the Czar says, 'To lead,

you must make some fear you, some admire and respect you, and others like you.' Besides, you are the best one of them."

After trying out her speech in the mirror a dozen times and once in front of dad, she was ready. "You think the language is okay dad, that our words will reach them?"

"Yes, I think we wrote a very good speech. They will especially like the part you quote from the Czar's lesser known writings." Jane nodded.

She put on a white dress, white stockings, and purple platform Mary Jane's. The last touch was curling her hair. *That would get their attention.*

Most were surprised when Sally Irvington didn't run for president. In fact, she wasn't even in the club anymore. However, Jane wasn't surprised. Jane knew Sally was a dirty liar who had cheated on tests. She told the principal about her cheating, and he found the evidence in Sally's locker. The liar denied it of course, thought Jane.

She made the last speech of the three candidates, and like a minister with her flock, she thrust her hands to the heavens. During her speech, students nodded in agreement, hissed at the mention of teachers, and cheered the mention of the Czar.

> *Patrioteers! In this new day, we face challenges like never before. We have been exploited, fellow students, by lazy and corrupt teachers.*
>
> *In spite of this horrible oppression, we have risen up against those who have encircled us, certain teachers would pit us against everything we hold dear. Entrenched teachers who refuse to move aside and let the newly indoctrinated teachers take control, would force us to break the codes of morality for their filthy ends. Teachers who confuse us with their words and lead us into the dark night of uncertainty*

*against the dictates of the Czar. As your president, I will bring certitude back.*

*The evil teachers fill our heads with what they euphemistically call 'knowledge,' encouraging us to think too much and tempting us with their cult of individuality.*

*THAT is not love. That is the hatred of the overeducated. Join with me, your new president, to fight against oppression in support of the true power of restraint of thought. We must rise up, humbly, as TRUE PATRIOTEERS!*

As she finished her speech, a banner unfurled above and behind her.

## Patrioteers United!

She won in a landslide despite many of the students not understanding much of her speech. Jane didn't understand it all either, but if the Czar and her dad wrote some of it, it must be worthwhile. The following week for her acceptance speech, Jane presented The Czar of Education's <u>Six Dicta for a Just and Productive Society</u>.

"Please stand while I read The Six Dicta." All the Patrioteers stood.

*1. Work is love of nation and all love is of nation.*
*2. The highest purpose is to help the nation fight against all foes, foreign and domestic.*
*3. Desire for what one does not possess kills the spirit. Acceptance is virtue; discontent means death.*
*4. Waste of resources leads to moral turpitude. Selfishly using resources to reduce one's own perceived suffering damages the nation.*

*5. Obedience in your heart, your head, and to your leaders is peace of mind. Questioning and disobeying is the path to suffering.*

*6. All dicta must be adhered to for the betterment of society and the security of its people.*

As the president of the Patrioteers' Club, Jane could help boost a student's rating, say from a B to an A. If they helped her get information about what was happening in the school and what students were doing, she would put in a good word for them with Principal Sklar. This network of patronage grew based on the perception of Jane's connections to the Insiders and her actual contacts with the principal and other important figures in the school.

"Principal Sklar."

"Yes Jane, may I help you?"

"I checked the footage on the Eduardo Martinez incident."

"And?"

"And one of the boys involved, Robert Isaac, didn't wear a mask of any kind and clearly he was involved in the assault."

"I guess it's time to deal with young Bobby," said the Principal.

"May I suggest, sir, that you get him to inform on the other two boys, the ones wearing masks, and have them expelled as examples."

"What about young Mr. Isaac."

"He's the weak link, sir. He was following the others. Besides, we might be able to use him again."

"Very good, Jane. I like the way you think." Principal Sklar wrote a note. "Give this note to his teacher in the remedial math class, and I'll deal with this."

"Yes sir."

Another student who came to Jane's attention was Clarissa Tyler, a student who Milly Sims said was making out behind the school.

"Principal Sklar, did Milly Sims talk to you about the illegal touching on school property?"

"Yes, Jane." He shook his head. "Making out behind the school. The rules are clearly posted yet some people choose to ignore them. It has been handled." He clasped his hands together and looked up from his papers. "It might do you well to stay in touch with Milly Sims. She seems so desperate to be popular that she will do almost anything. Perhaps she can assist us in some capacity later."

"Yes sir."

For all of her work monitoring the students her last three years at the high school, and as president of the Patrioteers, the administration offered Jane a deal. "Jane," said Principal Sklar. "Next year there will be an opening at the Reverend Manpower Academy as a content delivery specialist, and they have recruited you. You see, they are getting rid of the old teachers who teach with the old methods. The teachers who adhere to the teachings of the Czar, like you, will replace them. Of course, you must first finish your final year here and then start in the fall."

"Thank you, sir! What will I be teaching?"

"Your two strongest subjects, of course, computer technology and math. You already have college credit in both."

Jane's breath and heart quickened like a teenage girl out on a date with the dreamiest boy in school.

The principal continued. "They can give you a good salary and a faculty apartment to use that is close to the Academy. You will be doing all of Angeltown a great deal of good at that prestigious academy."

There is still more I can do to influence the students about the ways of the Czar through education, thought Jane. She responded confidently. "I accept." *I will not be there long. Other offers will be coming any day now.*

#

# Chapter 5
# Czar World

*Under the leadership of the Education Czar, students now have choices. They can take the path of the miscreant to Truancy Prison, or they can be the empty vessel, ready to receive whatever life requires of them.*
Office of the Czar of Education

"Hey Theo, thanks for inviting me to Czar World, I guess," said Chava. "At least I get to skip history class."

He shrugged. "If I want to keep my triple A rating, I have to go, so thanks for keeping me company." He rubbed his long, thin hands together as he talked. "And aren't you curious about the place? All of humanity's attempts to ignore what's going on in the real world crammed into one amusement park?" He frowned. "Besides, we couldn't afford to go on our own. So, why not?"

"Right, why not. Otherwise, we might not get to have the 'The Most Joyous Experience of a Lifetime,'" she said using air quotes.

Theo left with Chava on the 8 am transport from their school for the forty-minute ride to Czar World. The bus was bluish gray with white lettering on it that read:

## Compliments of the **Governet**

Highly rated students from Belmont High were on the bus and each AAA student could invite one guest. Theo invited Chava. *She's cool and smart and...cute,* he admitted to himself.

There were thirty students in all, mostly well dressed in slacks and button up short sleeve shirts with a few who wore t-shirts promoting their membership in math club, chess club, and propaganda club.

Most of the students were white, then Asian, and Latinos. None were African, except Theo who could claim African status on the *Decennial Body Count of Angeltown* with his father being a refugee from Tunisia. There were also two Black Americans, a boy and a girl, who sat together.

The bus rode on the elevated, specially constructed Czar World Expressway over redundant areas of Angeltown with gutted streets, collapsed buildings, vermin, and blight. It was the only road that led people from the still occupied regions of Angeltown and Saint Bernard to the theme park.

"Think of it this way," Theo said. "It's a trip to an exhibit of exotic animals. And you have a full spectrum of wildlife to gaze at."

"You mean the other patrons." She smiled. "Thanks Theo, you know exactly what to say."

Unconsciously, he leaned in closer to Chava. Chava didn't lean away. He pulled out the family phone he was given to use for the day. "I was reading up on Czar World on the Invisinet, our friend Larry showed me the search engine. Anyway, I found this article." He tapped on his phone. "You won't believe it." He tried to open the site but he couldn't connect to it. After a minute, he gave up. "The shuttle must be blocking the signal to my private network. Oh, well."

"Oh, no. Now you have to tell me, Theo." She punched his shoulder. "Just give me the highlights."

"Okay." He looked at her and his hands and face became animated as he talked. "There were three pandemics in the park before it was Czar World, the measles pandemic that occurred every five years since the year 2000 but was covered up by the media, the Covid-19 pandemic that couldn't be silenced, and shut the park down for a full year and nature punished the park owners for," he paused, "'failure to learn' with the 2035 American Flu pandemic with over 1000 deaths that lead to the park shutting down. The rumor is that the Governet created the last pandemic to take the park over."

"Wow. That's…I don't know. Diabolical," said Chava.

Theo grinned. "At least they didn't have to kill the former CEOs mafia style like in those old gangster films."

"Don't you watch anything other than horror and gangster films?"

"Why would I?"

Chava rolled her eyes.

They exited the bus and as they entered the park, they were bombarded with yellow, pink and purple decorations, banners, backdrops and characters.

A yellow and purple *Wally the Education Walrus* assaulted them with his cheer and goofy baritone as they entered, "Happy education to you!" he said with a big smile glued on his face. "Please join us for our lunchtime jamboree!"

A buxom blonde in pink over six feet tall dressed up in a sheep costume grabbed Chava around the shoulders as another sheep girl, a brunette, took a photo of them. The tall blonde looked at Chava, grabbed her hands with her sheep mittens and said, "Let's be friends; I can send you the photos!" Chava twisted her wrists outward and adeptly removed the gigantic girl's hands from hers. The girl frowned and put a mitten to her pursed lips.

Chava caught up to Theo who was watching. "What was that!?" she asked him.

"Molly, the Model Sheep. I read about her in their online brochure." He shook his head. "Where did you learn to do that maneuver with your arms?"

"My dad. He's always showing me how to defend myself. That sheep is lucky I didn't hit her in the stomach."

*We're lucky too.* Theo looked around. *You never know who's watching, and they wouldn't like people assaulting the workers,* he thought.

Chava frowned. "I think my dad wanted a boy."

"No way. Girls are much cooler." *Why the hell did I say that?*

"I don't think so."

After passing the entrance, they walked toward the main outdoor stage and saw one of the more popular groups in Czar World, at least with the parents, *The Bunny Rabbit Boys*. Chava and Theo stood just outside the tent and watched.

The group featured 16-22 year old boys dressed up like bunnies, each representing one of the Czar's six dictums. They wore fuzzy pink, purple and baby blue rabbit outfits, with big ears, feet and hands. Their noses had a prosthetic piece with large whiskers that took them at least two hours to attach every morning.

They hopped onto "The Stage of a Thousand Lights" under a gigantic peak marquee tent measuring over one-hundred feet in diameter, and after a minute of *hilarious hopping,* they jumped into song, a call and response chant:

Bunny 1: *Hop to it!*

Other bunnies: *Hop to it!*

*Do what is right!*

*Hop to it!*

*Do it with delight!*

*Delight!*

*Hop to it!*

*Hop to it!*

Bunny 1: *Don't resist what they tell you to do…*

Others: *Oooooh, oooooh*

*Do it now, don't put up a fight.*

*Oooooh, oooooh*

*Do it with delight, find that inner light, sanctify your sight…*

Bunny 2: *Work makes you free, so follow me.*

He gestured for the audience to follow him.

All the bunnies gathered in the center of the stage, hopping on cue and sang, *hop to it!*

Theo and Chava looked at each other, shook their heads, and walked away to explore more of Czar World.

Inside the park was *Apocalypse World* with its ride, 'Noah's Ark.' It was a boat, fifty feet long swinging on a giant pendulum, back and forth, back and forth. Devout passengers filled the boat and had a religious experience. Shouts of *Hallelujah! Amen! God Saves!* and other exhalations of religious fervor were heard all over the park if you listened for them. Theo and Chava walked over to see what the excitement was.

At the end of the ride, a god-like voice boomed out, "We have arrived; humanity is saved."

One patron shouted, "Mississippi Hell!" as they exited the ride.

Chava looked at Theo. "Mississippi Hell?"

"I think it's an exultation of religious fervor."

"Okay. What's Mississippi?"

"It's a state in the former Confederacy." He noticed Chava's confused face. "I'll explain that later. I wouldn't know about the state either if I hadn't found an old book about President Lincoln in the basement of the library."

"Lincoln?" she asked.

"I'll explain that later, too." He pointed at the ride. "Pretty amazing."

"Grotesque is what it is."

"Well, they gave us tickets for three free rides. See anything you want to try?" asked Theo.

Chava walked over to a three by four foot, free-standing map of the park and Theo followed. See skimmed her finger over it, stopped, and looked at Theo.
"There's a train around the park we could ride. I've never been on one before."

"Sure." Theo nodded and his afro waved back and forth. "I've never been on a train either."

Chava pointed past him. "That way."

At the Central Avenue Depot, Theo gave a young man their tickets. He was dressed in a Czar World uniform consisting of a purple shirt and shoes, yellow belt and hat that read *Czar World* in pink to match the pants. Theo looked at the worker's ID badge. "Simon, is there a better side of the train where we can see more of the attractions."

"Both sides are good." Simon looked around, leaned in, and whispered to Theo. "The left side is definitely better."

"Thank you." Theo said.

By 9:30 am they only had two other passengers in their car; people had yet to make it to this part of the park. Moreover, attendance had dropped since the park had opened due to rising temperatures throughout the year, The Sterilization, and the closing of parts of Angeltown.

Theo sat and Chava sat in opposing seats all the way to the left of the train.

He leaned forward to talk. "According to the book on Lincoln, he used to ride the train to different towns and make speeches out the back of what they called the caboose," said Theo.

"Caboose? What kind of the name is that?"

Theo shrugged. "I don't know."

"And how do you find all these books, anyway? I have never seen anything about cabooses in our history books."

"Promise you won't tell?"

"Who am I going to tell Theo? My parents?"

"Right. So, one of the keepers of the books at the library is part of an informal network of librarians who trade rare books back and forth and," Theo stopped before revealing his name, "and I asked this keeper one day about where Angeltown got its name, and they said, something like, 'you really want to know?'"

"And?"

"They started sharing history books with me."

The train started to move. It went about thirty feet and curved to left to start its big oval around the park. First they rode though a forested track with large trees and ferns on each side. The recorded conductor called out, "Please keep your arms and legs inside the train at all times. The next stop is *Salvation Island Station.*"

"Theo, have you ever seen so many trees?"

"Only in the movies." He reached out and ripped off sliver

of a fern leaf and sniffed it. He handed it to Chava.

"That's real. How are they able to grow all these plants?"

"I don't know."

"What, you haven't read about it in a book?"

"Hey!" Theo got up out of his seat and sat next to Chava and tickled her for a moment.

"Cut it out, Theo!" He stopped and his face turned red.

He pointed his thumb behind him. "I can go back—"

"Stay here, goofy."

They rode past Sheepland, home to Molly the Model Sheep. In the field they saw sheep dancing to a ballet composed by Justin Bieber, Ode to Bovidae in D minor, a Ballet for Sheep and Lambs. Behind the ballet, one sheep stood at an electronic whiteboard explaining an educational concept to the lambs who were sitting at desks writing and watching their teacher.

After the pink and purple festooned Salvation Island Station the next stop was *Constable's Station.* It had the only two roller coasters left on the West cost: *Death Row* that spun you around in combinations of loops and corkscrews until you couldn't wait to get out and *Psycho Cat,* based on the Governet's popular cartoon character, that leads you up and down hills and ends with you suspended upside down with your head facing the ground. They drop you and before you crash headfirst, the ride stops and flips you over and you land with your feet on the ground. In the cartoon, no matter what happened to Psycho Cat, it would land on its feet. Outside the ride was an animatronic puppet of the popular cartoon character covering its eyes and mewing its catchphrase, *Mississippi Hell!* every time the attraction stopped with the riders landing feet first, averting disaster.

"Well, that must be where the patrons got that exultation from, a cartoon. Unbelievable," said Theo.

Chava rolled her eyes. "No wonder I never heard it before."

The last stop before they ended back at *Central Avenue, USA* was *Illusion Land Station* with its hall of mirrors that distorted reality, mazes where visitors got lost, Hologram Mansion where each room had different holograms and illusions that you could look at, and the requisite shops, carnival games, and food stands.

The train stopped and Theo grabbed Chava's attention. "Let's check out the hall of mirrors." He ran off the train, and Chava shrugged and followed.

"Where are we going?" she asked.

Theo pointed at the sign. "The Hall of Mirrors. I read about on their website. It sounds interesting."

"What kind of ride is it?"

"It's not a ride. I'll have to show you."

They walked to the entrance and Theo gave the worker two tickets.

"Sir, please wait for other patrons to get further into the hall. We like our guest to have the experience on their own." He paused and looked at them with a grin. "Are you together?"

"Oh, we're just friends, right Theo?"

He nodded. "Yea, Chava is my buddy." He put his arm around her shoulders, squeezed, and quickly let go.

There was a ring tone from the entrance and the young man let them in.

The entrance led to a narrow hallway that reached a wall where they encountered two mirrors. One made you look taller, and the other made you look short and squished. Chava caught on immediately. "You take the left one and I'll take the right one," she said.

The left mirror made the bean stalk Theo look like a squat balloon with a head attached and the right mirror made Chava look like she was walking on stilts.

"Ha, I'm taller than you!" she said.

"Oh yea, switch!"

They switched mirrors. Theo looked like a tall, skinny, water starved tree, and Chava looked like a huge pear with an accentuated, round bottom. "Hey, my a...butt isn't that big!"

Theo leaned to his left and took a look. *It looks proportional to me.* Theo thought.

Chava grabbed his chin and force his view forward, toward the mirrors. "Stop staring, Theo!"

"Ow, okay!" *What a grip!*

*Does he really think of me...that way?*

Theo broke the tension. "Look, a hall to the right and the left. Which one should we take?"

Chava moved off. "The left one, of course."

They walked around enjoying, laughing and gasping at the different mirrors. The final mirror, curved one-way glass, had sensors behind it that scanned them head to toe and mixed their images as they stood in front of it, Chava with an afro, Theo with breasts that made his face turn red, Chava with thin arms and her muscular legs and Theo's wider nose and long neck. They laughed the loudest when Theo had Chava's purple page-boy haircut.

"Now that's a look. Why not try it?" Chava said.

*Better than suddenly having breasts.* "Maybe when I come back as a woman in my next life."

They started to exit. "You believe that stuff?" Chava asked him.

"Not really, but it's fun to think about."

"My Grandma Chava was a real believer in reincarnation."

"Interesting. What's your grandmother like?"

Chava stopped and was nearly in tears. "She passed away a few months ago." She cried.

Theo put his arm around her. "I'm sorry."

They both took deep breaths and after a couple of minutes, Theo removed his arm and they walked toward the entrance of the park. "I think the lunchtime show is going to start soon, so we better get some seats and free eats," said Theo. He looked at Chava. "If you're up to it."

Chava shrugged and kept walking.

They entered the area with the main stage they had visited earlier and waited for the lunchtime show. Theo put their lunch vouchers on the corner of the table and they received their food with a cherry flavored soda, Red Madness. "Could we have some water too," Theo asked the server. She nodded and soon brought out four balls of water for them, two centimeters in diameter, on a tray. Theo pushed his soda aside.

"You don't like Red Madness soda?" Chava asked.

"My mom loves it. That's all we have in the house half the time."

Chava took a gulp. "Well, I like it." She wiped her remaining tears on her sleeve and chuckled. "Well, this is an education. I'll give you that."

Theo took a ball of water into his mouth.

Chava watched Theo move the ball around his mouth then swallow. *That's what you do.* She tried it. *Oh, weird, squishy.* It dissolved.

Theo took Chava's hand. "Thank you for sharing with me."

Chava sniffled and nodded.

While Theo and Chava were eating peas and potatoes with their processed bird patties, a mixture of turkey, chicken, pigeon, whatever bird the caterer could get, the Patrioteers' Club started their performance.

Before talking, Theo looked around to see if he was being

monitored. "What do you think of this place?"

Chava wriggled in her skin. "It's surreal."

"It's a fantasy land."

"Is reality so bad that we have to create a fake one to get through the next day."

Theo shrugged. "For some. Wouldn't you like to forget your problems for a day?"

"I can't." Chava frowned and lowered her head.

They sat quietly for a moment, then several flash cannons exploded on the stage. An attractive seventeen-year-old female came out dressed in a dazzling white dress with matching cowgirl boots. Her dark hair flowed back and forth in synch with the tassels from her jacket and the skirt of her dress as she gyrated her body back and forth.

"Who's the singer in the sequined dress out front?" asked Theo. "She looks familiar."

"She should be. She's the one who does the announcements on Friday at school and sometimes sings at assemblies."

"What's her name?" Theo asked. Chava shrugged.

At that moment, Jane Caitlin Winston belted out the title of the song, "I will be singing *Angeltown, America's City*." The audience gasped and cheered. On the giant screen behind Jane appeared the title of the song. As she sang, the lyrics flashed above her head.

Chava got Theo's attention then pointed behind him to a QR code that had the words, *Today's Program* above it.

He took out his phone and aimed it at the code a few feet away. The schedule of events opened on his screen and he read the names as he scrolled to *Special Guest Performer, Jane Caitlin Winston, Patrioteer President and Former Governet Spokes-Model will be singing.* He showed the phone to Chava who shook her head.

Jane said, "This song is for the guests from high schools all over Angeltown who have joined us today." Then Jane put on her soft, cloying voice. "Unburden yourself." She winked coyly, and started prancing around the stage, microphone in hand. "Share your greatest desires." The backing music rose. She started singing in a powerful and lovely voice that made the audience jump to attention.

> *Some people want to stand out in a crowd*
> *they fight the norms and their voice is too loud*
> *they struggle every day; they struggle every night*
> *give in to your fate; don't put up a fight*

The Bunny Rabbit Boys hopped onto the stage dressed up as members of the Truancy Squad with badges, fake guns, hand cuffs, and army boots. A wave of approval swept over the crowd. The house lights dimmed creating a special effect called *artificial darkness* under the tent as purple lights from the foot of the stage suddenly flashed on and explored the performers' bodies, scanning back and forth. Jane started the chorus.

> *Work and breath, everything for the nation*
> *be with the crowd or be sent to damnation*
> *or you will end in bad situation*
> *there is no need for another creation*

Jane sang the chorus twice then went into another verse.

Theo felt a twinge of anxiety ripple throughout his body and missed some of the lyrics. "Though normal," the school psychopathologist in a sex-reduction workshop once told him, "these *hormonal reactions to stress* must be tamped down at all costs."

Theo and his male friends simply called it "horniness", and it was brought on by Jane's dancing. He tried to put it out of his mind. *I remember her from those State Auto-Defense ads when I was a kid. She's trouble*. Near the end of the song, it occurred to Theo that it was a warning to him and those who want to change the way things are. If he ever had doubts, he knew more than ever that the rally had to happen.

Most of the crowd was enraptured and stood in applause during the song. Chava was too nauseated by the canned sounds of the music clashing with the nationalistic lyrics to notice much else. It was all in good fun, the people thought, and they laughed and cheered at the sexual lunges by the male dancers towards the females who had joined Jane on the stage. Theo groaned in disgust at the dance and his own conflicted urges regarding Jane.

After a dance break with more prancing and lunging and one more verse and chorus, the song came to a crashing end of cymbals, power chords, and a loud thud. A deadly silence followed. The lights rose and the artificial darkness was gone. Then a robotic voice came over the loudspeakers. "Lunch is over. Proceed to your afternoon fun." Theo and Chava got up.

"That was nauseating." Chava turned to Theo. "Want to check out the lagoon?" Theo nodded.

They walked to the Lagoon near the middle of the park. People were milling about, eating their lunch on picnic tables, rowing in the lagoon, and other than a few students, everyone was white.

Chava turned to Theo. "I feel so out of place here."

Theo looked around for cameras then nodded his head. "This place certainly wasn't created for the likes of us. And that song. Is that how people feel?"

Chava grabbed his hand and squeezed. "You have nothing to prove. You do more to help people in school than any teacher ever has."

"Thanks," he said. He looked at her. "Let's get out of here."

They walked toward the early shuttle that brought them to their school and held hands on the way back, letting go as the shuttle stopped outside Belmont High Nanomed Academy. They exited.

"I have to go meet about the rally with some of the guys later. Wanna come?" asked Theo.

Chava grinned. "Thanks Theo. I better go back home and spend time with my mom."

"How's she doing?"

"Well you know…"

"Got it. If you want to talk about…it…I'm here for you." *Don't say cancer, man.*

Chava's eyes watered. "Thanks."

Theo gave her a hug and went in for a kiss. *Not the right time.* He slid his head to the left and kissed her on the right cheek instead.

---

When Jane arrived at home after her performance, she turned on her tablet: thirty messages from admirers. Jane smiled.

#

# Chapter 6
# The Benz Family Leaves Angeltown

*Angeltown contraction, along with The Sterilization of the Outsiders, means more for everyone and a better tomorrow.* Secretary of Happiness, Internal Memo

Fire Inspector Richard Houseman greeted Lieutenant Gomez at a fire in East Hollywood. "Lieutenant, there are two bodies inside. It looks like there was a spark in their cooker and something flammable, like paper, caught." Houseman looked at his notes. "The couple living there, Rita and Maxwell Benz," he looked up, "are charred beyond recognition." He tapped his note pad into his hand. "Smelled like barbecued pork ribs."

"Too bad we can't get ribs anymore," said Lieutenant Gomez.

"I have a source if you'd like a hookup."

Gomez ignored the comment. "Do you suspect any foul play?"

"These cookers have a history of failure, and if the wiring in the house isn't up to spec, it can lead to sparks and in the case of the couple here, death. Bad luck and bad wiring, I'd say."

Gomez waved over Detective Van Heimlich of the SADF.

"Look up the Benz family, the victims, see if there are any red flags."

"Yes, sir." Detective Van Heimlich left to look for witnesses.

Gomez looked at the remains of the house. "Anything look strange about the pattern of the fire?"

"You mean why didn't it burn the house on the right and the left?"

"Correct."

"We thought of that. It seems the cinder blocks on one side and bricks on the other stopped the fire from spreading." He noted the Lieutenant's furrowed brow of disbelief. "And we'll look into it."

"Who called it in?"

"I couldn't tell you," said Houseman. Gomez frowned. "The call was anonymous."

"And where was the call from?"

"We couldn't track it."

---

As Fire Inspector Houseman and Lieutenant Gomez discussed yet another Angeltown fire, Rita and Maxwell Benz rode their overstuffed motorcycle with sidecar and saddlebags into the San Bernardino Mountains, now officially called Saint Bernard. They bought land under a pseudonym for their escape from the city, and the seller didn't ask questions after they offered to pay full asking price.

After a slow, wobbly ride up the mountains on the uneven road, they made it to their Balch Camp property. Maxwell was stout, handsome like a rugged woodsman, balding, and reliable. He was handy and mechanical, a must in the wilds north of Angeltown. Rita was five four with an average build and light brown hair. Her intellect was superior. She could have been a grandmaster in chess or the Chinese strategy game Go. She chose instead to be a master computer hacker, "For the good of society, of course," she would say. The truth was she liked the pay at first, then she liked sticking it to the Governet.

Rita pulled off the strap that held their tent to the back of the motorcycle. "Let's set up the house first and then we can place our belongings inside."

"Of course," he said. "First things first."

After they propped up their yurt with the central pole and outer stakes, five meters in diameter and three meters high, they turned on their mini-satellite dish and checked the connection on their laptops to the Governet and Inivisinet.

"I have a connection," said Max.

"Me too."

They rolled out their six solar panels on a large rock in a clearing and connected to their computers. Exhausted, they fell asleep on their sponge like, air pocket mattress.

They woke up with the sun and ate dried fruit and nuts with a little water and planted seeds for a future food source. "Let's set up the traps," said Max. Mainly they were hoping to catch rabbit and squirrel but could also prepare birds and other small mammals for meals.

They hung their moisture collectors to gather water from fog that came off the ocean from the west. The irony of the rising temperatures is that while it decimated the planet it led to increased evaporation of the oceans that the Benz family collected in the mountains as the saturated clouds floated past.

Maxwell was constantly worried, and thus he asked his wife on more than one occasion, "Do you think they will be able to track us here?"

"You mean the cyber branch of the SADF? I don't see how.

We're dead, remember?"

"Right. But I got wind on the Invisinet that the five banks we worked with on cyber security are cooperating with the Governet on tracking down hackers." What Max referred to was their work with The Belgian Trust Bank, Hitachi Global, Alibaba Confederated Bank, The German Central Bank, and the Soros International Bank.

"My love, do you think I would leave a trace to us?" asked Rita.

"No. And you never got caught before. So why would it be different now?"

"Correct, and remember when Cyber Activist THX1138 helped us bounce our signal off the Governet's own satellites. Brilliant!"

"That should do it, I guess."

Rita and Maxwell brought down the Universal Cloud with other hackers in 2034, and they knew they had to leave Angeltown, lest they be arrested and killed.

Rita and Max had seen too much suffering at the hands of those they served to continue. The banking cartels now controlled the sale of human body parts, taking over after the Czar and his goons in the Governet shut down the organ cartels. It was a boom market with organs from desperate, scrabbling people regularly selling to the wealthy who couldn't adapt to the heating climate and contaminated environment ravaging the poor. Bodies had been cleaned for their meat, but fortunately, there were enough feral cats and wild pigeons to eat for protein. Insects, once ridiculed as a source of food in the time before history, were now a staple.

The Benz family faked their own deaths using two corpses they got from skid row through an SADF connection, someone Rita had helped recoup over one million pieces that had been stolen from them during a net scam. The agent put Rita and Maxwell in contact with two characters who would do anything for money, the Williams Brothers. For an agreed upon price, the Brothers brought bodies and put them in the family kitchen, near the cooker. The couple did the rest. Thus, Rita and Maxwell were able to fake their own deaths and not harm any living individual in the process.

During the time of The Sterilization, the birth rates collapsed. Almost no one outside of Saint Bernard was conceiving, so Rita and Max had not planned on having a child.

"Max, I'm not having my period."

He grabbed her hand and touched her forehead to check for fever. "Are you sick, too much physical activity, stress?"

She shook her head. "What kind of son did Evelyn Benz raise?"

He shrugged.

"Remember when I hypothesized that there was something in the air, or the water that sterilized women in Angeltown?"

"Yes."

"Well, perhaps the effects on me wore off and—"

"You're pregnant? What, amazing!" He jumped up and did a little jig. Then he kissed Rita what seemed to her one hundred times and squeezed her tight, then he grabbed her hands and looked into her eyes. "You're sure?"

"What else could it be. It fits. We left Angeltown a year ago, I had my period once a month, and I haven't had one for more than six weeks."

"But maybe you're late." Max said. "I hope you're not late. Honey, this is great. Let's get started with your diet and exercise and what are you going to listen to, or read, that's important, I better learn about being a midwife, and—"

"Max, shh, please calm down. You're more excited than I

am. Let's wait a couple more months to make sure it's happening before we get our hopes up."

Maxwell became nurse, mid-wife, and home birth attendant for his son's birth. They didn't even know what to name him until Maxwell looked around their land, saw wild artichoke growing everywhere, and said, "Let's call him Artichoke."

Rita gave Max a big kiss. "That's a great name, Max! My man Max," she said, smiling.

Artichoke, Artie, was born with hair and a smile. Only after seeing his balding dad's bearded visage did he start to cry. Soon, Max's beard had become Artie's favorite plaything, and he tugged on it endlessly.

Artie was breast fed until one day before his first birthday when he bit down on his mother's breast, slapped her nipple with his tiny hand, and said, "no!"

Rita held back her scream. "Ow, okay little guy. I get it. Time to ween you, eh?" She tickled his little toes. Rita saved milk for a while and Artie took some now and again, but he no longer collected it from the breast. Tiny brown haired, dark-eyed Artie ran around with bare feet and seldom got even a scratch. He would bruise and get cuts, but he healed rapidly. They lived without purpose except to care for each other. Then Artichoke started to ask questions.

---

"Well Artie, we left Angeltown because we didn't like what was happening in the city," Maxwell told his precocious four-year-old son. "We didn't like the environment and there wasn't enough open space for us."

"Like the forest?" asked Artie.

"Yes. Like in the forest."

"Okay," said Artichoke. Clearly satisfied with the answer,

he ran off to play in the garden with his mother. Artie liked hiking and exploring, but most of all, he liked learning with Rita, especially about the computers, the "little mind machine" as his mother called it.

"Mom, what is the world?" Artie asked after seeing the world on the Governet.

"We live on a planet called Earth. That's what we call the world. Earth is big to us, but small in the universe."

"The universe?"

"That's everything we can conceive of beyond Earth, the stars, the planets, the other solar systems—"

"The moon?" Artichoke asked.

"Yes, and our moon."

"So the Earth is small?"

"Compared to the universe, yes, but not compared to the moon."

"So…to a squirrel, we're big, but an insect is small."

"Yes."

Artie grew up without the social pressures of other children and their taunts. And without TV, he learned about the world firsthand without the propaganda. "Artie," mom said, "remember that not everything you read on the computer is true."

"But how do I know when it's true?"

*Oh, boy,* thought Rita. "You ask questions, like does this sound true? And then you see if someone else says that same thing."

Artie scrunched up his face.

"I guess you need an example. What if I told you whales were originally wolves?"

Artie giggled. "You mean those big swimming mammals were once doggies. No way!" He brushed the idea away with a wave of his hand.

"You're good not to believe me." She smiled. "But what if I insisted?"

"I don't know. I could say, prove it."

"Okay." Rita opened a computer sitting on her lap and quickly searched sites on the Invisinet that talked about whales coming from *doggies.* She showed Artie. "This one is from the French Oceanography Institute, here's an article from Doctor Ramona Grijalva from the University of Mexico, and…" She stopped and looked at Artie who was staring up at her. "That's all." Artie grabbed the computer and started reading.

There were no kids or teachers around to tell him what his limits were or what was expected of him. *Mom and dad are all I need*, thought Artie.

"Mom, can we play some number games?" asked Artie, now eight years old.

"Sure, sweetheart," she said, "but first, I want to talk to you about your latest lines of code for *Teddy.*" Teddy was a coding language named for his toy bear that Artichoke was writing. So far he only used it for programs that created mazes in different shapes on the computer.

"What is it mother?" asked Artie with a serious look on his face.

His mother grabbed him and gave him a big hug. "It's nothing dear, nothing at all. I was only going to say that your coding language is perfect. You could remove this section here," she pointed at the screen and circled a line of code, "and have the same outcome."

"No mom, it's a single repeat to verify the first pass, don't you see?" said Artie.

"Now I see it! But I haven't shown you when to use that yet," she said with pride. "How did you figure that out?"

"I just saw it." Coding was as easy to Artie as breathing was to other kids. Even though Rita's IQ was a recorded 170, she knew that it wasn't long until Artie would understand things about computing that she hadn't conceived of.

"Artie, did we get much water from the collectors? The clouds were heavy last night."

"Some, but it looked dirty. Can we clean it, or should we give it to the plants?"

"Have your dad check it. Perhaps it just looks dirty, but it's still okay to drink."

"I could check it."

"Artie, you were going to study some Spanish first. Spanish being banned is even more reason to learn it," she reminded him.

Artie smiled, "Si, entiendo mi madre." He looked over to his dad. "Max!" he shouted. His dad, who was fixing a tear in the tent, turned to look. "Maxwell, por favor, chequea a la agua, es limpio o no?"

Max laughed and answered in mock seriousness, bowing slightly, "Si señor Artie." With that, he finished a few more stitches and walked to where the water collectors were concentrated.

Rita yelled out, "And honey, can you check our solar array."

"Yes, my love." Max had to keep himself useful, only having an IQ of 140.

They hacked into the Governet to produce all of Artie's birth records and place them in the required databases, including a Social Security number, just in case. Artie was officially an orphan left at some now defunct church so there was no question about his parents. They hid his personal files in a separate partition that could be accessed at any moment if required. Cyber detectives would only be able to find it if they searched for it, and even then, there were no irregularities, so it looked just like a regular entry.

Artichoke learned exponentially. At first, Rita was uncertain that taking a black-market supplement to enhance the intelligence of her fetus was a good idea. However, both Rita and Max thought that if they were going to have a child in this terrible world, they were going to give the child all the advantages possible. That meant boosting his brain growth, neural activity, and synapse production with whatever supplements were available. Max figured that Artie must have an IQ of around 200. Experts would later confirm that estimate.

"Artie, are you ready to help out the family with a new task?" asked his father. "Take this card writer, it's old and that's why the SADF Cyber Division can't track it, and stick this card in." His dad gave him a blank plastic halo-card with a chip and a magnetic strip. Artichoke already knew how to do this, but he played along. His mom had shown him months before. "Is it in the recorder, son?" his dad questioned.

"Yep," Artie replied.

"Now, your mom already got into the corporate database of Prestup Pharmaceuticals and accessed their corporate credit account. They travel a lot to Russia, and they won't miss a few hundred pieces spent on miscellaneous expenses overseas." *And by the time they do miss it, if they do, it will be untraceable.* Artie put in the card and looked at the laptop screen, then clicked the downloading application, clicked on the halo card, and hit enter. In an instant, five hundred pieces were added. After ten seconds, the card popped out and they had shopping money.

Soon after, Artichoke started riding with his dad on the family-engineered hybrid motorbike (biofuel and solar with sidecar) from their Balch Camp land to Crabtree about once a month. They caught or grew most everything else they needed.

They always cut Artichoke's wild hair before each trip.

"Time to cut your hair, Artie. We don't want to draw attention to ourselves," mother said. Maxwell was now nearly bald and he preferred to shave his head. He blended in well with the rural California biker survivalists with his reddish beard and clean scalp.

Max and Artie communicated with headsets in their helmets on the slow drive down the mountain, and Artichoke enjoyed this time alone with dad.

"Max," asked Artie, "if time isn't constant, why do we measure it."

"Great question," his dad encouraged, being careful to stay on the winding, corrugated road. "We measure time as a social convention so that things happen on a schedule humans understand."

His questions became more complex over time. "If the computer isn't like a brain, what is it? Can it be better than a brain?" asked Artichoke.

Max swerved to avoid a boulder in the road. "Great question. So far, the brain is the most complex system in the known universe. Nothing else is close. Perhaps someday you will create a computer that can think."

Some young boys imagine themselves shooting a winning goal or being the first man on Mars, but Artichoke imagined himself in a white coat with safety goggles and gloves on, creating a supercomputer that calculated faster than any computer ever before, a thinking computer.

As part of his research into biocomputing, a topic that fascinated Artie, he asked questions about the meaning of life and cognition. "How do we know we are conscious?" he asked his dad on another one of their rides.

"Dr. Tononi says that consciousness comes from awareness of existence and this awareness is based on responses to stimuli and the creation of new neural pathways in the brain, more or less.

However, I don't think we can know what consciousness is," his father said.

By the age of ten, Artichoke had lost interest in the talks; he had surpassed his dad's knowledge of most things except for a few subjects like Freud and Flemish painters, topics Artichoke found no use for but his dad loved. He preferred silence, a chance to let his mind explore. *Is there a physical limit to a computer's speed, can we put nanoprobes inside our brain that can implant memories, how can we use DNA for computing?*

Artichoke had increasingly become dedicated to his mom's teachings. To sate her son's curiosity, Rita hacked into the science databases at M.I.T. and Berkeley for her son to browse, and she collected over 200,000 books for him on a reading tablet. "Why don't you read Henry the Fifth, Artichoke?" his mother asked. "You like history."

"What use is Shakespeare?!" *What a waste.*

His teacher, mom, didn't mind. "Shakespeare isn't essential to your education," said mom. "Work with your programming language for now if you want. You have an hour."

After an hour of reading and playing with the lines of code, Artichoke and Rita walked around the scrub land. They had set a line of jute twine as a hand-hold to help guide them as they walked the maze looking at their dozen traps. One small rabbit was all they had, but three other traps were sprung, the bait gone. Dad was tending to what was left of the garden, a few carrots and a couple of potatoes, some wild greens was all he could gather, but that was enough for dinner. The next day, it was on to Crabtree for the every-few weeks shopping trip. This time, they had to pick up more clothes for Artie left for them at the diner in Crabtree that they had ordered from a fake account.

Maxwell strapped Artie into the sidecar, checked the fuel

lines and the solar cells, tested the mini-satellite and searched for radio stations. He knew his son was bored talking to him during the hour trip down the mountain, so he came up with a solution. He leaned over to talk to Artie who already had his helmet on, one they had to order for him to travel with his dad. "Hey Artie, mind if I listen to the radio? I downloaded Doctor Asthana's lecture you were reading about on the potential of biocomputing. Want to listen to that?" Artie reached out from his sidecar and gave his dad a hug. Maxwell smiled. "I guess that's a yes."

Father and son made it to Crabtree and back in time for a late afternoon lunch and a game of Constellations with Rita. Dad was clever, even if he wasn't as smart as his wife and son, and he won his fair share of games. Rita was the master of moving the stars and creating gravity wells to trap her opponents or propel her spaceship to victory, but Artie was catching up and was soon beating them most games. Once he mastered the game, he became bored and spent all his free time working on his research in programming and supercomputing. Thinking back, he wished he had spent more time with his parents and less with computers.

#

# Chapter 7
# The Rally

*There are dangerous elements in society that need to be pacified, and thus I have directed the Truancy Corporation of America to send members of their Truancy Squad into every high school in the nation to protect the students from these elements.*
Education Czar, October 14, 2050

    Eighteen-year-old senior Thelonious Babar, student leader of the United Students of Angeltown (U.S.A.), led a walkout on the final day of the school year, May 14, 2053 in the largest school district in the nation. All the middle and high schools that were left in Angeltown had students walk out, the Belmont High Nanomed Academy where Theo enrolled, had the most students at the rally. The elementary schools had all been closed because no students in the city, outside the Center, were born less than thirteen years ago.

    "I wonder why no one else is in class today," Senior Patrioteers President Jane Winston said to herself. "This might be the best math class ever."

    Theo had a AAA rating, but he had many friends who lost brothers and sisters to Truancy Prison for *failure to learn* in a one size fits all test and curriculum regimen. So he started U.S.A and organized the protest with fellow students.

    "Leave the tests to the sheep!" shouted students in Mr. Carr's algebra class as they walked out when the testing tablets were placed on their desks. Even Bob walked out that day; more than anything because he hated Mr. Carr for bullying him for struggling at math.

The students took different routes to the library and left at different times in the morning. They traveled in groups of no more than threes, usually in singles or pairs. All ethnicities in the schools were represented at the rally and all gender preferences, or no preference at all. Some went directly to the rally, being too afraid to go to school and walk out. Some, after being dropped off, walked toward the library instead of into school. Students who lived further away left their homes early and took city buses; the money for the transportation was donated from the Emma Goldman Underground Copy Center and students with extra pocket change.

Some students went because *it was cool*, some were genuinely angry, and others, like Francis, were desperate and did not know what else to do. Theo was sick of it all, the loss of an education and the *fascist regime of the Czar*. Whatever the motivation, the walkout started as a success.

Most students wore black arm bands to symbolize "the death of education" as Theo and Francis agreed would be the theme of the day, and a few students volunteered to hand some out as people arrived. Those who arrived early sat on the low wall that separated the walkways from the drying trees in the once lush garden outside the Central Library. They sat fidgeting with eyes wandering in case of trouble and paced up and down the walkways. A few sat in silence and read, or pretended to read, or chatted about nothing with other students.

Theo didn't show up to class that day. He went directly to the library and arrived at eight in the morning as the others came. He carried a pass he forged that read, "Thelonious Babar is excused from class to do his final term paper research," so he was able to stroll leisurely and wait outside the library that wouldn't open until ten. Theo also carried his *AAA Student Standing Card* in case he was stopped and questioned. That had worked in the past when he had been pulled over. However, it was not needed that day. In fact, there was less security than usual when he arrived. He saw Chin sitting on the wall where the fountain was dried up and out of service. Theo sat next to him as he took deep breaths and tried to stay calm.

"Hi," said Chin. "My mom thinks I'm in class. I'll be in trouble, but…" Theo nodded and smiled.

Most Angeltown teachers went on with the testing and gave the absent students a zero as instructed by administration. They assumed it was laziness and moral turpitude keeping students away. "Damn student's. They never used to be this lazy and non-compliant," said Mr. Carr.

Jane's teacher was glad that two of her best students showed up and she could give them college math problems while she browsed Ray's Pawnshop on the Governet for new earrings.

More than two hundred students had arrived by 9 am. The diverse crowd eventually reached about five hundred students all crammed into the garden by 10 am. There were no police barriers to blockade the rally. Everything was going as planned and better than expected.

Students chanted and waved signs that read, "This is the real test!", "Bring back Art", "No more Truancy Prison" and "No test is the best test".

Theo had learned an ancient song from Uncle Caesar, *This Land is Your Land,* by a man named Woodie Guthrie. The whole leadership of the U.S.A. learned the song. As more people gathered, they sang the song from the time before history and people quickly caught on by reading the pieces of paper with the lyrics on them that were passed around to the crowd. By the time the last verse was sung, most of the people had joined the throng.

There were cheers, grins, and dancing all around. Thelonious got on the top step leading into the library to speak.

Francis was slightly behind him on his left and other close friends and recruiters were to his right.

Theo waved his palms upward to encourage the crowd to yell their chants louder. "Louder, louder, louder!" The shouting echoed off the walls of the library and buildings that surrounded the long, rectangular park, and it seemed to Theo to go on forever. Finally, the crowd quieted. Thelonious trembled inside, but his voice was calm, clear and direct.

> *Thank you all for coming. Before I speak, I have a former Patrioteer from BNHS here to talk to you.* There were a smattering of boos. *Be fair. Everyone can grow, and we must be open to all allies. So please give a warm hand to the brave, strong and intelligent, Sally Irvington.*

Theo gave Sally the megaphone. She pressed the button and there was a lot of feedback and static as she started to speak. Her brown hair was long and braided back and she wore white shorts and a t-shirt that said *SMILE* on the front with a big smiley face. She finally moved the megaphone away from her face and the feedback subsided.

> *Hello everyone. Some of you know me as that miss know-it-all in your math class or the girl who was always sickeningly nice to everyone.*

*You got that right,* yelled a boy from the crowd. A few students chuckled.

> *Well, I learned that there is more to life than grades and triple A status and the Patrioteers Club. I learned from Theo, from all of you, that many are suffering, and if one suffers, we all suffer. And I want to make sure that I don't regret not trying to make a real change in my school, for everyone, not just lead fake cheers of loyalty.* Sally started to cry.

Theo approached and gave her a hug. The students cheered.

He took the megaphone from her and talked into it. "Give it up for Sally, and everyone who came today!" shouted Theo. There was wild applause with a few die-hard skeptics booing, and Sally walked back into the crowd greeted by mostly smiles and pats on the back. Now it was Theo's turn.

> *Friends, our lives are in danger, and we have the opportunity today to unite as citizens of this city. We must unite against the greedy, selfish, hateful, misanthropic elements of Angeltown, The Insiders, the Czar, and his ilk!*

Some students in the crowd gasped, for it was unheard of to say anything against the Czar. Other people shouted approval. Bob leaned over to explain to his friend what *misanthrope* meant. She nodded and grabbed his hand.

> *We must not turn on one another, collaborate with the Contributors who sell us for a few pieces. We must reach out to neighbors, students AND teachers, who have been scapegoated far too long for the economic trouble the elites have created.*

The crowd clapped though a few booed the mention of teachers. Theo paused to look out at the ever expanding crowd. *They are hearing his, their, message.* He briefly turned and nodded at Francis who gave him a thumbs up.

> *We must take free speech back, and today is the first step. Education is less and less accessible. Our neighbors, brothers and sisters are being put in prison in record numbers.*

Some in the crowd were tearing up, others were angry, some cheering. Chava arrived late after helping her father at home. She wore jean shorts and a plain gray t-shirt, and was out of breath from running. She cheered from the back of the long walkway to the library entrance and pumped her fist. "Go Theo!"

> *Teachers are being scapegoated and blamed for a lack of resources, low wages, and a curriculum they are forced to use that stunts their teaching and our learning. Education is creating compliant students who learn to parrot the words of the oppressors and learn to oppress their own families and friends. We demand today that school becomes a place of learning once more and not a place of control. So from today we will...*

The sound of a firecracker exploding in the distance grew, echoed around the park, then made a hallow thud like nail hammered into a melon as the bullet split Theo's head. The projectile exited the back of his skull spewing blood and brains behind the target. Theo Babar, leader of the USA, was dead. The SADF sniper had a draft of his speech and knew when to shoot to make the point the Czar of Education intended: stop independent student action.

More than two dozen Angeltown Police assaulted the crowd from the right and left of the garden, over the walls and past the trees. Crack teams from the Truancy Squad and the State Auto-Defense Force joined them along with a squadron of mini-attack drones that had been waiting above. Bob and his date were subdued with Nanomed Stun Gloves (repurposed defibrillation paddles) that gave bodies up to 25,000 volt shocks. Francis was cudgeled bloody with batons to the head and legs. Chin ducked into a scrub and exited the park after the police passed his position. However, his friend and classmate Nancy flopped like a fish on a ship deck inside a barb-hooked police net. Sally was lucky to only be tackled and thrown into a van on 5th Street as she nearly escaped. Others were scooped into the beds of two dump trucks that roared up the steps from Flower Street followed by several large police wagons, trapping most of the protestors in the gardens.

The scoops of the trucks smashed bodies, severed limbs, and if the protestors were lucky, only left their bodies severely bruised. Limbs, heads, and bruised bodies were all mixed together in the truck beds. Those who could stand were put on display in front of the world on the nightly news. The Governet showed the story to the world only after the initial chaos and bloody take-down of the rally. Angeltown authorities had created the story of the events for the media. And the media broadcast the *official report* as gospel.

Chava's instincts took over. She swallowed her pain and grief when Thelonious was killed, turned away from the library entrance, and started running. She ducked her head, trying not to be seen by the drones or the police forces. She heard the trucks coming toward her from Flower Street. In her high-top sneakers, she moved left and saw a chance to escape.

Chava squeezed into a long-slotted storm drain on the edge of the courtyard and covered the front with branches from dead trees. Moments later, the trucks rumbled by. She curled back like a trapped animal as she heard the swarm of drones buzz past. She froze in terror, and her mind drifted.

---

All the kids in school thought Chava was Mexican. White kids would taunt her by shouting *Chaaaava Chaaaaavez!* They didn't know she was named after her mother's mother, Chava Cohen, and that Chava means 'alive', 'living' and 'animal' in Hebrew.

Her grandmother moved to Angeltown from Israel during the depopulation of the Middle East. The International Resettlement Organization helped move her Grandmother Chava to Angeltown in 2039. Otherwise, she may never have escaped the rampaging desert sands.

Grandma Chava was tiny, prematurely wrinkled and bent forward. "My Little Chava, how are you today? Would you like a story?" Her grandmother loved her more than anyone ever had, so Little Chava couldn't hate her name. When Chava was feeling down about herself, Grandma would cheer her up, "Remember how you helped that stray dog in the back yard, snuck it food? And I know you stand up to bullies for the smaller kids." Grandma said, "You are a good person who helps all creatures." Little Chava smiled at the praise.

Grandma read books in Hebrew to her granddaughter even though Little Chava didn't understand them at first. *Elvis the Camel* was one of her favorites, a story of an injured Camel that was helped by a family that found him. While too simple for her in English, it was the right level to help her learn Hebrew.

Her Grandma Chava had died the same year Chava entered high school. She still cries at the loss, and it sometimes comforts her to remember what she used to say, "You never lose someone if they are in your heart."

---

Chava shielded her face while the police marched over and past her and imagined grandma telling her about sneaking over the fence to visit her neighbors in Israel, the stories of the wall coming down were the land had dried up, the last flowers she picked from her garden, the stories of the Palestinian boy she had once loved and the respectable Rabbi she married. "Who knows who one wants to marry when you're only twelve?" Grandma Chava said. Little Chava knew one thing. She knew she was never going to marry anyone who loved her less than grandma had.

As her mind wandered, she heard a voice ring out, "Get out of there, come down RIGHT NOW…" She jolted to attention to realize the voice was calling from a few yards away. Peaking her eyes out from the sewage drain and through the branches, Chava could see a boy no older than eight who had foolishly climbed a ten foot tall tree as he tried to get away. He was a little Black kid she recognized from her neighborhood, a child Chava never paid attention to. The boy was crying and shaking and as he got out of the tree. The goliath officer put his gun to the boy's forehead and pulled the trigger. "Damn, making me shoot him," the White officer mumbled under his breath as he turned away.

Chava pushed herself back into the sewer. She was numb, stunned at the bombardment of her senses, the smells of the gas, the stench of the sewer, the smell of the earth, the air, the concrete. Her chest tightened as she gasped for air.

Cracks of gun fire and gas canisters being shot into the crowd punched her eardrums, then came the screams. Chava started to differentiate the screams, putting them into categories, from blood curdling to terrified to a shouted grunt of someone being hit in the stomach, hundreds of varieties, hundreds of voices.

Chava moved away from the carnage. Her hips and legs scraped on the cement as she wriggled side to side, inching backwards down the drain. *My damn hips!* "Ugh." She writhed into a larger opening and landed in the main, fifty-four-inch diameter 5th Street sewer. She was covered in excreta slurried from the library and surrounding buildings and marinated in a penetrating stench. Fortunately, the bumps and scrapes were only minor.

She was able to stand her bruised, five-foot-four body in a bent position. The pungency of feces and flesh churned Chava's stomach, and she bent over, ready to vomit. Nothing came out. She scanned left and right, barely perceiving the passageway in the faint light sifting through small vents from the street above.

Chava turned right and shuffled one foot before the other toward Pershing Square searching for a large crawl space to exit the sewer along the way. On her right, streams of light came down from the street. She saw a rusted ladder illuminated by holes of a manhole cover above. Here was her chance to leave the tunnel. She climbed up the ten feet to the two-hundred-pound drain cover. It didn't budge, even a little. She pushed and pushed with no effect but to bruise her shoulder.

Chava, stooped over, trudged onward for what seem further than the five kilometers she ran at school to a narrow drain that branched off to the right. With nowhere else to go, she slithered her way on her elbows and knees down the twenty-four inch diameter tube, anticipating that this led to the park at Pershing Square. After more scraping and bruising, she arrived at an eight inch high, three feet wide drain opening with faint light coming through the slots.

She turned her head to the left to squeeze it out of the slot. Once her head was out, she flattened her shoulders to get the past the opening. Like a baby out of a womb reaching for the fresh air, she sidled forward. Her hips stuck in the opening. *Damn my hips!* Chava wiggled partway out. She took deep breaths for the final push. *If Grandma Chava could survive war, death of her family, and interrogation by the resettlement agency, I...can...*"get ouuut!"

Chava collapsed with bruised hips and legs onto a cement slab near a storm drain. Her eyes adjusted to the darkness of the garage basement. She sat up and leaned against a wall. Chava no longer felt the pain of her body but the pain of loss and grief at the death of Theo. She sobbed.

In the darkness, she saw the contours of the parking garage basement: cement supports, a hint of a staircase, faint white lines on the cement near her. *Pershing Square.* Her chest rose and fell as she breathed slowly like she would on a long distance run. Chava relaxed, sat against the wall, and cried herself to sleep.

She woke hours later curled on the cement floor of the garage. Now the pain in her body enveloped her, her legs throbbed and a headache had her skull in a vice. *I need water. I need home.*

Thoughts of her family, father and his mother, compelled her to move. And the fear of death, worse, of prison, propelled her. She was shaking from the day's brutal events. *Oh Theo!* She never had seen anyone killed nor heard such screams. Chava had been protected from these realities.

Home was miles away. She skulked, sidestepping like a vertical crab while clinging with her back to the cement walls. Every breath ached. It was silent like the inside of a coffin. Chava inched up the stairs to ground level. The formerly lit downtown outside of Pershing Square garage was half-lit, and remnants of the sun created a brilliant orange halo on the horizon. A few lamps still burned in the cavernous downtown as the light dissolved into dark. Chava was shocked by the passage of time. *How many hours did I sleep?* she wondered.

A few offices remained in the city center: recovery businesses, investigators, security firms, eviction and reclamation specialists, and miscellaneous small offices that could still profit with cheap rents in a collapsing society. The Angeltown Transportation Division ran a few buses to downtown, but they would not be active after the attack at the library.

Chava left the lot, walked out to South Hill Street, and headed toward 8th. She bent her head in a futile attempt to hide the purple ends of her hair, a shining beacon in the dark, from the drones' and stalkers. She picked up her pace.

As she marched along, she stayed away from the few lights she saw. Since the banks had left the center of Angeltown, there were fewer patrols to avoid. The same was true about surveillance cameras; there was little left to watch over. Random people from Skid Row, the homeless or squatters, wandered the streets at night. Drones were used to spy on them.

On this night, most of the indigent had moved out of sight or had already been rounded up and placed in The Pits after the events at the library. Chava's eyes and ears scanned for any disturbance, for she knew some people would elude the SADF and feared they could overpower her without much difficulty.

When she heard a drone, Chava ducked and crouch in a vain attempt to avoid their cameras.

As she reached 8th Street, Chava heard a buzzing close to her head. She dove behind a trash heap and held her breath. The buzzing receded. She heard a thud from where a drones had gone.

"Let me go, let me go, I'll cut you!" shouted a man to no one as he flailed his short collapsible knife in the air. Then Chava heard an electrical *zap* and a scream echoing off the buildings. The man was stunned into silence. He had been stalking Chava, and in her fatigued state, she hadn't even noticed him. She shivered at the thought of what might have happened to her and was now at full alert.

The drones flew off, and Chava waited until she heard them no more before moving. She knew that the SADF would arrive soon to take the stunned man to The Pits; she had to move. The drones she feared may have saved her life. Chava was sweating, her pulse was racing and her head throbbed, but she had no time to feel her pain if she were to get away.

Chava veered and ran south toward 9th Street on the edge of the occupied corridor. Like a bad dream, she was stuck in mud as she ran, breathing heavily. *There must have been a pollution cloud through here earlier.* She ran to the right across what was once a parking lot and into a space between two abandoned buildings and waited, quietly listening. Chava heard a loud heartbeat, tensed her muscles and gazed around. Finally, she realized it was blood pounding in her ears.

She jumped at the loud rumbling horn of an air raid siren

followed by a marine horn, the siren of an SADF cruiser passing on the street she had just crossed. She assumed they must be coming from Rampart, the fourth version of the infamous police station and torture facility. Chava had to make sure she didn't cross their return route, so she would have to avoid 8th Street. When she heard the siren wind down as they picked up the man trapped in the barbed net, she went out the other end of the lot and ran down Olive as fast as she could. She ran, and dodged garbage, car carcasses, cement remains of roadways, and other debris.

Chava went south, away from Skid Row and the wanderers and also away from the SADF. In a few short blocks, she was in uninhabited land, a part of Angeltown that had no electricity, no water, no habitable buildings, and plenty of rubble, vermin, and creeping flora. The sun had gone, and what remained was the inkiness of an unoccupied part of Angeltown. Chava stopped running and got her bearings.

---

*"Chavez!" shouted her coach. "Why did you stop running? You might be the best miler on the team, but if you run against Saint Francis, they will crush you! Get out there and run another mile...run, run, run!"*

The further Chava got from 8th Street, the more relaxed she felt. *Don't relax.* She was elated what seemed like minutes ago at the library, and it all went wrong. *The wrong reached out in all its wretchedness and killed hope, killed...Theo.* She sighed. *I have to keep going.*

She smelled the foul air, listened to the scurrying rats, raccoons, and feral cats, and adjusted to the darkness as a half-moon filtered through the pollution. Chava felt a sharp stab into her stomach and a rattling thud of wood. "Damn it!" she grunted and doubled over. She held her stomach. There was no blood, just a gasping for air and the lingering pain as if being hit in the stomach by a rock.

Chava reached forward. She had been poked by the limb that was sticking out of a fallen tree. In her anger, she grabbed a protruding branch and kicked it with her left leg. It cracked. She kicked it again, and the branch snapped off into her hands. It was light and strong, about five feet long. She used this stick to find her way in the dim light. It bounced off the trunk as she crept forward. She veered left to circumvent the tree, tapping along the way as she moved around it. Chava tripped over a piece of concrete, nearly falling. She briefly stopped, sobbed, sucked in some air and advanced.

After thirty minutes of navigating concrete, trash, metal scraps, burnt out cars, and other detritus, Chava hit something that gave out a dull metallic ring. She groped forward into blackness and touched a chain-linked fence. Chava had come across the remains of the 110 freeway. Most of it was collapsed with a few segments of ramps and roadway remaining. It was officially off limits years ago as the Insiders shut down parts of Angeltown they no longer deemed viable.

Chava bent over and put her hands on her knees. *Damn! I'm not going around!* Chava remembered seeing the fence along 8th Street Place. It was at least ten feet tall, but there was no wire on the fence. She could pass around it, but she would risk being seen by drones, the SADF, or the Truancy Squad. She had seen them far too often these days, and they showed little mercy.

Fueled by anger, Chava threw her walking stick up toward the other side of the fence. It hit the top, and she side-stepped it on its return journey. She moved back a couple of feet, careful to reach out her foot so she didn't trip over anything. Then she jumped forward and heaved the stick. It was silent so long that Chava thought the stick had stuck on the fence. Eventually, she heard a faint sound of wood rattling back and forth.

She grabbed the fence and started to climb. It dug into her fingers and her legs cramped at the exertion. She tried to take large strides; her body tensed and rebelled in agony. After a few feet, she slipped downwards. She could handle the pain, but if her legs cramped up, she would never make it home. She stretched and punched her muscles to relieve the cramps. She thought about her father's devout mother. *Grandma Chavez, pray for me now.*

On the next attempt, she dug her shoes into the links of the fence and kept moving upwards. She grunted with each hand-hold and footstep and used her powerful legs to propel her. After six steady lunges, she felt the top of the fence. No wire. She pushed against the fence, bounced up, and swung her legs over the top. Chava stopped her momentum before flying over the other side.

She maneuvered her body so she hung downward near the freeway debris, and then jumped. Her left leg hit the edge of a concrete roadway and her right leg hit the dirt. She fell back and was braced by the fence as it caught her. *My shoes are useless*, she was thinking as she tested her left ankle. It gave her a slight twinge when she stepped on it, but she could walk.

Chava smelled something horrible, like a dead rat in sewage. The odor belonged to her. She felt around and touched the concrete roadway. There was a sharp edge with rebar sticking out. She moved carefully, avoiding the rebar and crawled up on top of the slab. She scraped her hands and knees on the surface, reached out, and found the stick. She wheezed air into her lungs.

Chava scuttled along the side of the fence on her right, and she reached a paved roadway that marked her return to the occupied corridor. She sighed at the sight of lights that shone up ahead in occupied apartments near her home. She clung to the shadows and continued.

The rally at the Angeltown Central Library appeared to be a total shock, a terrorist plot fiendishly planned by the worst elements of society: North Mexican revolutionaries, anti-government mongrels, armed sub-humans (ASH), and failing students. The rank and file of the State Auto-Defense Forces, the Truancy Squad, and the Angeltown Unified School District Police were caught off guard. However, the top brass under the leadership of the Czar of Education planned every detail of *Operation Early Graduation:* the timing of the assault, the weapons used, and the tactical plan for eliminating the threat. The takedown crushed all opposition to future educational reforms from the Czar, including the soon to be implemented work-study program.

Afterward, the Angeltown security forces were directed to investigate the particulars of the rally. How could the protest subvert the security forces with all the electronic surveillance in Angeltown? How did they coordinate the walkout? And most of all, who were the leaders?

Millions of pieces were spent and hours of Governet footage were scanned and entered into data bases for clues as to who the leadership of the rally was and who was involved the uprising. After the protests, the Czar banned all use of paper, the "tool of riots and unrest." The Czar declared protest a capital crime. The attack on the students wasn't broadcast on the television, the radio, nor the Governet, and the murder of the leaders was not in the news.

After the initial chaos and bloody take-down of the rally, surviving students were cleaned up and displayed in front of the world on the nightly news before being sent to prison. Angeltown authorities had created the story of the events for the media. And the media broadcast the *official report* as gospel. This show played on international news channels for months, with warnings to the public such as "look for any strange behavior", "confiscate all suspicious and out of place pieces and scraps of paper" and "parents and teachers, monitor your children and students' behavior closely." Clouds of smoke were seen for weeks afterward from official paper burning sites.

---

Commander Gorn of the SADF video-conferenced with Lieutenant Gross, coordinator of *Operation Early Graduation* on their direct VPN connection. "Lieutenant, what's the status on the aftermath of the rally?"

"Commander Gorn. The information from your source panned out beautifully, and most of the subversives from the rally have been captured or otherwise delt with."

"That was a brilliant idea helping the rally commence as planned, and even better, having the Czar's Office secretly distribute flyers for the rally in all the classrooms in Angeltown through a few well-placed operatives."

"It is our duty to expose as many terrorists as possible," said Gross.

"Indeed! I think you've earned a promotion." Gross smiled. Gorn took out a rare Guamanian cigar from a box made with Brazilian rosewood. "How long until you have all the undesirables from the rally in custody, Lieutenant?"

"Within a month, sir."

#

# Chapter 8
# Teachers

*Dedicated to a man of God and the people: God bless you Reverend Manpower.*
Plaque outside the Reverend Christ Manpower High School.

*I will meet the Czar one day, and we will fix the education system together.*
Jane Caitlin Winston

On the last day of high school before Jane's speech for winning student of the year, Jane was called to Principal Sklar's office. He took her hand and gave her an envelope. "Here's your assignment for the Reverend Manpower Academy." Jane jumped inside. *I can't believe it, a chance to leave home and make a difference.*

"Thank you Principal Sklar. How can I ever repay you?"

"No need. I've got a new job on the inside, in Saint Bernard, working with the Czar's Office monitoring school improvement, partial thanks to your contribution to our work here." He smiled at Jane. *You know, I'm going to miss her, but somehow I think I'll be safer with the Insiders. Things will only getting worse here.* "My wife and I will be moving away tomorrow."

Jane got home and opened the envelop that contained a disk

with the description of her job. She would start going to staff meetings in a week, so she better get planning. She would have her own apartment furnished by the school and be given special security clearance.

She went to talk to dad. "Daddy, I have so much to tell you. I have found a job, a teaching job, one with good pay, and roo—"

"But you have barely graduated high school, how could you—"

"You always told me to befriend the right people, and Principal Sklar recommended me; it seems I got the job."

"When do you start?"

"I start teaching in a couple of months, but we have meetings next week and I have planning to do and I need to pack my things so I can move into my new apartment down the street from the school."

"What school are you teaching at, Jane?"

"That's the great thing Daddy; it's the Reverend Manpower Academy."

Chuck nodded and sighed. "Your mother will be devastated, but at least you will be at a good school."

Jane smiled, *I know.* "Let me tell her right away." She skipped to her mother's study where Mallory sat in the dark and stared out the tinted windows. Jane stopped at the door before entering. *Gee, I haven't skipped in years.*

---

Harry Campos, lanky, glasses, short curly hair, approached Jane Caitlin Winston after her first day of teachers' meetings at the Reverend Manpower Academy.

"Jane, right?" he reached out his hand, smiling amiably.

"Yes." She allowed him the privilege of shaking the tips of her fingers.

"Just wanted to let you know that we're a team and we are here to help, if you need. Not trying to presume or anything…"

Jane smiled falsely, "Thank you, you're so kind."

"Harold. Call me Harry," he answered.

"Harry, how could I forget?" Jane said as sincerely as she was able.

"Well, good luck. See you when classes start." Harry walked toward his residence.

Jane waited to make sure they weren't walking the same direction, and then walked off toward her new home.

Jane couldn't believe her luck, and she almost skipped again. To teach at Reverend Manpower Academy and unknown to her, to be paid double that of Harry and the other teachers. All she had to do in exchange was monitor student activity on her special network tablet. "Jane," said principal Manpower, the reverend's fifty-two year old daughter and executor of her father's estate, "we need your help making sure this is a safe place for everyone. So we have assigned you some extra responsibilities. In exchange, you will teach only one section of government and one section of computer technology."

Jane looked up and said, "That is very generous, Principle Manpower."

"Call me Mabel," she said, patting Jane's hand. "Oh, and before you leave today, visit the nurse. You need to leave a blood sample." Then Principal Manpower lied for the first time since her father died. "Every teacher has to leave a sample."

---

Harry, who once taught poetry and English literature, was relegated to teaching business English and computer basics. He knew the Education Czar thought poetry was immoral, but Harry desired to ready poetry to Jane, like he used to with his ex-wife. He approached her one Friday after the end of the school day.

Jane guarded against distractions and unwanted solicitations. She tensed up when she saw him approach with a piece of paper in hand, ready to read. *Does he like me?* She paused to regain her composure and quickly recited the dictums in her mind in short form: *work, purpose, spirit, morality, truth and security.* After remembering her purpose to lead a humble life in service to the Czar, Jane coldly addressed Harry. "Harry, paper is not allowed. Next week then." She gathered herself, straightening her skirt, and left.

Harry had been in love before, married, but his wife left him to move into the City Center to live with a Contributor. He thought he had loved his wife. He loved how beautiful, no sexy, his wife was. But his wife always thought she could do better, and used her malice and other assets to trade up for a wealthier, more powerful model. "Harry, you'll never be more than a…Harry," Mitzi told him when she left. "How could I fall for such an ugly creep like you?" But Harry knew. *You fell for me long enough to get out of the Rampart slums. Then you traded up.*

There were things much more important going on than pining over a young woman at thirty-two years of age. Was he in so much grief that he had to prey on younger women and not find a woman his own age? Jane was pretty, and not stupid, but she was also uncaring. Like society.

One day Harry entreated her. "You could come over for some tea, or dinner or we could just take a walk."

*Oh no, I can't, I just can't. What if I like him?* She closed her eyes and focused on her purpose. "Harry, you're nice," she said, "and you are not bad looking, but I can't. Who knows how long I will be teaching here? I have a future beyond this school that doesn't include you. But we can still talk, if you need."

Harry never met with Jane again; he turned his energies into writing tragic and apocalyptic poetry and teaching his classes. Even so, Jane thought of him every once in a while. Harry was the first to court her. *But we were ill matched...ill matched indeed.*

Moreover, Jane had to learn about the new surveillance tablet she had, how to use it to track students' devices, the movement, their contacts, actions and behavior as she was hired to do. Key words such as *cheat*, *steal* and *hide* as well as words like *free, speech, elections, vote, democracy, freedom, thought, individuality, independence, revolt, protest, march,* and many more had to be traced. *That list is so long. Good thing I have it on the software,* Jane thought.

Jane would go to Principal Manpower's office every week for an update on her classes and other work.

"Jane, how are the classes going, more importantly, how is your other job going?" asked Principal Manpower.

"Perfect," said Jane. "I am glad I can make a difference.

"So are we," she said to Jane as she patted her hand.

Jane's apartment was an oasis where she could relax, work on her classes, write speeches and send out letters to the Czar of Education over her Governet laptop about how to improve education in Angeltown. She worked at her dining table next to a display of the only physical book she owned resting on a stand, "Diary of a Young Girl." She picked it up at the closing of the Glendale Public Library when she was nine because she liked the title. Jane knew the "Diary of a Young Girl" was just a book, but she still felt bad for Anne, the main character. It was so clever the way the author got into the mind of a young girl. *I wish I could write like that.* Everything else she read was on the Governet, whether it was entertainment, history, reports, or news.

On the first day of school, Jane put on her ankle-length beige skirt and purple top. She tied her long hair into a ponytail and put on her glasses. She didn't need to wear glasses, her eyes were perfect, but this pair would pick up any illegal wireless signals in the classroom and indicate where the culprits were.

Jane stood in a large auditorium of two-hundred seats and looked at the students from below. She placed her bag on the desk in front of her, pulled her tablet out, and tapped the center of the screen. She had one hundred students on her roster for her 9th Grade class. However, when she looked at the seating chart on her screen, thirty-seven seats were empty.

Her job was to keep the kids on task. "Students!" Jane belted out with the help of a special voice augmenting collar around her neck connected to the room's hidden speakers. "You must keep your eyes and minds on the task at hand, and not let anything distract you: not the noises in the room, not the other students, not the sensations in your body. Nothing. You are assets, and we are investing in you. Make sure our investment pays off. Moreover, if you use any wireless devices other than your tablets, we will know. And when we find out, you will be expelled."

Jane looked around the room at the nervous students. "Do you understand?" Some of them raised their hands. "Do NOT raise your hands, tap the appropriate response into your tablet." On every tablet on their desks appeared two buttons, a "YES" and "NO" selection. "Do you UNDERSTAND!" she reiterated. The students quickly clicked the *yes* button.

Classes now used the new software Quicklearn, and operated under the new mandates of monastical silence in the class as dictated by the Czar of Education.

She clicked on the menu that said, "Report." A table with the names of the thirty-seven absent students appeared on the left with comments on the right about why they were not in class.

The same message appeared thirty-seven times: Missing.

*Hmm, I wonder why they are missing.* She continued, "Attendance is down, so we expect more from those who are here." She looked around the room. "Do you understand?" Only one button appeared on the screen as their choice. It read, Yes.

A few students murmured aloud, "Yes."

"If you answered aloud, you clearly do not understand. You will be responding to me through the computer only. No speaking is allowed in class. If you wish to talk to me, type me a message or send me a digital video file." Again she asked, "Do you understand?" Only one voice responded aloud. The rest of the students clicked their *yes* button. Jane tapped a few keys on her tablet and a message appeared on the screen of the student who was talking: "You have been put on notice." The message was automatically sent to the principal's office and the student's guardian at home.

"Now hit the start button and get started," announced Jane. A large button filled the center of their tablet screens. Every student hit start with auditory comment.

Ms. Winston stood erect in the front of the room as the students started tapping on their tablets. She moved her eyes between the tablet and the students and slowly wandered around the room, watching to see which students concentrated as she walked by. After a few minutes, a name flashed red on her tablet, indicating that the student had gone under the 90% time on task threshold. Ms. Winston tapped the name, and a message was instantly sent to the student. In the student's earpiece a voice spoke out, "You have gone below the *time on task* thresh-hold and are in danger of being expelled." He picked up his pace and started to answer some of the questions incorrectly just to keep up with the required productivity.

Several of the male students got messages in their earpieces, "Keep your eyes on your work," as their eyes wandered to look at Ms. Winston as she slowly sidled by the young men. In disbelief, they looked back at their tablets. There were only two students who got expelled during the semester, one female for *failure to learn* and one male who could not keep his eyes on task. Otherwise, most of the days were the same: a teaching journey with a new curriculum.

It was similar in her politics class. "Remember, time not on task is time for the forces of madness and criminality to set in," Jane often stated.

At home, Jane ran the diagnostics for her class and produced a spread sheet that indicated their ratings. She noticed that two of the students had a C rating and were close to being expelled. She sent out the standard message to their media devices, and their parents and guardians would receive the message that night. The Woman in Pink would appear on their television, tablet, computer, phone or holographic belt.

The Woman in Pink had a stern face and was dressed in her favorite furry pink suit that she had designed with a frilly light-pink shirt along with her Czar World pink hair, "Dear parents and guardians of students in the Angeltown Unified School District. This message is to inform you that your child is close to being expelled for *failure to learn.* Please be advised that this would mean grave consequences for your child if they were expelled. It could mean truancy prison, or worse." Then her voice changed to a friendly, syrupy, singsongy tone, a smile on her face with her right hand raised and fingers wiggling, "Thank you for your time. Tootles."

Jane unwrapped and put her dinner dish with salad and chicken in the cooker, a metal cylinder about a foot high with a clear dome top and hit the cook button. The salad remained cool on the plate while the chicken was hot. *Strange, I never used to like chicken when my mother served it.*

She sat down at the table between the living room couch and the small kitchen area. As she ate, she looked at the updates to the computer software Quicklearn with the news channel on in the background. The Czar was talking about further closures of parts of Angeltown. In accordance with Czar Law 51, all citizens with have to evacuate the following areas: Crenshaw, Leimert Park and Parkview neighborhoods by tomorrow, August 30th. Failure to leave the areas immediately will lead to arrest.

Then there was also an interview with the engineers at the *Coso II Geothermal Park* about the secure future of energy for the City Center, Saint Bernard.

She checked the four other channels that the Governet ran. She turned on Middle Eastern Hunt on the Game Show Channel and touched the side of her tablet, enlarging the show on the white wall next to the table on the opposite side of the room.

Currently on the show, there was a chase over rocks with a man, tan with a long beard, who was running along a jagged mountain side. He looked down and the camera panned to show a deep chasm. Thirty-feet above him was the top of the cliff. Two men with guns ran onto the screen and looked around. "Martin!" shouted one man.

*I like Martin,* Jane thought.

The man who spoke clearly outranked Martin. He pointed to the right, "Look over there, I'll check over here."

Martin's legs look even bigger than before, thought Jane. *He must work out a lot.*

His body was bullet shaped and his arms thick, like pythons. Every muscle bulged and his veins popped. The camera followed Martin. Suddenly the angle cut to Martin's point of view as he ran.

The view got close to the ground. *He must be on all fours,*

Jane imagined. Jane felt a sense of vertigo as she looked over the cliff with Martin. Jane was startled with a shout of, "There you are!" from Martin. Out of the lower left corner of the screen she saw a man in terror. Then the camera bumped, clanked and shook as it smashed up against the rocks.

Again the shot changed, this time to a longer shot of Martin scurrying down the rocks like a mountain goat.

He's so fast, thought Jane.

Martin started to move toward the suspect, "Okay Ahab…" The man cut in. "My name is NOT Ahab, I'm Raul, from Dove City!" Martin kept advancing, "Sure Ahab, time to turn yourself in."

Cut to a commercial: "This show brought to you by Powerlock Security, featuring the Cell 32 Gate. Criminals come in, but they never leave. Good against cars, armored vehicles, and even crazed footmen. In chromium black. Available on Governet.org.

Back on *Middle Eastern Hunt,* Martin quickly advanced on the suspect. On the screen, a question appeared: "Should Martin throw Ahab off the cliff, lift him up and carry him to justice, or kill him there?" Jane never knew what to answer in these cases. They are all good choices, and she's sure the real Ahab did something really bad like rape someone or murder a family. Now she regretted not turning it on when she got home.

"The vote is in!" said the announcer. "It's a tie, 37% for kill him there, 37% throw him off the cliff and 26% for take him in. That's much higher for *take him in* than I predicted. This ought to be special," the announcer shouted. Arms flailed between Martin and Ahab, until Martin knocked Ahab's arms away, grabbed him by the neck and lifted him up. He did all this while balancing on the edge of the cliff. Jane started sweating all over, and her heart raced watching Martin's demonstration of strength. Martin was crushing the man's trachea while lifting him over the cliff edge. Just as Ahab was about to breathe his last breath, Martin dropped him. The camera followed the man down the cliff until he was out of sight.

After a five second pause, the announcer spoke, "Stay tuned for bonus footage of Martin demonstrating how to subdue a suspect."

Wow, thought Jane. That was really something. The show came back on and Martin, as advertised, demonstrated how to take down suspects who were armed with knives, clubs and even swords. Afterwards, the announcer spoke, "On the next episode, Martin and Captain Brick take down a gang of fifteen of Mohammad's most dangerous men, on Middle Eastern Hunt!"

After the show, Jane put her plate and utensils in the Zapper, a small metallic box just large enough for one dinner setting. It zapped her dishes clean with a minimum of water use. Then, she laid out her clothes for another day, put on her pajamas, recited the six dicta and went to sleep.

> *Jane walked toward the school, and with each step she was farther away from her goal. Harry exited the school and walked toward her, holding paper in the air. Light poured out of the pages. Jane shielded her face with her hands and arms from the blinding brightness.*
> *Martin appeared out of nowhere at her side, poised to defend her honor. Harry stretched out his hands and pointed toward Jane. Dozens of students ran at her. Martin intervened and punched and punched this band of ruffians, each one flying out of sight with one blow. Eventually, he faced off with Harry. Martin punch him in the stomach, over and over and Harry laughed loudly with each blow. "Sir Martin, you are not worth*

*my words, you indelicate brute. As for your maiden there,"* Harry pointed at Jane, *"You can have her."*

# Chapter 9
# Artie and Dad Take a Trip

*From this day forward, the Internet will no longer be a tool for the subversives, radicals, and terrorists to use to undermine the goals of this great nation. Today, the Internet dies and the Governet takes over.*
The Education Czar, February 14, 2035

Artie and his dad packed for another trip to Crabtree. They brought their reusable mesh hemp bags, two fake-leather saddle bags, a credit card with five hundred pieces loaded onto it, their riding helmets, and goggles. They looked like hippie steampunk explorers. "Ready to go Artie?"

"Sure, dad."

"It's almost your mom's birthday. Maybe we can find some wildflowers, mint, or rosemary to bring back for her."

"Can we look for lizards?"

"If we have time, perhaps on the way back at Roger's Crossing."

"Okay." Artie knew that if dad didn't come through this time, he would make sure they got to look for lizards on the next trip.

Artie was in the sidecar and dad started the motorcycle with the biofuel ignition that gave out a slight roar like the guttural sound of a wild cat on the prowl. Their solar batteries were fully charged, so the journey would be quiet, like a stealthy Interceptor X2500 at one-tenth the price. The military green motorcycle had two solar panels over the polymetal containers on the left and right of the vehicle. There was a tank to the left side opposite the sidecar that contained biofuel and a micro-satellite dish three inches in diameter just behind the driver's seat. They were on their way.

Max pointed out a scraggly coyote on the side of the road jumping up and down in an apparent attempt to catch a rat he had his eyes on for breakfast. It was nice they could still see some wildlife that they weren't eating for supper. Otherwise, the trip down was uneventful with dad listening to satellite radio, whatever he could access, though he preferred *holopop*. Artie listened to a lecture on using DNA for data storage. They both listened through their helmets.

They arrived at Crabtree at 6 a.m., and they parked behind a local bar in an alley out of sight from the main road where they had parked the vehicle safely before. Then they went to breakfast. They would be long gone up to their Balch Camp compound before the bar opened.

What Maxwell failed to realize on this trip was that this was the morning after Saint Patrick's Day, still a must-celebrated holiday for drunks. A man using the alley to relieve himself on his way home saw their vehicle. "What the hell is that?" he said. He stumbled and turned to show his friend who was still in the bar settling their tab. Then he looked back to gape at the strangest motorbike he had ever seen. The man brought out his phone to take a photo, sending it up to the Citizen Cloud to his *Buddy Network* and *Plain Folks* accounts. He had to take a couple of photographs to get it right. He laughed and shouted, "Happy Saint Patty's Day", forgetting that it was the morning after the holiday.

Max and Artie ate their scrub-fresh eggs with coffee, tea and water in Ted's Diner. They were in luck; they had wild turkey sausage that day. It cost them a pretty piece. Afterwards, they shopped at the general store, a combination grocery and hardware store named *Crabbies*.

Soon, the Cyber Division of the State Auto-Defense Force got a hold of the photo of the strange motorcycle and started to investigate. Warren turned his screen with the photo on it toward Barb who sat to his left chewing gum. "What you make of this, Barb?"

She stood and leaned over to get a good look. "Well, that is the darnedest thing. That doesn't look like any model of motorcycle I've ever seen."

"Me neither," said Warren. "I'm sending it up to investigations, let them figure it out."

Barb slouched back into her rolling office chair and stared at her screen. "That's what I would do."

The SADF tracked some irregularities at Ted's Diner near Outlaws' Bar where the motorcycle was found and also at *Crabbies* in Crabtree. It seemed that prepaid cards were being used, prepaid cards from corporate accounts, accounts that no one noticed such as the governor's office on immigration and pharmaceutical travel accounts.

Instead of risking a trip into the mountains where an unknown number of perpetrators might be holed up, the SADF waited for the next shopping trip of the criminal hackers. Then they would be notified by local merchants of the masterminds' arrival.

A month later on their next trip, the father and son were approached in the diner by two heavily armored SADF forcemen. They surrendered without complaint, not wanting to be killed as other hackers had been.

On July 4, 2047, the Rural Branch of the State Auto-Defense Force arrested Max and Artie Benz, two counterfeit masterminds with links to cyber theft.

Artie was in a small room at the former post office and his dad was in another room down the hall. "Here's the deal, Artie," said Doctor Lee, cyber investigator for the SADF. "Your parents are known cyber felons, and you are linked to criminal activity. They can do hard time in The Pits." Doctor Lee looked at Artichoke, "Do you know what The Pits are?" He slid his phone with a photo of Pit #1 over to Artichoke. "Do you understand?" he asked.

Artichoke nodded silently. For emphasis, Lee added, "The Pits are abandoned holes dug for high rises that were never built. The amenities are clay floors with cement walls, open toilets, dirt beds, with no shade nor protection from the elements of any kind, including the increasingly frequent pollution clouds." Artie sat, worn out and in shock. "Think about it," Lee said as took his phone he exited.

While he waited, Artichoke stared expressionless as he calculated the amount of energy you could save using DNA as a storage medium. Within ten minutes, Doctor Lee came back. "We came up with a deal for you," Lee explained as he showed Artie the tablet with the agreement on it for him to fingerprint. "You like computers, right?" Artichoke nodded. "In fact, you're a savant, a genius." Artichoke flushed. "You even wrote a virus that you inserted to the Citizens' Network cloud and have been designing your own computers since you were six."

Artichoke looked up, "How did you—"

"Your dad told us. Max is a pretty nice guy. It would be a shame to put him in The Pits with *real* bad guys." There was silence. "I will leave that for you to read over," Lee said as he pointed at the tablet. "I will be back in a few minutes." He stood to leave. "Do you want anything, soda, water, snacks?"

"No," Artie replied, focusing on the text in front of him. The agreement gave Artichoke a choice: enter Caltech University and commit to work at least five years in their cyber crime's department, or they would put him in juvenile detention for at least six years and also incarcerate his parents.

When Lee came back into the room, Artichoke handed the tablet back to him. Artichoke had circumvented the tablet's security and added some text to the agreement: *Rita and Maxwell Benz will be able to retain their land in Balch Camp and 20% of Mr. Artichoke Benz's salary will be deposited into a secure account for Rita and Maxwell Benz.*

Doctor Lee grinned after noticing the changes to the agreement. "I think Caltech will be very pleased to have you, even if you can't accomplish your goals of creating an AI system."

Artichoke was also impressed, "As my mother always says, it's good to do your homework, Doctor Lee."

"Your mother is a smart woman."

The conditions for their cooperation included that Rita was allowed to surrender safely when the SADF went to Balch Camp to arrest her. Moreover, they would not be required to turn in any of their collaborators from the Great Cloud Crash of the 2030s. Other than his wife Rita, Max didn't know anyone else involved.

After satellites verified that Rita Benz was the only one occupying the Balch Camp land, as Max had told them, Lieutenant Garcia and Doctor Lee rode up in their Caravan with Artichoke and Maxwell Benz in the second row of seats. They got out at the top of the road and looked down on the land. *That's a very impressive set up, water reclamation, solar power, gardens, shelter,* thought Lee.

"Quit gaping at the camp and call Mrs. Benz out," said

Garcia.

"I think we should have her husband do it." He gave the megaphone to Max. "Mr. Benz, tell your wife you're safe, Artie is safe, and that you have surrendered peacefully. As long as she comes out quietly without resisting, everything will be okay."

Max's voice echoed around the woods. "Honey, Artie and I are here with the SADF, and we're alright. Come on out, sweetheart."

After she saw the approaching SADF vehicle, Rita started downloading files into a server they had buried half a mile away while simultaneously uploading the data to a cloud account. She came out of the tent with her hands up. *They will confiscate the computers, likely find our Governet cloud account, but they won't find the server unless they dig up this whole mountain.*

"Alright, I'm coming out." She kept her hands up and walked the fifty yards to the dirt road where her family and the SADF waited.

"How did you find us?" she asked, with hands still raised.

"You can put your hands down Mrs. Benz," said Lee. "Your husband parked in the wrong spot on the wrong morning and someone sent a photo of the motorcycle to his *Plain Folks* account."

"And you geolocated it and from there it didn't take long for you to discover the use of fraudulent accounts," said Rita.

"That sums it up."

Rita wasn't mad, just disappointed that they were so easily tracked. "What's going to happen to us?"

"They're going to give us a deal," said Max.

"What's the deal?"

"You get to keep your land, you turn over all your computer devices, and you can remain here under watch," said

Lee.

"There's something you're not telling me. Why the free ride?"

"Your son will have to work for us in cyber security at Caltech—"

"You can't do that, it's against, I don't know, child labor laws."

"As you know, Mrs. Benz, those laws were rewritten to exclude children with extraordinary gifts whose work can be used for the betterment of society," said Gomez.

"So, child abuse."

"We are prepared to give Artie an unprecedented opportunity to work with computers at one of the best facilities in the world," said Lee.

Artie was standing quietly next to Lee who was stopping him from running to his mother.

"Are you okay with that sweetheart?" his mother asked.

"If I don't, they will send you to jail where, where, where you don't belong…where you will die."

She glared at Lee. "How dare you frighten our son like that!"

Artie struggled to get away and Lee let him go. Artie was crying as he hugged her close. "It's okay mom. It's only five years, and we'll be free. I even get to put some money away for you and dad. Please, mom, don't be mad."

Rita kept her venom in check. "If you are going to take him to work with you, you need to let him take his laptop. It has all his ideas, programming data, software, and other information he will need on the job, plus," she looked at Artie and scratched her nose, "family photos."

Garcia sighed. "We can't allow you to take the laptop. However, if Doctor Lee would be willing, he can transfer over any personal photos for you, after he investigates them of course."

"No problem, sir," said Lee.

Artie and Doctor Lee walked to the tent and stepped inside.

There were three laptops. "Okay Artichoke, which one has your photos?"

Artie pointed at a computer with *Turing Machine* written on the outside in purple ink derived from local wildflowers. He bent down in what looked like an attempt to tie his shoe as he sat on his bed. He snuck a mini-dive he had on his mattress, put it in the side of his left shoe, and tied it up.

"Turing, huh?" They started to walk back up the slope. "We've come a long way since Turing, still no AI though. I personally don't think computers will ever think like humans, but where would we be without them, right?"

Artie frowned and remained silent. Lee put the computer in the trunk, and they all got into the Caravan. They drove down the hill to Rampart where they were processed and spent the night in separate rooms. The next morning Artie went to Caltech to meet Doctor Asthana and Rita and Max were driven back to their land and released with Governet issued phones for emergencies, calls to each other, and a weekly meeting with Artie. Additionally, Rita and Maxwell were given GPS tattoos in case they decided to leave house arrest.

Artie was in Caltech University with people on average twice his age, and he would not be able to leave and visit Rita and Maxwell for at least five years as a condition of the family's plea. He was given a new wardrobe and stayed that night in his one-room apartment near the Caltech computer laboratory.

He woke up with the sun, two and a half hours before he was to meet Doctor Asthana. He stared at the ceiling and wrote code in his mind that could be used to defend against intruders into large databases and online software. Artie also envisioned a backdoor to enter such a system, one that only he could access. Two hours later, he quickly wrote down his coding notes on a pad left for him on a small, square dining table. He sighed and held back tears, changed into his slacks and shirt, and trudged two hundred unbearable yards to Caltech. As he approached the doors to the computer laboratory, his heart raced and his palms sweat.

He was recruited by Caltech to help develop a system, under various team leaders, to stop hackers. It takes a hacker to stop a hacker, they hypothesized. He was to work under the tutelage of the Director of Cyber Research, Doctor Asthana. Artie was just inside the entrance to the large four story, city block-sized monolith that housed one of the top computer research centers in the world, the Caltech Research Institute for Manufacturing and Engineering, when the Professor met him.

"Hello," said Doctor Asthana, not sure what to call this young man. "Should I call you Artichoke or—"

"Call me Mr. Benz."

*He's bitter. Be patient.* "Okay Mr. Benz." He pointed at the bench that had protective gear laid out on it. "Why don't you put on your lab coat and booties and take a head cap just in case, and I'll show you the facilities."

*Why don't I? Because I don't want to.* "Okay."

They put on their protective gear and walked down a long glass-encased hallway under sterile air and lights, created by Bezos Space Industries, engineered to kill foreign contaminants on surfaces but leave healthy skin bacteria alive. They arrived at a bright twenty by thirty foot room with two rows of six foot high cabinets on each wall and a twelve by fifteen foot white table in the middle of the room with storage bellow. The table had tools, magnifying lenses, areas for x-raying computers, components, and other devices.

"So, where's the supercomputers?" Artie asked.

"Upstairs, covering the expansive second floor. Our fastest supercomputer—"

"But they're not as fast as K-9 from Japan or Ohio State's Titan II."

Asthana smiled. "We're within one tenth of one percent of the fastest supercomputers."

"That's still a dozens of petaflops a second slower."

"If you put it that way, we have some catching up to do. Still, our computers get enough work to keep five of them running full time and we haven't found a problem we can't compute."

"What about predicting the temperature to one-hundredth of a degree for five years."

"No one can do that Mr. Benz." Asthana shook his head. "Why don't I show you your workstation."

Asthana turned to a lower cabinet along a wall directly in line with the door they entered and another door on the opposite wall. He pulled up a holokey, a round disk, he kept on a chain around his neck and put the edge up to the keyhole. A hologram emanated from the end of the key and perfectly filled the space that metal keys once filed. There was a clicking sound. After, Asthana put his right thumb on a keypad on the side of the cabinet, and the cabinet clicked open.

*Interesting, using new hologram tech and a basic thumb scan in combination,* thought Artie. "Is the holokey also print activated?"

Asthana grinned but didn't turn nor answer. He opened the cabinet and pulled out their latest micro-supercomputer.

"Oh," said Artie as Asthana turned around. "That's the Perugio laptop with electronic extendable display and, what is it, jellyfish DNA in the circuits to speed processing?" *Plus Signal*

*Area Scanning to block activity detection from unwelcome networks.*

"Uh, the public isn't supposed to know about the DNA, yet." He waved his hand in the air to brushed it off. "Good thing we have a press release coming out about it next week." Doctor Asthana looked at him. "Then we will deliver a million of these to the Central European States. Of course the Chinese think they can do better, and the Japanese would feel honor-bound to sell us similar technology, so they won't be buying."

"The Chinese have created similar technologies, but somehow, they can't get enough of the genetically modified jellyfish DNA." *Because you have an embargo against Chinese computer firms,* Artie thought.

"Don't believe everything you read on the Invisinet."

Artichoke looked at him sideways.

"We know about the Invisinet, the Invisible Net, Ar…Mr. Benz. We just haven't found a way to stop them, at least for more than a day."

As a user of the Invisinet, Artichoke looked down and away from Doctor Asthana to avoid his glance.

"Perhaps you can help with that," said the professor.

*Why would I?*

"Well, let me show you the configuration of this—"

"How about I just look around Perugio and ask questions when I have some?" asked Artie.

"Okay. I know you have classes coming up, and I am charged with giving you an independent study's course. This can be your first assignment."

*I hope the homework is harder than this,* he thought.

"Perhaps you would like to look at your new residence."

"Can I take Perugio with me?"

"I'm sorry, Mr. Benz. That computer has to stay in the lab.

We expect you to do your programming and research here."

Other than working on security protocols for their LAN, they enrolled Artichoke into PhD courses in computer technologies. His ultimate goal was to create software that was self-aware. He had been planning it for three years and wanted to try out some ideas now that he was working in a world class computer lab at Caltech.

On many days during the year, Artie was exhausted after working all night in the lab. One morning, he closed his Perugio and wandered through the decontamination hallway, and past the security doors, hoping he might use the computer at home. He pressed his palm print on the scanner to exit the supercomputer facility with the laptop. It was almost 8 am. He ran into Doctor Asthana who was just arriving.

"Artie, you didn't stay up all night, did you?"

"Yeah, I was working on something."

"You're always working on something. Go and get some rest." Then the professor noticed the laptop. "Mr. Benz, you can't take that with you, you know the rules."

Artichoke, usually good tempered, moved the computer out of the Professor's reach. "It's my private work, and I can't show anyone, yet."

"I'm sure by now you know the security protocols and what would happen if you left the campus, just past your apartment, with that computer: an alarm would go off and your parole will be revoked. That goes for any unauthorized visitors as well." Asthana laughed, "Besides, you and your mother are probably the only ones that could fully understand your work."

The mention of Artichoke's mother made him bristle. But he remembered what his dad used to say. *Don't let your enemies use your emotions against you.* Artie paused a minute. "What if I want to order pizza?"

"It won't be a problem getting in a delivery. Besides, you could use to put on some weight."

Artie put on a weary smile and said, "Thank you professor," he held up the computer, "I need this just in case I think of something else."

The professor patted Artie on the back. " Go ahead, take it, if it helps you with your work. Just know that we will monitor your activity."

"I would be disappointed if you weren't."

He still couldn't bear the two hundred yards to his one room apartment. Angeltown was so noisy and smelly. The cement hurt his feet. But he would make do, for his parents. He entered the guest house, unlocked the door on the left and fell onto the bed on the right. He wasn't hungry. He would eat later that day after his feverish sleep.

After a helping of almond butter on crackers, he looked at the family photos that Doctor Lee had approved and put on Artie's university drive for him to have. Most of the photos were of Rita that Max took. Then there were pictures of Artie, and a few of dad, the land, a rainbow, a rattle snake, the motorcycle, and photos of trees.

The photos weren't clues, they weren't embedded with lines of code or passwords. Doctor Lee would have discovered any out of place characters embedded in photos. No, the photos themselves were mnemonic devices. Artie turned off his Wi-Fi connection to the university network and the Governet and after putting the photos in the order his mother had him memorize over the last year, typed forty-three lines of code in under six minutes. He hit save.

He had created an upload to the Invisinet Wi-Fi server. He used this patch and connected to the server named SGmountain that was buried at Balch Camp. He downloaded the encrypted directory called "Happy Days in the Mountains" that his mother had left for him to an external one-inch by three-inch drive he had with him from Balch Camp that he had hidden inside his shoe. Using a key of forty-two alphanumeric strokes, he unencrypted the directory and found it contained hacking software, viruses, tracking tools, and ways to break into personal computers as a work around to connect to larger computers' directories and backdoors into the Governet. Most importantly, it contained a program, *deadzone,* written by his mother used to check for unwanted spybots and exobots inside and outside an active network and blocked their snooping. This would allow him to work outside the watchful eye of Doctor Asthana and Caltech.

    His breathing increased and his throat dried. Worried that his activity even off the university server might be tracked, he opened the program. He scanned his network for non-conforming electronic signals and found none. He finished and only found his broad movements and location of the laptop were tracked when he was off the university server. *Was letting me take the laptop a test?*

    Artie closed the directory and it re-encrypted itself onto the external drive with new key that only he could access: a key encrypted inside a key. He put the drive in a plastic sandwich bag, sealed it shut, and submerged it in a jar of almond butter he had in the refrigerator. After disconnecting the link, he connected back to his partition on the university server.

    Every night he worked off the server, exploring the actions of what his dad called "the police state", and he used *deadzone* each time for his off network activities. He hacked into the Angeltown education site and found new educational directives from the Czar of Education. Students were going to be used as test subjects of some kind, yet to be determined. And, according to the

Czar, students were soon to be used to track each other's activities and find 'subversives.'

Artie knew the risk of being caught, despite working through his family's hidden server and the Governet's own satellites. His story about *just being curious* wouldn't hold up if they caught him in action. His mother told Artie stories over games of Constellations about a pawnshop downtown that supplied their camp with some of their electronic devices. So he ordered a special delivery from Ray's Pawn Shop's secure page on the Invisinet of an advanced tablet, had it wrapped in a pizza box, and delivered by a young man disguised as a pizza delivery driver. Once he received the Archimedes Tablet, the most advanced Ray had, he immediately improved its speed and memory to meet his new computing goals.

#

# Chapter 10
# Home Life

*Privatizing Instruction of Underserved Students Act of 2052 guarantees that all students will get the chance to serve the greater good through restructured educational institutions.*
Education Czar press conference, June 2052

    Chava scurried past the empty apartment complex behind her house. The low moon created long shadows like bodies strewn along the sides of the buildings. A familiar route now terrified her.
    She took her key out of her jean shorts, slowly opened the screen door to the small back room, walked to the back door, and unlocked the bolt. Her grandmother wheeled up immediately in her chair from the kitchen.
    "It's past eleven! Where have you been…are you okay?" she said in a quiet yet forceful voice. Her grandmother's eyes bulged at Chava's appearance. Grandma Alma, her dad's mother, inspected her.
    "No," Chava shook with tears, fright, and cold. "Did you see it, grandma, did you see what happened?"
    "Never mind that for now," Grandma Chavez said, holding her granddaughter's hands. "You need to take off those dirty clothes, wash. Now go quietly, Manuel esta dormiendo. I bring you

some clothes."

Chava looked down on grandma and smiled through the tears. She trudged to the back and into the make-shift, wooden-planked shower with a barrel once used by monks to crush grapes with their feet on top and a chain that portioned out a bucket of water with each yank. It was one of her dad's better inventions.

She took off her clothes and started to feel all the pain of the scrapes, cuts, and bruises of the day's journey. She planted her feet and gave the chain a quick tug, soaking herself. She lathered up with the Nanomed enzymatic all-in-one body wash that dad would get free samples of at the black market. It stung her flesh, and the dissipated sweat gave her chills. She felt the soap eating away the dirt, and she stood and cried, alone and naked.

"Estas bien, Chava?" said grandma who had rolled out onto the platform to the shower.

"Yes…si, grandma!" she answered. She wasn't.

After righting herself, she pulled the chain and rinsed off. She stepped out of the shower and grabbed the towel grandma had left on the vegetable crate outside and wrapped it around herself. Her grandma was sitting in her chair at the screen door.

"Aqui nieta, toma," grandma said as she handed Chava some clean clothes: underwear, shorts, and a t-shirt.

Chava dried off and put on her fresh clothes. Then she went inside the safety of her home. As Chava entered the house, Grandma grabbed her hand, rolled into the small dining area, and set Chava in a chair. The small house was slightly under eight-hundred square feet. It had one main room that had a bed shared by Chava's father and grandmother, a small room on the side for Chava's mattress, a kitchenette with a two-burner stove and an ice box, two wardrobes for closets, and a front entrance and back porch.

Chava was glad to see Grandma Chavez, but she was no

substitute for Grandma Cohen. Chava felt ashamed for thinking this and started to cry louder. Grandma Chavez brought her some water. Chava kept crying. "Let me get you some cool tea." said Grandma.

Chava heard a grunt from the bed as her dad, Manuel, was getting up. Since Angeltown College had closed, her family was forced to move into this tiny house. Manuel was keeping odd hours, trying to make sense of life and find any kind of piece work. Fortunately, he was paid a little pension, had a few pieces left in an account and a little insurance from the Czar when his wife died. And Manuel was, after all, an experience survivor.

With no phone, no rent, small payments for the little utilities they used, they were alive.

"Chava, que pasó mi hija?" he said, his voice weak from stress and lack of sleep. He hugged her fiercely.

She was embarrassed that she had learned more Hebrew than Spanish, and Chava turned into her six-year-old self, "It was terrible papa. People were hurt, my friends, other students…" Chava faded off.

"Chava, I heard, something terrible happened."

She wept and her body shook.

He held her and brushed her hair out of her eyes. "Are you okay? Were you hurt?" Just then, her grandmother rolled back into the dining area with a cup of sun-steeped mint tea and laid it beside Chava on the oval shaped linoleum table. Manuel stood straight and his muscles groaned when he sat in a metal chair next to Chava.

"Thank you," Chava said, sobbing, looking down. She put her hands around the mug. Again, she thought of Grandma Cohen. "Thank you," looking at Grandma Alma's face, "you have always been kind." Chava immediately thought it an odd thing to say, though it was true. Only after her mother's death, and they were forced to move, did she get to know dad's mom.

Her dad kept looking at Chava with a combination of pleading and concern. "You're okay though, right?" ending his question with a faint smile of hope. "Do you want to talk about what happened?"

"No. What's the use?" Chava looked at him and saw him for the first time since she got home, "Oh, papa." She wrapped her arms around him and squeezed, not wanting to let go. "Ooomph!" said her father from her hard squeeze. His straight metal chair tilted back, and he quickly stabilized it. She relaxed in his embrace. He pet her head and she fell asleep.

---

Chava slept until noon the next day. Manny offered her some water when she woke. "That was quite a sleep. I didn't know if you were going to get up."

Chava smelled the eggs and onions coming from the kitchen.

"You want to go down to the market with me, we can look for some shirts for you? The ones you have are getting old, and it always helps to start fresh with a new shirt," her dad said.

"Thanks dad, I think I'll have whatever Grandma is cooking and have a run."

"Thank your Grandma; that's the second breakfast she's cooked today."

"I will."

He kissed Chava on the cheek and headed out with his hiking pack in case he found some bargains at the market.

When Chava wasn't sleeping, she was running early in the morning, 1, 2, 5, 10 miles a day. She became obsessed with running over the uneven terrain, rubble, remains of houses, and wore out her shoes. One day when she got home, her dad had a surprise for her.

"Look what my son got for you, Chava," said Grandma, anxiously awaiting her reaction.

Chava saw the running shoes. "Oh, papa! But how did you—"

"All I did was trade in that old leather jacket that I never wear anymore." Her dad had loved that jacket with the serpent in the eagles talon's and the name *Los Grandes de Nogales* on it.

"But dad, you said you would never trade your prized jacket, are you sure?"

"Too late for that, hija. Try them on," he said.

She put them on. "Perfect!"

"I couldn't get them in purple, but a shoe's a shoe, right? They're well made; a friend at the market told me. He wears them all the time."

Chava gave him a big hug and kiss on the cheek. "The white is great." She ran out the door to try them.

Grandma looked at Manny and smiled, "Mi hijo, tu eres un papa bien!"

"Gracias, Mama."

Chava kept running throughout the fall and she missed the semester at school and the rest of the school year. She knew that she could never go back, that a degree meant nothing, that school was just a place of suffering. She lost one of her only friends, and she may never know why. *Theo wanted better lives for students, and they killed him for it.* She wanted to cry every time she thought of him.

Over the next months, she started to think of Theo as a hero, not as a victim. Theo made the world a better place. She, on the other hand, barely made it through classes, ran on the track team, and made dinner for her dad, and her mom when she was alive.

She ran more and more each day, at least seven miles each time. She was certain that she could win a medal if there were still running competitions. Her dad gave her more self-defense lessons out back after the sun went down. It helped pass the time and it gave Manuel a sense of pride. "Remember mi hija, you have the vulnerable parts of the body." He nodded to her. "Those are…"

Chava pantomimed kicking her dad as she called out the areas, "The groin; the knee, any of the body's at joints; the head and neck area, temples, throat, car…car…"

Manuel point to the spot on his neck. "Carotid artery. If cut and bleeding, that artery can cause death, so be careful."

She kicked high enough to hit him in the head if he had been in range.

"Woh, you've been practicing your kicks." He smiled. "But those high kicks aren't practical. They leave you vulnerable to someone grabbing you. And a strong man will take advantage."

Manuel waved his hand in front of his eyes.

"Right, the eyes," she said.

"Those are the main ones, but the ankle and top of the foot can debilitate an attacker." He put out his foot and let Chava feign a stomp to the foot and ankle.

"And remember what my Kenpo teacher Doctor Ngowe used to say, the best self-defense technique is?"

"Running."

"And mi hija, you have mastered the running part of the training."

She clasped her hands together and bowed. "Yes, sensei."

The new year came and it was February, nine months since the rally.

Chava and dad started working on the garden together with

whatever seeds would grow in the dry, hard soil with little water. Spring didn't mean much anymore, just a time of year. There was only one season left, dry and hot. They collected all the water they could when it did rain, and it was barely enough to sustain them, especially now that Manuel had set up a make-shift gravity powered misting system to cool their tiny home. They didn't know how they used to live without it. More than ever, they had to use filters and iodine to make the water potable.

Manuel began to trade for a book or paper at the black market, and that helped pass the time. Reading made Chava miss Theo. She would read to Grandma Chavez and her dad at night instead of watching the television, which they no longer owned. Once they were done, dad would trade the book for the next one.

Some of the books were strange like, *The Hitchhiker's Guide to the Galaxy.* Grandma understood most of the English, and she liked to hear her granddaughter's voice. However, dad loved hearing that one; he had fond memories of it when he was a kid. The book talked about the galaxy, how to travel, what the meaning of life was. Chava didn't understand that at all, but it made her dad laugh. Dad tried to explain, but it didn't translate to their current life situation.

Chava's favorite that she read that spring was *The Day of the Locust,* a history of Angeltown when they made movies that played in theaters. She also liked the detective novels that Theo read, especially Easy Rawlins. Grandma preferred *A Room with a View* because of the romance. Chava found it so foreign, all those costumes and strange customs, and she couldn't engage with the book. All three of them enjoyed *Alice in Wonderland.* Chava would act that one out for them. She would bow like a thespian after her dramatic reading of certain passages.

*'Cheshire Puss,' she began, rather timidly, as she did not at all*

> *know whether it would like the name: however, it only grinned a little wider. 'Come, it's pleased so far,' thought Alice, and she went on. 'Would you tell me, please, which way I ought to go from here?'*
> *'That depends a good deal on where you want to get to,' said the Cat.*
> *'I don't much care where—' said Alice.*
> *'Then it doesn't matter which way you go,' said the Cat.*
> *'—so long as I get SOMEWHERE,' Alice added as an explanation.*
> *'Oh, you're sure to do that,' said the Cat, 'if you only walk long enough.'*

They clapped and laughed at the dramatic readings. Sometimes, Chava couldn't get through them because of her own laughter, and sometimes, dad would read the Cheshire Cat role with his low baritone. They were sad when they finally traded that one in, but Chava had drawn a few pictures to help them remember the best parts of the book.

With no school to occupy her time, Chava joined her dad collecting scrap and traveling to the Grand Black Market to trade. The Market was about forty-five minutes away on foot, and it took an hour when they pulled their cart to pick up or trade something large. Usually, they carried a couple of backpacks full of items to trade or sell.

More and more of Manuel's personal belongings and scavenged items from the apartment building behind their house, and other abandoned buildings in their neighborhood, were traded for necessities of life and survival. Recently, they had traded some copper wire, a sink, and two dozen floor tiles for a more efficient water collector based on collectors employed in African desert cities that took hydrogen and oxygen from the air to create water.

That was one trip in which they needed the cart.

They left for the market at 6:15 am before the sun was fully up on a Monday, though all days of the week were now the same. Chava brought her Belmont High Dragons t-shirt and her sleeveless, dark blue jersey from the school's track team that had the number eleven on the front and the words *state champion* on the back. Her dad carried their penultimate toilet seat and a deadbolt scavenged from the neighborhood. He kept the last toilet seat at home as a backup.

The market was housed in large, high-ceilinged building on Broadway that resembled a small airplane hangar and had been an upscale food market before the 2030 collapse. Now it was a repurposed lifeline for people holding on for tomorrow.

"Dad, we should get some seeds, see if we can grow anything. I mean, the rainy month is coming up."

Chava entered the market with her dad and was amazed at the stacks of t-shirts, bikes and all the individual parts, human powered appliances of all kinds like washing machines and dish washers, solar powered fans and scooters, toys, games, computers at least fifteen years old, phones, small consumer drones most which could barely make it around the block, almost one of everything you wanted, or didn't want, all stacked up in crazy heaps or artfully displayed in arrays on tables.

Chava found a table with plants and seeds. She browsed the herbs, flowers, and individually packaged seeds specially selected to grow in the hot and dry climate of Angeltown. "Dad, what do you think of these." She pointed at the yarrow flowers and seeds.

The proprietor of the stand walked to where they were looking. "They're not very pretty compared to roses," Manuel said.

"You're not wrong there, sir," said the stout Black man in light blue coveralls. "But you won't get a rose growing in this climate. And I think the yarrow can be quite lovely when you don't get much other flowers."

Manuel pursed his lips. "You decide honey, I'm going to look for some gutters." He walked off toward Sam's table of plastics and plumbing.

The proprietor of the plants and seeds looked at Manuel walk off and addressed Chava. "Did you know that the yarrow flower makes a very delicious spice for your potatoes and turnips?"

"Okay." She paused, then unfurled her Belmont Dragons t-shirt. "What can you give me for this?"

The man took the shirt, held it up to his nose and sniffed. Then he inspected it for holes. "It's a bit small for most of the people that come by here." *But I hear the school is closing, and this could be a rare commodity.* "But let's see." He inspected his selection of seeds. He grabbed packets as he talked. "You can't go wrong with yarrow seeds. Once they start growing, they're like weeds. You can bring the extra here for trade. And lavender adds a unique flavor, and you can make a refreshing tea with it." He grabbed a packet of mustard greens. "These are the best greens for the dry climate. They go good with yarrow too." He looked at Chava. "You don't need any agave do you?" he asked, looking at the dozen small plants he had on his table.

Chava laughed. "That's one thing we have plenty of out back."

"Right," he said. "Okay, I have some Japanese sunflowers, they're like regular sunflowers but don't grow so tall and still give you quite a big flower."

Chava pointed to the corner of the table. "How about a pair of those clearly used, old tech sunglasses thrown in."

"No can do. That would bust me."

Chava unfolded her running jersey with the number eleven on front. "It's clean, you can't even smell that I wore it, unless you're a dog…sorry, bad joke. But really, it also says 'State Champion' on the back." She turned it to show him.

"You were a state champion?"

"Yes, cross country. I was one of the milers."

"Okay. Since you're such a sincere young woman, why not." *Besides, no one is taking these glasses, and I just diversified my portfolio.* The man took the jersey and t-shirt and placed them carefully on the corner of one of his two long tables covered with his wares. He then put the seeds in a plastic bag for her. Chava put on the glasses and walked off.

She hurried over to see her dad who was haggling, trying to trade his toilet seat.

"I need at least one plastic gutter, twelve feet long, and a collection bucket, with a cover," her dad said. "A thirty gallon bucket."

The woman, Sam, bartering with Chava's dad, shook her head and noticed the girl jog up. She looked at her and pointed at him. "This your dad? Talk some sense into him, will ya? I don't have any twelve foot gutters, just ten and shorter."

Chava glanced at Sam's table full of gutters, buckets, filters, tools, and connectors. "I see an eight foot gutter and a four foot gutter. Throw in the connectors and we have a deal."

"We're going to lose six inches that way, Chava." said her dad.

"But it's a good deal," said the vendor.

"Alright, with the connectors." Manual handed over the toilet seat and took the gutters. Chava put her seeds into the bucket and carried it.

At home, they assessed their day over some water and tea with Manuel's mother.

"How are you Grandma Alma?" asked Chava.

"Bien. I am just glad you are back, I get so worried."

"You're granddaughter is a born negotiator. She got us two lengths of gutter, just the sizes we needed."

"Well, you said you needed a four foot and an eight foot length, so now you don't have to cut them. Besides, you found the toilet seat."

"You're a team," said Alma, tapping her son's hand.

He smiled and knocked mugs with Chava and his mother.

"You know you could have gotten more for your school shirt. They will be closing it down soon; those shirts are going to be rare."

"Daddy, that place is just a bad memory. I'm glad to be done with it." She sorted out the packets of seeds and thought of how to plant them in the back. "After learning to read and write and do a little math, school just became another style of prison."

He was relieved that they had moved two years ago and were harder to find, but Manuel was still concerned about the safety of his daughter. He asked, "Chava, aren't you afraid that the Truancy Squad will come after you for not going to class?"

"To them, I don't even exist, and for all they know, I'm dead."

"I hope you're right."

Chava took the seeds out back and dug four troughs, the mustard greens closest to the shower to get the most run off, then the sunflowers, yarrow, and the lavender. They were planted to the side of the rows of turnips and potatoes that they had planted the previous year. She gave the seeds what water they could spare and hoped for rain.

The next morning, Chava enjoyed an egg and a small potato and some dark, over-steeped tea. Still, it was refreshing.

As she finished, her dad came out of the kitchen carrying two thin polyfiber aprons and handed one to Chava.

"What's this for, dad?"

"Chava," her dad said, "I trapped a pigeon in the back yard, and you're old enough and ready to pluck your own bird."

She bit her lower lip. "Really, dad?"

"Yes, if we are going to eat what's available, birds are a good place to start." Manuel gave Chava an apron and took her out back where he had set up a stump with the dead pigeon on it. Next to the stump he had set their best knife on a fruit crate.

"Pluck the feathers off onto the ground."

Chava put on gloves and started to pluck. At first, she made a face of disgust, thinking that cleaning the pigeon gross. However, she understood the necessity of it and started to enjoy it.

"On the chest, you can rub them off. They come off easily."

Chava turned the bird over and started to rub off the feathers.

"Good. Take your time and don't worry if you miss something. You can clean that up later."

"What about the wings?"

"Finish plucking the body."

Chava was slow, but careful, and she got most of the feathers off in one pass.

She cut off the wings and feet.

"Make sure you don't cut off any meat you might want." Her father pointed.

"Oops." Chava smiled. *This is fun!*

Her father leaned over and pointed. "Hey, you're pretty good at this!"

"For a girl?"

Manuel frowned. "Chava, you know that's not what I think. You can do anything you want."

"Even pee standing up?"

"Chava!" He laughed. "Very funny. Now," he pointed at the head. Time to gut it.

She finished cleaning and gutting the insides as her father instructed.

He smiled. "Now rinse the body off and we have meat later, or tomorrow if we let it cook over night in our solar oven."

Chava put three inches of water in a bucket and dipped the pigeon in a few times until the blood had rinsed off. "Thanks, dad."

"One more thing Chava. Eating the guts can make you sick, but a dog or a raccoon can eat them without getting ill. So we can save the guts and try to catch a raccoon or—"

"A cute little raccoon? Daddy!"

"Okay, okay. But a raccoon would make a good meal." She glared at him "Okay, I'll toss it down the road at the fence."

Manuel started to run with Chava at night, but only short distances. Then he would challenge her to a game of chess, winning each time. But every time they played, she got closer to beating that trickster dad of hers. Grandma watched in silence, just glad that they got along so well. In her family growing up, it wasn't always that way.

In April, Manuel was going to take a trip to Ray's, the infamous pawn shop, to look for a present for Grandma, more iodine tablets for their water filter, and whatever else they might use. Chava begged to come along, and although it was dangerous, she was allowed to go. "If you were a boy, I wouldn't hesitate, and you're sixteen, so why not."

It was a nearly two hour walk, so they left some food and old-time magazines in Spanish they found at the market for Grandma, and set out. Manuel carried a jug of water for them to share.

So much had been shut down, even in the habitable zone. It was barely dawn, but the world was already burning due to the raging sun. They stuck to the shadows and wore hats, and still the chance of being burnt was present. While they stayed in the shadows, they were careful not to cross any blind corners without looking around them and used a mirror attached to a pole to check. If the sun didn't kill them, an ambush could.

They passed the recently burnt out Uptown Dresses shop that had been closed years earlier, staying on the other side of the street. They both could smell the embers of the recent fire that smoldered from the basement of the long abandoned store.

Father and daughter saw a few stray cats and dogs and Manuel made sure they stayed clear of them. They passed an elder hostel that now had been taken over by vagrants who looked scaly and cracked like snakes. The residents hissed and flailed their hands into the air like insane mimes on the sides of decaying buildings as Manny and Chava passed. They saw people who were lost with no place to go; they hunkered down and avoided eye contact. "Get away from us!" they shouted as they ran away from Chava and her dad.

Every large building they passed appeared to have one or two occupants and dozens of unoccupied offices. Two had signs with numbers or web addresses: *Bail Bonds, Loans on the Cheap,* and some had advertising, *"Looking for intelligence enhancements? Call 4y9 from our website or buy them directly online."* They kept walking with their empty packs on their backs and as neutral a gaze as they could manage on their faces.

On the trip, they discussed the books they had read together but avoided topics like Chava's future, what career goals she had, and anything that would remind them of their dire situation. And

Manuel only broached the tragedy at the library to make sure his daughter was okay emotionally. *It must have been so hard,* he thought. Chava still didn't know how to make sense of that day and stopped trying.

They did, however, discuss water purification, electricity generation, and urban/solar survival gear. They had to live through the next day to have a future. They also learned that talking for two hours was harder than they thought it would be, and eventually just made observations about their route as a way to keep their senses keen.

Finally, they arrived at Ray's Pawn Shop. Ray was supposedly over one hundred, but he looked in his fifties. No one knew how old he really was. Ray was short, under five foot six, thin, and hearty. Rumors were that Ray took some of his own pharmaceutical inventory to stop aging. Whatever the case, he was able to keep his store open by not ripping anyone off and limiting his dealings with murderous thugs.

Manuel waved at the camera outside over the entranceway, "It's me Ray."

There was a buzzing sound, and Manuel opened the door, nodded his head for Chava to go in, then followed her. Ray's was a cramped corner store with items stacked from floor to ceiling in what used to be a convenience store.

The first thing Chava noted was the cool inside, only eighty-five, she thought. Then she noticed the rows and rows of stuff. Goods were stacked on bookshelves, in cabinets, and on top and inside desks. But it didn't look haphazard, it was visually appealing somehow. There were tools, hammers, nails, screws, rulers, two pairs of binoculars, a locked jewelry case, old clocks, suitcases, a saxophone, a tool chest with no tools in it, a few jackets, a couple of hats, hundreds of ties, a few televisions, and on and on.

"Mr. Chavez!" shouted Ray, "And this must be the daughter you always go on about." He looked her over, trying not to be inappropriate, as if he knew what that meant. He continued, "She looks healthy enough." He quickly looked back to Manuel, "What can I get for you?"

"Well Ray," he said as Chava looked around the tiny store in amazement, "I'm looking for a gift for my mother who is eighty-four tomorrow."

"Wow, there aren't many people that old these days, except perhaps the Insiders. But I wouldn't know," Ray said, putting his hand on his chin in thought. "Let me see, does she wear jewelry? I've got these fake pearls…"

"No, she doesn't" said Manuel. "How about something like canned fish?"

"Nope, I don't get much fish these days, only lab grown," Ray says, pinching his nose in disgust. "I do have some canned rabbit meat," Ray added. "It's locally grown, or captured or something. I like it. And the producers sell it at a good rate if I buy it in bulk. I could let you have a dozen cans."

Manuel wasn't convinced, "I'll take two cans and try it, but that's all." Manuel focused back on the task, looked at Ray and explained, "I need something unique, Ray, but obviously, not too expensive."

"I have just the thing." Ray turned to the shelves directly behind him and pulled out a tray of half inch sized disks, and from the haphazard writing on the discs, they were clearly bootlegged. "Your mother is from North Mexico, right?"

"Mexico," Manuel corrected.

"Okay," Ray responded with his hands up, conceding the point. "She's eighty-four, I have just the thing." He pulled out a disk and put it on the counter, "John Gabriel," he said with the

English pronunciation, "he was really popular when your mom—"

"Alma."

Ray continued, "When Alma was young. I hear this Gabriel was quite popular with the mujeres."

"Ray," said Manuel, "we have nothing to play it on."

Ray pulled out a little player from under the counter. "I have just the thing for you." Ray held up his hand to stop Manuel from speaking. I can throw this in for free. I get these for a pinch of *nutmeg*." Nutmeg was the latest in street drugs, and Ray felt embarrassed for saying that he sold it with Chava there. "No one has music anymore, but I have a few of these things."

Manuel hesitated.

Ray increased his offer, "How about I add something for your daughter, a bonus, only one-hundred pieces for the whole lot." He sized up Chava, "So, you know what music you like?" He asked her. "No, of course you don't." He rifled through his circular disks, speaking to himself, "Brittney Spears…" he looked at Chava. "Nope. Taylor Swift, no, Arianna Grande? How the hell…" he caught himself, "How did that get in there? Too bad there's no X or Siouxsie and the Banshees, they were REAL women," he reminisced with his hand over his chest in respect. He addressed Chava, looking at her purple hair, "You kind of remind me of her, Siouxsie…You won't find those artists anymore." He picked up a disk and held it to the light, "This will do. Good old Joan Jett for—"

"Chava," she said.

"Joan Jett for Chava Chavez," he repeated.

As good as Ray was at remembering his merchandise, he was terrible at remembering names. Faces, fine. Names? There were too many to remember and as soon as you remember one, they were gone. Again, Ray was lost in memory.

Manuel broke his trance, "Ray? You said a hundred, for the

disks, the rabbit, and the player…"

Ray look up, calculating the costs. *The player was free from a junkie, the disks, hell, no one wanted them anymore, so selling two was great. The rabbit, that was the cost: fifty pieces. Still, twenty pieces profit for fifteen minutes of work for a nice man and his daughter. Why not.* He'd make it up on the criminals and junkies.

Ray reached under the counter and pulled up the scanner with eye pieces like binoculars. He put it on the tray of disks. Ray tapped the top. "Give it a second, Manny. You know how old this thing is?" After about a minute, it beeped. Manuel bent down with his eyes on the lenses and closed them for a second, then opened them wide. A concentrated beam of light crossed his eyes vertically, horizontally then vertically again. The scan was done. The funds had been safely deposited.

Chava was admiring the survival gear, the boots, the anti-contamination pills, water purifying pills, solar protective gear with solar-powered air cooling. *That must cost a piece or two.*

"Ray, do you have any like this in my size?" she asked, holding up a pair of off road running shoes. Ray looked down at her feet, "Size six, seven?" he said.

"Six," she responded.

"Oh, those are hard to get. But I know someone who can make a pair, custom," he added.

As Manuel was packing up his bag, Ray leaned over to Chava and gave her the disk, "You want to play track one, *Bad Reputation*." he told Chava under her breath so Manuel wouldn't hear. "It might lift your spirits." *Or it might blow your mind.*

"Thanks Ray," said Manuel.

"You need a little water for the road. I get a good deal. You can cover me later," Ray said as he gave Chava two golf-ball-sized balls of water specially wrapped in a dissolvable polymer. *It's not good business if your customers die*, he thought. "Just put the ball in your mouth and it will dissolve over time and keep you hydrated for three hours. And don't worry, the skin is coated: no bacteria can live on it."

"Thanks again, Ray," said Manuel as he exited.

"Yea, thanks," added Chava. She followed her dad outside.

---

Five minutes after Chava and Manuel left, Martin from the off the books SADF special squad arrived.

"Ray, buddy!" shouted Martin. Ray motioned to him to keep it quiet. Martin continued, "I hear that the Williams brothers are looking to acquire a drone. I also heard Darnell Daft was shooting down drones again, got a big one. And there is only one guy left in Angeltown that can move such merchandise." Ray averted his eyes. Martin raised his voice, "That's YOU Ray. So where's the drone?" Martin flicked a pair of cuffs in his hands.

"There's still room in The Pits, Ray."

"Okay, but you have to let me slide. I'm too old for prison," whined Ray. "I have it in the back."

Martin paused to think before he spoke. "Here's what we're going to do Ray. Keep the drone, and when the Williams brothers come for it, and they will come for it, you signal me and I'll be right down."

Ray shivered. "They'll kill me Martin, you know what they do."

"Not if you signal me, Ray."

Ray thought about The Pits and decided to take his chances with Martin. "Okay," said Ray.

---

Having the water helped Chava and Manuel on the way

back home. Other than the sun burning down on them even hotter than the trip down to Ray's, their journey back was uneventful. The benefit of the heat and sun was that people stayed in the shade, making traveling less dangerous.

"Me encanta la musica, mi buen hijo!" exclaimed Alma as she kissed her son on the cheek. Chava liked the music alright, but she liked even more that they were happy together that night. As they listened to Juan Gabriel, they ate some rabbit and potatoes from the garden with some garlic. They drank reclaimed water they gathered from the night air. Moreover, "El conejo no era tan mal."

#

# Chapter 11
# Jane's New Assignment

*Education is not preparation for life; education is life itself. The Education Czar is the Life Giver.*
The Office of the Education Czar's Daily Word

Jane was startled by a loud knock on her front door in the early afternoon during the one month summer break. "Jane Winston," the man insisted, "we are from the Education Department to give you your assignment for the next year." He held up his badge to the security camera above the door. It read, "Office of Education, Angeltown Division." Jane had seen these badges before when she signed up to teach classes the first time. She let them in.

The man, a trim former acrobat from the Eastern European States, was wearing a purple suit with a white tie and black shoes. The tall, voluptuous, thirty-five-year-old woman was wearing a furry, hot-pink suit with pink shoes and a stern look on her face. He was carrying a purple folder, a small phlebotomy bag for collecting blood, and the woman was holding a dark brown briefcase.

Jane directed them toward the white couch that faced her large combination computer monitor and television. Jane sat on a straight-backed white chair near the couch. She held her composure and didn't react to the presence of the well know confidant of the Czar of Education, the Woman in Pink.

The Woman in Pink took the lead with her newly dyed blonde hair curled up high on top of her head like upside down ice cream cone. She spoke in a sickly sweet tone of someone trying to act concerned but unable to care. "First, we have some sad news to tell you. Your parents are dead. Suicide. That's such a sad thing for a young girl."

Jane was not sad after hearing the news; she no longer cared what happened to her parents. Her only concerned was her new life, not her parents' death. She straightened her spine on her chair. "Would you like some tea?" She inquired.

In unison, they curtly responded, "No."

"Today, you will renew your commitment to the Czar. You have helped us in the past, and you will continue your work as a content delivery specialist at The Reverend Manpower Academy."

Jane bowed her head. "I am ready to serve."

The Woman in Pink pointed her hand to the man and he laid his purple folder and medical kit on the white table in front of Jane. "Here are the terms," he asserted, "just as they were before, with a bonus for results."

Jane reached for the folder. The woman interrupted, placing her hand on it. "There is no need to look at that now. We are certain you will comply."

Jane nodded. The woman put her briefcase on the table and opened the lid toward Jane, hiding the contents. Jane sat with her hands clasped on her lap and her ankles crossed.

The woman brought out a hand-held retinal scanning device. It was a Citizenet Com5000 plasma phone, six by three inches, but twice the thickness of a regular CitizenNet phone, with a protruding eye scope at the top for scanning retina. She also brought out a light-box, six by eight inches, three inches high. The sides were translucent white and the bottom featured a series of wires, transistors and circuits to record, store, and transmit every print.

"Before we get started, my assistant, Flex, will take a blood sample from you."

Jane stuck out her right arm and otherwise sat erect.

Flex laid out the kit to take her blood. He sterilized her right arm with Nanomed ointment and drew the blood before Jane noticed he was taking it. He carefully put the blood in a vial and put it in his bag.

The Woman in Pink floated around the white table in her a tight pink skirt and six-inch pink heels, barely leaving a mark on the white carpet, and grabbed the retinal scanner. From behind, she put her left index finger on the crown of Jane's head, freezing her head in place. The woman bent slightly and put but the retinal scanner on the table in front on Jane. "Bend over and put your eyes on the lenses." Jane covered the lenses with her eyes. "Blink three times," the woman said in a voice for a child. Jane did as she was told. After a moment, The Woman in Pink removed the device from the table and looked at the readout. The device read, *within parameters.*

After she put the retinal scanner back in her case, the woman brought out the light-box palm scanner. The woman placed Jane's right, then left hand on the top of the scanner and recorded both palm prints.

The information was sent through the Governet router *Photon* to their decision databank. Then the woman grabbed Jane's arm and led her back to the chair to sit. "Now, hold your head still as we ask you a few questions," instructed the woman. She put her hands at the sides of Jane's head. "Don't move, or we will have to get the neck immobilizer." Jane dutifully held her head straight.

The woman put a small tablet on the table, pointed the camera toward Jane and hit record. The man pulled out a small handheld device from the inner left pocket of his jacket, held it vertically and perfectly still to focus on Jane's left eye. The woman commanded, "Hold your head still." The man read the bottom of the handheld device. "No Deception."

The Woman started, "Are you ready?"

Jane sat erect. "Yes, let's start with your questions."

The woman sat back down. "Will you fulfill your duties faithfully to the Czar?"

"Yes."

The scanner read, 'No Deception.'

"Will you follow the curriculum in all its detail and never deviate?"

"Yes."

The scanner read, 'No Deception.'

"What will you do if a student isn't working?"

"I wouldn't sit and talk with them. I will have them surrender their tablet and dismiss them. This is about doing what is right."

"During your classes, what will you do if students don't perform to the required standard?"

"They will be dismissed."

"What with you do if you catch a student using paper in the classroom?"

"I will call security and have them removed."

After fifteen minutes of questioning, Jane received her teaching assignment for the next school year. She would be teaching in a gymnasium in Angel Heights, not far from the Rampart Station. Jane's pieces could be given to her subcutaneously or put into a Governet account to be accessed using her palm-print or retinal scan.

"We will take our leave," said the Woman in Pink.

"Yes, quite," said the man. The front door automatically shut behind them.

After they left, Jane sighed and turned on the nightly news on her Governet television. A man sat at an empty desk with a logo of the Czar on the screen, the eagle with talons clutching lightning bolts and a quiver of arrows. The picture changed as the stories changed.

*Today's top story: The education Czar is concerned about the increase in truancy in Angeltown, and plans to get to the bottom of this as soon as possible.*

The Czar spoke: *While truancy is on the rise, the students that remain have had increased success with the new Quick Learn Ultra-targeted Software. We expect a record graduation rate.*

The camera switched back to the reporter: *A new report from the Czar of Education indicates a 20% increase in sustainability and continued growth in the energy sector. New closings of the Angeltown district will be announced soon in an effort to increase productivity. More news after the interview with our own Martin, star of 'The Middle Eastern Hunt.' Remember that the enemy is nowhere and everywhere. This interview is brought to you by Drone Max, the first name in drone technology.*

Jane was so excited to see her hero, Martin, that she was sweating from every part of her body. She would certainly have to take a cold shower after this.

"So Martin, what do you attribute to the show's success?"

"Well," said Martin, "justice is brought into homes all over Angeltown and the sovereignty, and there isn't a lot of justice these days."

"There's no need to be modest, people watch the show for you—"

"If I am the reason people watch these stories of justice, then I am a happy man. What people don't see is the hard work behind the scenes, tracking these dirtbags, what that takes and all."

Jane got chills when Martin used the word, *dirtbags.*

"How long does it take you to produce one of these shows?"

"Sometimes a week, sometimes a month, it depends on the case. Some cases are obvious, others are not so easy."

"Before we go Martin, can you show us your famous pose for the ladies out there."

Martin leaned forward into the microphone, "And for the guys too, am I right?"

Martin stood up, ripped off his detachable pant legs and flexed his abs, legs, and arm muscles with a dull-witted yet threatening grin on his face.

Jane clapped enthusiastically like a girl getting a puppy for Christmas.

Before the next show began, the Theme Song for Czar World, *This land is ours; take it and make it,* played and names of neighborhoods appeared on the screen with a voice over. "Due to cutbacks, these areas of Angeltown will be closed starting Monday." A list of six neighborhoods scrolled from the bottom and exited the top of the screen.

---

After the short summer break, Jane was back in the classroom monitoring the students. In her earphone she heard, "Check the boy in row five, seat nine." Jane walked up the aisle and she saw a boy with his head tilted over, not moving, with his eyes closed. Instead of approaching the boy to see what was wrong, Jane tapped her tablet and 1000 volts shocked Thomas McTavish from his chair for one second. He jolt up, opened his eyes temporarily then collapsed, falling out of his seat. The school's security force, having been called when the boy lost consciousness, picked him up and took him out.

"Faking seizures will NOT get you out of your work," shouted Jane's amplified voice. A few of the students snickered as the collapsed boy was taken out. Most students cringed, hoping it didn't happen to them.

"Now back to your lessons!" she screamed.

The first lesson they received on their tablets was Lesson Alpha: Working for the Insiders. It taught the importance of the Insiders and how everyone must work for their benefit, most of all, the Contributors, the highest class of Insiders.

The lessons came with a warning for teachers: *If you fail to follow the programmed curriculum and labor portion, if you veer off script to improvise no matter what was happening to your students, if you provided extra help outside of the given program, or if you in anyway deviate from the educational plan, you could be fired, fined, and arrested.*

The public, so the media said, was sick and tired of certain teachers who thought they knew best how to help their students. Teachers would now do exactly what was required of them to be employed; those who didn't had almost all been removed and teaching was a respectable profession once again. Jane Caitlin Winston was a pure follower of the Czar. She was never sullied by her own needs and desires.

In education as in life, there had to be winners and losers. Grades and test scores didn't motivate students as well as they had in the past, college was out of sight for most students, and jobs were few to non-existent. No, Truancy Prison was the final solution to the problem of students refusing to learn.

When not working on the Quick Learn curriculum, the students learned how to gather GPS and personal data on their fellow students, collate and code it, put it into a spread sheet and Jane would send it to the SADF. This was *training for a future in computers* the students were told. They learned how to track signals from phones, tablets, belt buckles and other communication devices and map daily travel of signals given a nine digit ID. They used the extension to the Governet's education software, "Quick Learn Tracker," for their exercises.

 One task the students worked on was tracking people that had been scanned at the May 14, 2053 United Students of Angeltown school protest and terrorist attack. This lead to the arrests of the leaders of the rally from the Angeltown high schools, those who weren't killed on the spot. An estimated 12% were still not apprehended at the time the program began. The apprehension rate improved as Jane's students started working with the software, and the students who excelled at tracking focused on this work. The student-workers were not told why they were tracking students, just that this was practice for future jobs.

 Cameras had recorded faces from all over the library grounds. Jane's students collected the pictures, identified some of the students through face recognition programs, and sent them to the SADF to be stored and sent into a tracking loop. Every month, the percent of students not caught went down, and Jane was praised for the success her student's had in their capture.
After a few months of using the Quick Learn Tracker, the number not caught was down to one percent, and now the students scanned the footage frame by frame, bit by bit, every one of over three thousand images. An especially illusive suspect was spotted. In the picture, a swirling flash of purple hair and the side of a girl's face at the end of the Central Library's Maguire Gardens was caught on camera. The image of the girl with purple hair was marked and sent to the SADF tracking lab at Rampart.

*Who is that*, thought SADF Plebe Jooseppi (Joe) Hankala, a rotund, short man with dyed, short blonde hair. He was updating the security protocols for entrance into Rampart when the photo of a girl with purple hair appeared on his screen. He worked in a cramped converted storage room with three computers lined up, side-by-side with large 34 inch wide monitors. He was the only one in the section at the time, and he moved his bulk freely around the space.

Most of the pictures sent to Officer Hankala to be analyzed were easy to identify with standard searches and facial recognition, and he knew he would make quick work of this job. He typed purple for hair in the Angeltown school yearbook database, clicked the box for female and for age typed 12-18 to cover his bases. Then Plebe Hankala, clicked *search*.

After a couple of minutes, there was a beep from his computer signaling the search results. He furrowed his brow. There were no class photos of girls in junior high or high school with purple hair in the past year. He expanded his search to all the schools in California. As he waited, he clicked his halo-belt. It projected a hologram from his oversized belt buckle of a child running in a room with what they once called a "Christmas tree." People still celebrated all sorts of holidays, there just weren't a lot of trees to go around, and they couldn't be used for such frivolities as ornament hangers. A woman came onto the picture and hugged the boy. She waved her hand in a welcoming gesture offscreen. "Come on Joe," the woman said. "Come here and play with your brother."

The same beep came out of a speaker overhead. The search of California revealed no school records for the purple-haired girl. He had one more idea. He attempted to open the database of truants for the past year and a bright orange text pulsated on his screen that read *Access Denied.* A second later, a loud screeching horn came out of the overhead speakers. He quickly hit the *Abort Application* key on his computer and the software closed.

Now Hankala would have to disappoint his boss, something he hated to do. He liked his Captain; he wasn't bad for a military sort. But because he "worked his way up from the bottom of the SADF" to make Captain, he was often quick to strike out at even the slightest tinge of failure.

He switched to visual talk mode and connected to his supervisor upstairs. The screen in Captain Ranken's office flashed a message and the computer vocalized it, "The scanning room needs your assistance." The Captain answered it by double tapping a visual communication icon on his computer.

Plebe Hankala's face appeared sheepishly on the monitor. "Yes, Plebe, how have you failed now?" asked Captain Ranken.

Hankala frowned. "Captain," I am sending you a packet with a photo of a girl who doesn't appear on any student databases in the city or state. Perhaps she is a dropout. We don't have much."

"Why is this girl so important, Plebe?" the Captain wondered.

"She is a girl from the May 14th rally that we can't identify. One of a dozen. I think we can track her by her hair," he said, worried. *I couldn't be demoted from Plebe, could I?*

"Okay, plebe, consider it handled."

"If I may make a suggestion, we could look into those students who haven't attended class recently, the truants, and track her that way. I tried, but I don't have access to those files."

"No one can access those files. The whole system has collapse and recent truancy records have vanished. They're trying to rebuild it, but for now we have to use the footage from the library." Ranken disconnected.

The Captain looked at the material on his screen. He pushed the corner of his small monitor, and a wall across from his desk lit up. The image featured the side of a girl's face and her purple hair with a cap of black hair on top centered among fleeing students. The Captain inspected the side of her face. He touched the wall projection and activated the document menu. He then selected a box called *Analysis* that featured the incident report.

*Location: Central Library, Angeltown, 630 W. 5th Street.*
*Time of Incident: 10:17 AM, May 14, 2053*
*Suspect: unknown*
*Gender: female*
*Age: 12-18*
*Weight: Estimated, 100 lbs*
*Race: Southern European, Middle Eastern*
*Hair: Black and purple*
*Eyes: Unknown*
*Skin: Olive/Tan*
*Height: 5 feet to 5 feet 5 inches*
*Clothes: Jean shorts, gray t-shirt*
*Behavior: Running away from the speakers' podium and library entrance.*
*Motives: unknown*
*Affiliations: unknown*
*Address: unknown*
*Associates: unknown*

Ranken looked again at the photo on the wall. He started at the center of the screen where the purple-haired girl was located and scanned around her counter-clockwise and saw in order: a tree, sidewalk, planter, legs, body, head…He stopped and tapped the head and a light-ring appeared around it. It was a boy her age looking at her as she ran. He tapped the head and a button appeared on the screen that read, "Search." He clicked the button and another dialogue box appeared with selections: Angeltown, Southern California, California, United States. The State Auto-Defense Force did not have access to worldwide data for their searches. Ranken checked the box for Angeltown and the one for Southern California, just in case.

Another selection box appeared for various databases: school, work, government, suspicious persons, and ALL. He selected 'school'. *ALL could take ALL day.* Then he hit 'enter.' Ranken closed the large wall screen and minimized the screen on his desktop. He opened the folder with information on the May 14th riot. They had made a lot of progress recently, and they were near a conclusion of the case.

Ranken recognized the name: Darnell Dwight Daft. He knew he had seen that face before. As Ranken waited for the young man's file, the computer let out a ring and opened up the data on young Mr. Daft.

*Daft, age 18, white, 5 foot 10, 160 lbs, recent Truancy Squad drop out, part time employed recovering scrap, pliant witness, given 5 years' probation for attending a political rally and cooperating with authorities on the case.*

"Perfect," Ranken said aloud. Then he thought to himself, *we can get this baboso to confess to anything, and he won't have any qualms about turning in anyone*. He pushed a red button on his desk to call the second lieutenant, commander of the extraction squad.

Ranken sent the data with Daft's address and particulars to Lieutenant Gomez. The address was in Westlake Park. *Why haven't they bulldozed that place?* the Lieutenant thought. The data also said, "Darnell Dwight Daft was harmless with few prospects and few skills other than shooting down drones with 22 rifles." *That's quite a feat, considering the gun's lack of power.*

They never did find Daft's gun, but they know it was him shooting down drones.

When Gomez and a uniformed officer turned onto his street, Darnell was waiting outside for them with his hands interlocked over his head; the young man had an uncanny knack for knowing when the SADF was coming for him. Lieutenant Gomez said as if ordering take out, "You can put your hands down Darnell. We just want your help with something."

Gomez took off his optical sunglasses and the officer watched Daft carefully. "Here, put these on," he motioned toward the kid. Darnell put on the glasses. Gomez then tapped the side of the glasses and a picture slowly faded up from black to show the photo of the girl with the purple hair.

"Do you know this girl?" asked Gomez.

After mouthing a few words under his breath, Darnell said, "Yeah, I've seen her at Belmont Academy, but I don't know her name…"

Gomez took the glasses off Darnell's face, making him flinch. Then Gomez patted him on the back, making him jump. "Keep on helping us Darnell, and we will keep helping you. That's how this works. Come with us." They drove to Rampart IV. The station had been destroyed twice in rioting and once in a massive fire, only to be rebuilt. This time, it was a fortress that people were afraid to approach. The police, with the cooperation of the media, had been spreading rumors about torture, killings, and other atrocities going on inside the station, and the people still living in the neighborhood wanted nothing to do with it.

If you didn't pass a fingerprint and badge scan when entering the armored compound, 2.5 inch traffic spikes stopped your vehicle from entering. Gomez presented his badge and pressed his left thumb on the scanner. Then he pointed his middle finger up at the camera for his fellow SADF members. The rank and file laughed, if they noticed it at all, and the higher ups relied on Gomez too much to do anything about his miscreant nature.

"Hey Triple D," shouted a detective as Darnell entered the new Technology Augmented Police Station, TAPS. The technology center of the station had an open floor plan with desks as barriers segmenting off the departments: theft, cybercrime, homicides, fraud, and so on. Video displays covered almost every inch of wall space around the edges of the floor.

"Hey," Darnell said sheepishly to no one in particular. He was brought over to a large monitor near the center of the room. Detective Kendo, unaware that the expensive antique Jerry Garcia tie he wore was a fake, had the photos of the Belmont High Nanomed Academy yearbook, years 2052-53, open. They started with the freshmen.

"Look at all the photos of the freshmen and tell me if you see this girl," said the detective.

After a quick scan of the photos, Darnell answered. "Nope."

"Are you sure?" the detective asked.

Darnell glared at him. "She was…unique looking, I know."

"Okay," said the detective. The same happened with the sophomores, the juniors and the seniors.

"She's not there, man. Can I go?"

Gomez grabbed his shoulder and made him cringe. "No Darnell, we're not done yet."

Gomez took Kendo aside. "What if she didn't have a class photo?"

"We could match school enrollment with the photos to find out what students were enrolled but didn't have a yearbook photo," she said.

"Sure. We could try," said Gomez.

"Why do want to find this girl anyway?" asked Darnell.

Gomez was ready with an answer. "She's missing and her parents want to find her. You could make them real happy if you could help us out."

Darnell bit his lip and nodded. "Hey, do you have all the photos from the yearbook, you know, the clubs and stuff?"

"Yes, Darnell, what do you mean?" asked Gomez.

"Show them to me," Darnell insisted.

Gomez shook his head. *A lot of good this will do.* The Lieutenant touched the monitor of his computer and tapped the screen twice. It went back to the title page.

"Go ahead," Gomez told Darnell, pointing at the screen. Darnell looked at the table of contents page and then scrolled to page twenty-four and looked around the screen. He pointed to a head, barely sticking in from the edge of the photo on the left side in the back of the track-team photo. Darnell touched the screen, "There."

"You sure?" asked Gomez.

"Yeah, it can't be anyone else."

"How do you know?"

"Cause I used to hang out and watch her run."

"That's perfectly understandable."

Darnell stood. "Yeah, can I go now?"

Gomez looked Darnell once over. "Have you seen this girl recently."

"Not recently, like…"

Gomez glared at him. "When did you see her, Darnell."

"I don't know, a long time ago, like."

"Why didn't you tell us you had seen her?"

Darnell avoid eye contact. "You didn't ask."

"Darnell, we allow you your freedom because you have been an upstanding citizen, until now." He gritted his teeth. "I guess we need to reopen your case—"

Darnell flinched.

"Where was this, Darnell? Where did you see her?"

"She was going into a house at 2nd and Park."

Gomez grinned. "That's near where you live, Darnell."

Darnell cowered as if Gomez was going to hit him. The Lieutenant pat him on the shoulder instead.

He handed Darnell to a detective be taken home. "Be a good boy, and go with this officer…and Darnell, keep this between us, and you might get those charges completely dropped."

Gomez sat down, opened a document on his computer, and started a criminal file on Chava Chavez.

#

# Chapter 12
# Work Study

*Our software is engineered for the individual needs of each educational environment. The package is flexible and scalable with students' complete lifecycle in mind.*
Director of the Educational Software Division for the Czar of Education

  Jane Winston taught civics and surveillance lessons in a large auditorium in a converted 4th Street mall. In the other areas of the building there was instruction for medical assistants and lab technicians with test subjects taken from the student population. The shiny white walls and ceilings in the lab area symbolized the purity and holiness of their mission: the protection of future generations.
  The lower-rated students were led off into a waiting room, a defunct women's clothier, and the higher-rated students were sent into the dressing rooms to change into hazmat suits. They had received training on how to inject serums, extract blood samples, and all the other skills required for the day's experiment. They walked down the sterilized corridor into the testing center, a former lingerie store, to a light, noninvasive soundtrack once called *elevator music*. Students who demonstrated they were more worthy by scoring higher on the tests and the classroom assignments, the A

and AAA students, were given the job of lab technicians. Lab techs were 'in demand,' they were led to believe, and the students considered this a great honor and opportunity.

The B and C rated students arrived from all over the area. They were separated from their peers in their school of origin to reduce experimental contamination. These students were instructed by the Nanomed technicians who were dressed in the bright pink hazmat suits to, "take off your shoes and clothes and put on the booties and robes for your lessons today. You can put your clothes in the lockers behind you."

The students obeyed without question. They were convinced that this was part of their training for work after having been told they were specially selected, given a mental acuity test, and a physical examination before becoming test subjects. The subjects sat on cream-colored disks two feet in diameter that emerged from slots in the wall.

The higher-rated students, the laboratory attendants, entered the room with boxes of syringes with filled with nanoprobes. A voice came from the PA system. "Students. You will now receive your nanoprobes. Sit still." The nanoprobes were injected.

The lower-rated students sat still on their disks as they were injected with nanoprobes to be examined later for the effects of their *training*. Today, inhalants were being tested on them. Each student-subject was brought to a sealed-tight, shower-sized box by one of student attendants. Once the box was sealed, air streamed in from ceiling vents, air from the most contaminated regions of Southern California with an increase in the pathogenic particles by a factor of ten, what one might receive walking through a pollution cloud without protection.

The student-researchers, directed by employees from

Nanomed, would then wait ten minutes (an alarm sounded when the time was up) and then take a blood sample and give the student-subjects a pulmonary test to check the oxygen and foreign particulate levels in their lungs and blood. A few students passed out soon after breathing in the contaminated air and were taken out by the Nanomed physician who declared loudly for all to hear, "Do not worry, everything will be okay." Those test subjects never came back.

Afterward, the lab-technicians gave half the subjects, the experimental group selected at random, an inhaler with chemical agents formulated to fight pollutants in the lungs. The other half of the group would get a placebo inhalant. The lab attendants assumed all subjects were getting the anti-pollutant agents and had no idea how to read the coded results of the experiment. Only the Nanomed technicians knew what the numbers meant.

The next day, a new set of low-rated students in the area were bused in for their *lessons*. The students who were learning the experimental techniques in the laboratory remained from day to day. The students who had been experimented on would return and be monitored for any health effects, with some sent home and others sent to The Center for End of Life Care (CELC). Before sending students home, a full DNA panel was taken from them and put on record for later investigation of those students who didn't become terminal.

Some of the students in the area were sent to different centers for other kinds of *biological training*. In one school, students were tested in extreme heat and high solar radiation conditions. Some students wore protective gear, and others wore a jump suit that provided no protection at all from solar radiation. Still another group of students were sent to a different lab and were given food that had been contaminated with mercury and lead. One group was given a suppository that would fight these toxins, and the other control group was given a placebo.

The Insiders were happy to donate financially to such research for the betterment of life on earth. All the data would be used to save the elite members of society and protect the future of the species.

Letters were sent to families explaining that their children had been killed in a viral terrorist attack and that their bodies were to be cremated for the safety of the other students and the population of Angeltown. Of course, the Governet showed stories of this terrorist attack on their news channel for over a month.

---

Artie could barely endure the walk from his one room apartment to the computer lab. And having never collaborated with anyone but his mom and dad on projects, he was not sure how to work with a team. The team leader, Professor Asthana, knew about Benz's history hacking the Citizen's Cloud. So he put Artichoke on the task of writing libraries and security protocols, under his supervision, to protect their network and computers from hackers.

"Mr. Benz," said Asthana who had checked on Artie's recent work. "What you wrote is great. I tried to hack into the computer, and it took me quite some time, more time than required to track someone who was making the attempt. The new hydrowall was quite effective, and it could be even more so. For example, somebody like you could still find a way in."

"Thanks Dr. Asthana."

"Your next step would be to make it impenetrable to you, or your mother."

Again, Artie didn't like him mentioning his mother.

"Tell me something about how do you write your code? You clearly studied several computer languages, I hear you even invented one. But how do you know what to write?"

"I just see it and write it," he explained. "Like Einstein saw space in a different way or Doctor Tao sees math arrange itself."

"Like Dr. Ramanujan knew a solution to math's enigmas without proofs," said Asthana. Artichoke perked up at this conversation. "Oh, we'll do the proofs, Artie." He pat him on the back. "Lucky, or perhaps not so lucky, lad."

"Not," Artie muttered to himself.

Artichoke missed the forest and his parents. And every two weeks, he looked at his paycheck to make sure Caltech wasn't cheating his parents of their 20% of his pay. He was allowed by the Governet to talk with them for 30 minutes once a week. They monitored his contact with them; he was not allowed to talk about his work at Caltech or he would be cut off. That happened once, the second time he talked to his mother he said, "I get to protect the whole system with…" Click. He never made that mistake again.

By the age of eighteen, Dr. A. Benz earned his PhD in Advanced System's Theory and Programming from CalTech, the youngest recipient ever. He passed his examinations armed with advanced knowledge from his studies and mother's lessons and learned all he needed on the job, from Doctor Asthana, and from the course books. "Congratulations Artie, or I should say, Dr. Benz," Professor Asthana said with pride and only the slightest hint of jealousy. "I think you are ready to explore your dissertation work, Doctor." Artichoke smiled briefly for the first time in years.

For his dissertation, Artie wrote what he thought could be the missing link between supercomputers and AI, *Fermat*. He researched the concept, tested computer speeds under various conditions, and worked on security protocols.

He also took on the job of improving the *Quick Learn Education Software* used all over Angeltown, and soon, the nation. His job was to maximize the reactiveness of the software to the student's family, personal history, and online profile. If put in the proper environment with the students connected to various cameras and sensors for heart rate, skin temperature, breath rate, the software could focus better on students' needs. Soon, Dr. Benz had created the Benz-Responsiveness Protocols used for educational software all over the nation.

Artie spent so much of his time working on his projects that he would forget to wash or eat for days, living off of expensive almond butter and crackers, one thing he could digest. "Are you okay, Dr. Benz?" asked a colleague from France, Dr. Marlibund, after seeing him nearly wretch into a waste basket.

"Yes, just nerves," he said, waving her off.

After a few months, *Quick Learn* was ready for the Citizen's Network *Universal Platform*. It was installed on every computer in every classroom in the state and some states outside of California.

Unfortunately, his parents never saw his work; they died when he turned eighteen, just before he received his diploma, apparently of the American Flu. Artichoke wasn't able to say goodbye to them. He found out they were dead when he noticed that the 20% reduction in his paycheck earmarked for his parents wasn't being removed.

After Dr. Benz learned of his parents death, he curled up on his bed every night shaking in anger and grief. They were his whole life for so many years. He was no longer interested in the long term goals of speedy computing, processing, and creating real AI. Besides, he was sure AI was decades off, if it were possible at all. He now made new plans for the educational software. Destroying the truancy records in Angeltown was easy compared to his next task.

He spent the next month finishing his special extra-responsive upgrade of the educational software for the schools. He had spent much of his time looking at the education architecture of the Angeltown Unified Schools since entering Caltech and had read about and learned everything he could about education and the Czar's Office, including material that was restricted to the public. It was just as well his parents weren't around to see this. Dr. Benz knew that he could no longer live being a part of the system that his parents had fought against.

    That summer, Artie was ready. He went to Dr. Marlibund to discuss the transfer of the maintenance of *Quick Learn* to her. "It won't take more than an hour a day, and there is a test program that checks the functionality every night. Nighty-nine percent of the time it just gives the all clear message in the morning."

    "Why me if it's so easy?"

    "I trust you, and I need to take time off; I just learned of my parents' death."

    She bit her lip. "Oh, sure. Sorry. No problem. Take your time away. I will handle it."

    Dr. Artichoke Benz knew his work at Caltech and with the *Quick Learn* software was helping the oppressive state, but he had no choice while his parents were alive. Now that his parents' were dead, threats of their incarceration no longer forced his compliance to the university, or the state. He felt sorry about what his leaving would do to Doctor Asthana who had treated him well and given him freedom to work on his own. However, he had no reason to stay at Caltech and finish the last year of his parole. So at 4:35 PM on August 31, 2054, Dr. Benz left the computer lab early. He never returned.

---

    Jane Winston taught her new data entry, civics, and patriotism class on Tuesday, September 1, 2054. She planned to work from home in a year, having saved up enough pieces to teach part time. She also knew that one day soon, she would be receiving an invitation to work with the Czar. In the meantime, she would continue her work for the SADF as a network communications specialist. She ran the education software Quick Learn as usual for data analysis and the education of her students.

Quick Learn had newly updated curriculum and software written using the Benz-Responsiveness Protocols. It adapted to the students' answers faster on this day than ever before. In addition, the lessons started to morph, as if they wrote themselves. Instead of getting the basic readings about loyalty, patriotism and faith, along with their time on the surveillance network, today they were getting messages about individuality, resistance, and rebellion. The software was honing in on the histories and records of each student. It's tendrils reached into the Governet, Angeltown school and truancy records, and the SADF.

As the students worked with the software, nearly invisible, pale parallel lines rotated around the screen. A periodic tone brought the students into focus, into a heightened suggestive state.

Instead of the standard material about the importance of the Czar of Education and how they keep Angeltown from ruin, the students started with lessons about the Constitution of 2032. But the lessons soon veered in a new direction, with each student getting different material targeted to his or her profile. The first question most students received, read aloud by a low, frog like voice into their earphones and printed on the screen in the new Constitution lesson was:

*Did you know there was an earlier Constitution?*

That confused the forty-eight students in the auditorium. First they weren't doing their surveillance tasks, and now this. They had never heard of an earlier Constitution. Most of the students hit the *no* button on the screen. A few, not wanting to look stupid, tapped *yes*.

*Have you heard of freedom of speech?*

Again, the same results.

There was a strange phrase:

*Congress shall make no laws abridging freedom of speech.*

*What's Congress*, thought the students who hadn't yet had all their curiosity drained out of them.

Jane only had the standard lessons on her tablet and was not given any feedback about student performance. Instead, all the students were scoring 100% in accuracy, speed, time on task, and eyes on task. She smiled with pride at these results.

The students glanced at Jane surreptitiously, but they said nothing. They looked at each other and shrugged, making sure not to be seen by the teacher although certainly the tablets' cameras would pick up their body movement and facial twitches. Then the quality of the messages in their ears became more sinister.

*You are being lied to.*

*You always wondered why your parents left you. They didn't. The Czar of Education killed your parents.*

Others got the message:

*Why are you tracking others the way you are tracked? Your sister was tracked (or brother, or friend). She was removed for refusing to learn. They were destroyed for resisting.*

These messages upset the students, made some of them shake, some teary eyed, some angry. Others had a rotating combination of emotions.

*You are hurting your own and the families of others in this room. You are hurting yourselves.*

The parallel lines kept spinning and the tone rang out again.

Pictures of dead bodies appeared on the screens. The bodies were stacked in piles. They could have been their parents, grandparents, cousins. They were in fact pictures of piles of Native Americans, Jews, Cambodians, Armenians, Indonesians, and other bodies. The students didn't understand; they had never seen anything like this before. Then videos of executions, lynchings of Black Americans, executions of Africans and Asians and many others were played on the screen.

The students were trained by the Czar and his educational forces to believe and not question what they saw. Most lacked the ability to discern truth from lies. *Seeing was believing* was how the Czar's forces trained the students. *Don't question what you see*, was the Czar's message. Now that message was being used against the Governet; students were seeing and believing.

*Do something…these are your people…all people…*

Once pliant students started to cry, shout, hit their desks. They stood up and threw tablets at the wall. After what seemed like hours, actually less than one minute, shy and docile Aaron Crown took his tablet and smacked a boy in front of him on the head, knocking him off his chair and into a stupor.

Chaos took over, for exactly 15.9 seconds. Then trimethylheptylpyran, Formula 18, spewed through the vents in the gymnasium to incapacitate the students. Jane collapsed like a rag doll onto the floor.

The office of the Education Czar used the remote cutoff switch to stop the tablets from accessing the program, and Quick Learn was shut down all over the nation.

---

Jane woke up fully clothed in her teaching suit in her new, dimly lit basement apartment. She lay on a firm, serviceable twin mattress. Jane squinted, trying to adjust to the low lighting from long, narrow window fourteen feet over the bed. Twenty feet cross the dark blue room sat a black writing table, a metal chair and a laptop computer attached to a wireless power supply. Otherwise, the room was empty. She scanned for her book, "A Diary of a Young Girl." It wasn't there. Jane put on her purple low-heeled shoes next to the bed, and after gaining her balance, she wandered around the room.

During the years since Jane was a child star in Angeltown, everything had changed. The only thing left in her hometown of Glendale were a few RVs off the grid and survivalist camps. Angeltown's population had collapsed like the rest of the world. The Sterilization meant that no new life was being born in the city, just old life dying.

Jane saw a door to a closet sized bathroom in the middle of the wall on her right. It opened to what was a shower and toilet room with a wash basin directly next to and below the showerhead. Clinging to the wall so she didn't fall, Jane tried the shower. Nothing. Jane didn't react with even the slightest surprise or disappointment at the lack of water.

She swayed back and forth as she moved toward the opening in the wall at the opposite end of the room from the bed. It led to a stark hallway, also midnight blue. In fact, the walls, the floors, and the ceiling were all midnight blue. The darkness of the room crushed in on her after her time in a sparkling white apartment.

She started down the dimly lit hallway and saw an opening on the left. There was a small table and a chair along with an instant food cooker on a counter to the right. More midnight blue. As she entered, she saw a nook used for a closet on her right. Her clothes were hanging neatly in the opening. Seven blouses, three jackets, three skirts, and three pairs of slacks were hung in the makeshift closet. The shelving underneath contained a few pairs of underwear, socks, two pairs of stockings, and a couple of t-shirts, all neatly stacked. There were also two pairs of pajamas with *Czar of Education* and *Angeltown Unified School District* written on the tops. To the right of the shelving were five pairs of shoes, four were heels of two to four inches with a pair of sandals. She collapsed into the metal chair, already exhausted.

She stared at the cooker. It was like one they had when she was a girl, not the newer model from her last apartment. *Was I ever a girl, I've been grown up so long...*

Jane heard a clanking and crash of metal from the end of the hallway past the kitchen area. Jane jumped at the noise then wearily got up out of the chair and slogged down the long hallway where the sound came from. *Strange*, wondered Jane, *where are the other rooms*? The hallway was a solid, wall to wall, a twenty-five foot narrow path without any doors or intersecting hallways. Jane reached the end where it opened up to a ten by six foot space. There was a steep wooden ladder on the left leading up to a two-by-four foot landing in front of a door fourteen feet up. To the right of the ladder was a metal air duct that led from the outside to the floor. There lay a three-foot square package wrapped in mylar. It was thin and bulging in the center, like a ravioli.

She looked at it a moment and saw on the top was a label that had the words *Spring Street* on it with an advertisement for *Ray's Pawn Shop* "supplier of the best water in Angeltown," on it. *That must be where I am, downtown, near Ray's.* Jane struggled up the ladder to the silver door. She had to get out and look around.

The thick, steel door didn't budge. There was a keypad on the door next to the chrome handle, but she did not have the code. Jane calmly accepted the outcome after a brief feeling of embarrassment over acting so inappropriately.

Jane maneuvered her way back down the ladder and looked at the package. She dragged it twenty-five feet back to the kitchen area and plopped it onto the table. On the long counter that held the cooker there was a drawer. In the drawer was one mug, one glass, one butter knife, one fork, one spoon, one plate and one bowl, all neatly organized. Next to the cooker was a small sink. Upon the wall to the left was a hard plastic rectangular cubby with slots like an old post office. In contained two kitchen towels.

Jane ripped and yanked at the corner of the package, pulling at various edges in an attempt to open it. Nothing. She grabbed the butter knife and tried to slice it open, getting angrier with every failed jab. "Damn it, damn it, damn it!" She threw the knife in frustration. It clanked around the floor. She put her hand to her mouth. She had never sworn in her life, even when fighting with her mother.

She gave up and slumped onto the chair once again. Only then did she notice that one of the corners of the mylar-wrapped mystery had the message, *Open Here,* with an arrow pointing toward the corner. She ripped it open and desperately reached in and pulled out one of the twelve meal packets from inside the bag and put it in the cooker.

Thirty seconds later there was a ding and a voice, "Wait, it's hot, wait, it's hot, wait, it's hot …" and a red light flashing on the top of the cooker. As she waited, she got the one bowl out of the cubby with the fork and spoon. After one minute, the green light flashed on the cooker, and she heard the words, "Safe, safe, safe" repeated three times.

The food fit perfectly in the bowl with no wasted space. She smelled a light odor of rosemary and garlic. There was chicken and carrots, exactly how her mother used to cook. For a moment, Jane almost felt sorry for her mother, almost empathized…almost. But she would never show such weakness as to feel sorry for herself. Jane expelled the disease-causing emotions until she was empty. *There is nothing different from the smell of the food to the time of day or color of the shoes I wear. They are just facts.* She put the wrapper in a chute on the wall, and it swooshed away.

Jane sat down with the bowl and engulfed the food. *I guess I like chicken.* A terrible thirst came over her; she panicked. She grabbed the mylar pouch, dug her hand in, then dumped the rest of the contents onto the table in desperation. The contents spilled out. Several balls, clear and gelatinous like jelly-fish bodies, rolled onto the table. They were the size of small plums and appeared to contain water. Jane, desperate to get at even a little water from the inside of the casing, put a ball in her mouth. The sheath around the water dissolved.

As the flaccid ball melted, she sensed the moisture entering her body and her blood. She experienced a sense of calm, something she had never felt before. Then she felt a rush of euphoria and forgot about her need to shower. She bolted upright and realized that she should look at the laptop in the other room.

On top of the computer was a note that read, "Jane Caitlin Winston: Confidential," with a password on the bottom. She sat in the chair, lifted the lid to the laptop, tapped in the password, and hit *enter*. Immediately, a digital video file started. The Woman in Pink, who had earlier taken Jane's retinal scan, appeared on the screen and talked straight into the camera with the voice of a sentencing judge.

*Jane Caitlin Winston: You have been found guilty of illegal distribution of illicit material and failure to control the learning environment. In light of recent events, we have closed your school and the others run by the Governet. Only Insiders' Academies in Saint Bernard will remain open. You will be supervising the remaining students digitally from your new residence.*

Oh my, thought Jane, I am a terrible person. She immediately returned to the calm and tranquil feeling that had been hitting her in waves. A large message that nearly filled the screen appeared as the Woman faded to black: 'CLICK HERE.' Jane obeyed.

The man in the purple suit came on the screen, speaking like a game-show host.

*Jane Caitlin Winston: We hope you are comfortable. The water is available for two minutes a day at every spout. We suggest you make the most of it.*

*You will start your assignment on Monday. You will supervise ninety-two students from 7 AM to 1 PM, Monday to Friday. You will be presenting new curricula from the Quick Learn II program.*

*If you wish to exit to the outside, which we recommend you do not, you must type in the code "czarisgood" onto the keypad and then press your right hand anywhere on the door. That will unlock the mechanism. You have to type in the code only once. In the future, just place your right palm on the door and it will open. In the meantime, familiarize yourself with the new educational program.*

---

Jane had lost the desire to leave the living quarters. Instead, she started looking at the new educational software. After a few minutes, Jane was exhausted and lay on her bed. She didn't have the will to put on her pajamas. She woke up the next morning, Saturday, sweating in her clothes and in need of a shower. *Where is the soap? How do I wash my hair?*

She walked to the open closet and got a fresh set of clothes and then went to the bathroom. She sat down to pee and made a face of disgust that the shower was next to the toilet. "Oh, gross!" She stood up and the toilet sucked her waste away.

*I need more water. I should shower first. But I need more water.* She looked to the sink and saw the outline of a metal box hidden in the wall. She pushed on it and the drawer slid outward. Inside she saw toothpaste and a toothbrush, bath wash, shampoo, conditioner and a hairbrush. No hair drier, but she did find a thin rolled up towel. Jane gritted her teeth, then grinned.

Jane took off her clothes, but before stepping in for her two-minute shower, she ran into the kitchen. She looked around for the water. She had left it on the table. It was gone. She panicked, but then looked at the cubby and saw that the balled water had been put inside along with the food packets, all neatly stacked. *How? I hadn't put the food away.* The kitchen area was now straightened and organized. It happened overnight, and Jane was almost certain she didn't do it.

The thought passed quickly, for she needed water. She grabbed a ball and put it in her mouth. After a moment, she realized she was standing alone and naked and quickly returned to the shower. She would have to be strategic. She got herself wet for ten seconds, then rubbed the body wash on and put some shampoo in her hair. Then she wet herself for twenty seconds more, scrubbing in the soaps. She felt strangely calm and at peace, with a clarity of thought.

After she was covered with lather, she turned on the water. She scrubbed and rubbed herself all-over clean and felt an intense feeling of dirt washing off her. The water stopped.

*Let's look outside.* The towel unrolled to a full size and was surprisingly absorbent. Jane dried off and put on some clean clothes. *No makeup, oh well.* She went down the hall, up the ladder to the door. She typed in the password, *czarisgood,* then looked at her right hand for a moment. *Amazing.* She smiled and placed the hand on the door then heard the 'click' of it unlocking.

Jane turned the handle, pushed, and walked outside. The Angeltown sun stabbed into her. She screamed in pain and immediately turned around and went back inside onto the platform. She was less panicked once she reached the bottom of the ladder. She would try at night. *No, I can't.* Okay, maybe she would try again later. She wondered what to do before then. The door shut and locked.

She went back to the computer and turned on the software to look at the instructions. She had to start the next session in two days.

She read the first screen after it opened: *By reading this, you are contractually prevented from illegal use of the program including copying the material for sale, distributing it to unlicensed users, or misuse of the material in anyway. Recent updates have fixed past software problems. Videos will be played and students will also read standard test questions and reply. Instructors will check scores and grade writing assignments. The Czar wishes you a great journey of learning.*

Jane's mind wandered and she relaxed. She thought of the story of the teenage girl in what was called Nazi occupied Europe. *The Nazis sounded terrible*, she mused. *Good thing we have the Czar to protect us from them. Where is that book of mine?*

*Tonight, I will go outside and look around. I wonder if someone misses me. I wonder where Harry is.* Jane briefly indulged the thought, then went numb. She needed more water. She took another dose and worked through some of the lessons in the updated Quick Learn II software. It was simple material for Ms. Winston. Besides, she had the answers on her screen.

Then she looked at the most important part, the management software: grading and total time on task. The only thing new was the constant tracking of students' locations, even when they weren't online. Jane knew it was for their safety.

On Monday, Jane still hadn't gone outside. She had everything she needed in her residence: water, food, clothes that she found cleaned themselves every week, a wall television with the five channels, and a job. She loved teaching and seeing students succeed every week was gratifying. She promised herself that she would soon leave her apartment and look around.

Months later Jane still hadn't gone outside, and it was almost her twenty-first birthday, January 7th. She renewed her promise to go out and get her bearings. The sun should go down early on Sunday and the buildings, assuming there were still buildings outside, would block the burning rays.

On Saturday, Jane looked up out her window. It was overcast at two in the afternoon. Jane put on her shoes and started down the hallway. She placed her hand on the door, and it unlocked with its loud click. She moved outside and saw the alley. To the right there was a brick wall and on the left was a street at the end of the alley. Her breathing was labored as she walked toward the road. She was determined to get to the street and gain her bearings. Her breath halted with each step.

She reached the street and looked left and recognized downtown Angeltown. Jane could barely breath as a dense pollution cloud came down the street at her. She turned and ran back toward her home, but not before the tailing edge of the cloud hit her. She coughed and gagged and struggled to make it back.

She slammed her hand on the door. It unlocked. She pulled it open and collapsed on the platform at the top of the ladder. Her breath was labored and she was covered in filth. Jane needed to take a shower, but she had already taken a shower that day. She didn't know how much time had passed, but after what she assumed was fifteen minutes, she got up and climbed down the ladder.

She clung to the wall on her right and made it to the kitchen area. She grabbed a washcloth and stumbled to the shower room and tore off her clothes. Her skin burned from the pollution. She turned the knob to the shower. Nothing came out. She went to the kitchen. No water came out of the sink. "I need more water!" The pollution was still burning into her skin.

Jane grabbed one of the five remaining balls of water from the cubby and slid to the floor, sobbing. She put it in her mouth as her body heaved up and down with her tears.

Minutes later, Jane jumped at the sound of running water in the other room. She rushed to the shower. Nothing. She slumped onto the toilet seat.

After that, Jane started to hear the voices.

#

# Chapter 13
# Doctor Benz

*All students must make the most of themselves in order to receive the most from their education. Students must be prepared for whatever career is granted them and make timely use of the opportunity when it is presented.*
The Czar of Education

After the *Quick Learn* software system went rogue, the SADF contacted their head of cyber-warfare defense, computer security, and anti-hacking technology, Dr. Lance Lee. He went with Sergeant Van Heimlich to talk to the software engineers at Caltech where *Quick Learn* was created.

They parked and entered the computer department. The detectives were followed all the way from the entrance to the lobby by cameras, listening devices, and lie detecting sensors that were programmed to detect visitors with ill intent by recording skin temperature, skin moisture, facial movements, and piloerections. They met Dr. Marlibund in the lobby, and after they put on booties and head coverings, she walked them to the cyber lab.

As they talked, they stood around a metal bench in an intensely-lit room that once contained Dr. Benz's workstation.

"Dr. Marlibund, very nice to meet you," said Van Heimlich. They shook hands.

"Can you explain what went wrong with the software, Doctor," said Lee.

"The software acted...*vengeful.* That is what it was," explained Dr. Marlibund. "But it wasn't by accident, it was by design."

"And you think Dr. Benz was involved?" asked the sergeant.

"Of course it was him. He worked around the clock and barely slept. He was the head programmer of *Quick Learn*, and he constantly upgraded it, though it was an already stable program." She thought a moment. "I thought he was just a loner with nothing else to do, a perfectionist trying to make a name."

*Dr. Benz is the kid I investigated a few years back,* thought Lee.

The sergeant addressed her, "Do you have the computer interface that Doctor Benz used to program the software?"

"No, it is missing too," she answered.

"Were you able to trace the last code Dr. Benz uploaded, the last changes he made to *Quick Learn*?" Lee asked.

"Well...I wish I could. He uploaded a wholly new version before disappearing, each packet had changes. Luckily there was only a broken nose in Chicago, a student stabbed with a pencil in Denver, several fights in the metropoles and of course the concussion case in Angeltown when the kid was hit with a tablet computer. It was unfortunate, but not fatal."

"Weren't you tracking him? How was he able to elude you so easily?" asked Lee.

"He used some sort of software to block our surveillance. Something sophisticated that we didn't detect until he was gone. We only watched his work on the software, the time he spent updating and improving the security. And his ability to block our tracking of his electronic movements allowed him to sneak out in the dark of night. He disappeared before we knew he was gone."

"There was no one guarding him?"

"He was a good kid, he got his PhD and always did what was asked of him." She frowned. "I guess we underestimated his desire to leave."

The sergeant asked, "Could there have been foul play?"

Dr. Marlibund thought on it. "No…who knows?" She looked around the lab area. "No, I think he was ready to stop."

"What makes you say that?"

"Well, he had finished his degree so young; he had nothing left to prove. His parents had died and he needed time off, so he asked me to do periodic checks on *Quick Learn* for him."

"Did you have any suspicion about his plans?" Lee asked.

"No idea. We only talked about work. In the months I knew him, he never told me anything personal."

*But he told you about his parents' deaths,* thought Lee.

The sergeant gave her his data card. "If you think of anything that might help, contact us. You can leave a message anytime. Thank you."

"Well," said the sergeant to Dr. Lee, "let's go look at his apartment in the guest house."

The sergeant and Dr. Lee left the massive computer tech department and walked toward the guest house. "So, Doctor Marlibund doesn't know about the suspect's criminal background as a hacker," said the sergeant.

Dr. Lee nodded. "Right."

They arrived at Dr. Benz's former residence, the first apartment on the left as they entered the building. It was a studio with the bed to the right of the door. To the left, there was a small kitchen area with a sink and a refrigerator. On the far right was an opening featuring a tiny living room with a wall mounted TV on one side with bits of it on the floor.

"The Doctor cut the TV's satellite unit right out," the sergeant said, scratching his head. Dr. Lee made a mental note. A pizza box was laid on the far corner of the couch. Lee put on polychloroprene gloves.

"Hey Sergeant, take a look at this." Lee picked up the box and inspected it. "There's no grease or cheese, or evidence of any kind there was ever a pizza in here."

Van Heimlich put on his gloves. "Let me look at that." He grabbed the box and carefully examined it for residue. "They used to deliver drugs in pizza boxes until the police caught on. I don't see any evidence of that. Let's get a dog down here to sniff around."

"Do you know of any pizza places still operating downtown?" asked Lee.

"He could have had it drone delivered, but you're right. There's no evidence there was pizza in that box." Van Heimlich placed it back on the couch where they had found it.

In the cupboard, there were jars upon jars of almond butter with *Kaiser Saltines* on the shelf next to them.

"Jeesh," exclaimed the sergeant pointing at the almond butter, "that stuff goes for hundreds of dollars a jar. How much were they paying this guy?" There were a few cloves of garlic on the shelves and nothing else. There was an open jar of almond butter, some eggs, some olive oil and a jar of "Atomic Salsa." The sergeant opened the jar, smelled it, and recoiled in pain. "Mississippi hell!" Then he noticed a label placed on the jar with handwriting that read: *Take in order to feel something.* He showed the message to Lee. "Man, this guy was really messed up. I guess lots of geniuses are," laughed the sergeant.

Dr. Lee looked at the message then at Van Heimlich. "Not any more messed up than the rest of us." Lee was looking at the bedroom and desk area. He collected a few fibers. A preliminary dusting of the bed, the light switch, and the desk, revealed no fingerprints. "Hey Sarge," he called out, "this guy must have worn gloves in his sleep. I don't see any fingerprints. Why would he hide them?" Then he answered his own question, "Paranoia, I supposed."

"Perhaps our good doctor didn't have fingerprints anymore," said the sergeant, "he had removed them somehow, like destroyed them somehow." He walked over to the stove to take a look and gave it a careful inspection. He saw nothing unusual. "Let's get the crime scene folks in here to vacuum that rug. Perhaps we'll get lucky." He looked around and added under his breath, "I doubt it."

As they exited the apartment, the sergeant called Lieutenant Garcia. "Hey Lieutenant…Nothing…No digital trace of this kid…Nope…Lee can give you a bit of a profile if you wish…His coworker Dr. Marlibund…she seemed honestly baffled…We're not far, see you soon." He hung up the phone.

They got in the car, and the sergeant turned to Dr. Lee. "Hey Doctor, you're a kind of genius like this Benz. What would lead him to leave, what is he after?"

"I'm well within one standard deviation from the norm in regards to intelligence, but thank you."

"Can you just answer the damn question?"

Lee grinned. "He found out about his parents' deaths, how we did nothing to help them even if there was little we could do."

"So what's he after?"

Lee's head was full of ideas. "Okay, say he blames us for his parents deaths, he doesn't like his work anymore, he's clearly got no friends, he's a loner—"

"What, are you a psychiatrist now?"

Lee rolled right over the comment. "It's part of our training in profiling hackers, saboteurs, and computer criminals. So, computer criminals are loners, often depressed. He wants to get away, but he sees no choice. He feels trapped in his circumstance. Suicide isn't out of the question."

"As the saying goes, what a waste." They drove off toward Rampart Station.

---

At two in the morning, Doctor Artichoke Benz had reached Chantry Flat Road and started his hike up to Sturtevant Falls Bridge. He carried a hiking pack and used a walking stick to reach the edge of the occupied corridor. He turned on his flashlight and shined it on the sign on top of the tall gate to unoccupied areas north of Angeltown. It read: *Warning: if you leave the occupied zone, you will be prosecuted. Exit at your own risk.* Artichoke spread the gap between the rusted, chained-linked metal gates and squeezed through.

The road was dominated by scrub oak hanging over it, mountain mahogany, and dry grasses growing up through the cracks of the former road. Artichoke wound his way through and up the scrub with his flashlight, scraping his arms with thorns along the way and snagging his bag on branches. *At least I had the sense to wear long pants.*

It was a trek of four miles of scrub, uphill, in the night heat of 95 degrees Fahrenheit. At least the scrub would make it difficult for the satellites and drones to track him, for now. And he chose the night of a full moon for his walk. He had walked eight miles to get to the gate. That was uphill and paved, though bumpy and full of deep potholes. He was already exhausted, but he wanted to make his statement, and the only way was to keep walking.

He had spent his time at Caltech sedentary, living in his

mind to tolerate his situation. He used to be like a goat in the forest with this parents, now he was gasping for air. Every one-hundred yards or so, he stopped to breathe. Every few stops, he found a branch to sit or lean on. His hiking shoes were holding up and luckily not hurting his feet; he had only been wearing them for a week, another purchase from Ray's. He thought he was halfway, but when he checked his tablet, he still had three miles left. He thought to lay down and get some sleep, but there was no place to rest without getting poked or stabbed by branches and thorns.

*I could light a match and set this whole place on fire, smoke them all out, increase the air pollution that half the people will get cancer from.* But Artichoke felt bad for the birds. The human condition wasn't their fault. He kept hearing sounds in the brush, and he assumed it was rabbits, rats, or squirrels. *There couldn't be bears out here still, could there? They were extinct, and if they did exist, they were higher up.* His mother had told him about the bears, how fierce they were.

He kept walking and daydreaming and stopping and drinking water and walking and two hours later, scraped and littered with leaves and thorns, he made it to the bridge. It was four in the morning. He was sweating but determined to end his work. He was on the top of a bridge with a steep cliff and there was a clearing in the vegetation. This place used to be heavily traveled. Now, no one came up there except the *random lunatic and suicide,* the SADF Mountain Division said on the Governet news service.

Artichoke took the work-station he commandeered from the Caltech lab out of his backpack, and he opened it for the last time. He put it next to the edge of the bridge, opened the lid, started it, and put his tablet in the pack. It took less than five seconds to boot. "Hello Dr. Benz," Rita said. He had named his computer for his mother and had given it an approximation of her voice. He started to relax, which allowed him to tear up for the first time since he learned about his parents' death and how they died. He composed himself. "Start the countdown," he said.

---

At 9 am in the supercomputer laboratory at Caltech, Dr. Marlibund got an alert from her computer. She heard three loud beeps and then an audio message with words appearing on the screen:

*Let's talk about your surrender.*

She walked over to her laptop and hit *replay*. There were three beeps followed by*: Let's talk about your surrender.*

Marlibund looked at her the computer screen. *What? That signal is coming from Artie's laptop!* She open the Search Signal software. *He's outside the occupied zone!* The doctor picked up the data card on the desk, flashed it across her phone and it dialed, "Hello, Sergeant Van Heimlich please…yes…I got a message from Dr. Benz…best you come to hear it…I'll look into it."

Dr. Lee and Sergeant Van Heimlich arrived at the computer lab within twenty minutes. She played them the message: *Let's talk about your surrender.*

The sergeant noted it was a female voice and scoffed at the message, "Us surrender? He's lost it. His life is over and he's playing games."

Dr. Lee joined in, "He might be delusional and really think he has the upper hand." Dr. Marlibund looked more circumspect. "Were you able to trace that message?"

"Yes, it's from Benz. He knows we can trace it. It's from the mountains just outside the occupied zone."

"What is he playing at?" asked the sergeant.

"I don't know."

Addressing Dr. Lee, Van Heimlich ordered, "Call Garcia to

send men out there to get the suspect."

"It will take some time," Lee said. "We could try to drop people in, but it's mountainous and between two rock outcroppings, full of mountain oaks, lots of shrubs too."

Frustrated, the sergeant commanded, "Make the call and let Garcia figure it out." He addressed Dr. Marlibund. "Whose voice is that?"

"We traced it to Jane Winston, a teacher who works on the Governet with students," she said. "It sounds like one sentence, but it is from more than one. Dr. Benz did a good job mixing it. But when I play it through our voice analyzing software, the different words have different attacks and decays. It is definitely assembled. The good news, maybe, is that the voice is from one conversation in the same location. "

"Why her?" the sergeant asked.

"Well," injected Lee, who had just got off the phone with Garcia. "Perhaps she represents something. She's a female, a teacher, she's young—"

"You have no idea, do you?"

"Well," said Lee, "I don't have a lot to go on."

"We should talk to her," said the sergeant. "In the meantime, Lieutenant Gomez will track down Benz and bring him into custody."

The computer beeped again: *Let's talk about your surrender.*

The sergeant looked puzzle. He had never in his seventeen years on the force been told to surrender by a criminal.

"Dr. Lee, do some profiling, will ya?" he commanded.

"It is puzzling," said Lee.

"Is that all you got? Really?" mocked Van Heimlich.

Dr. Lee answered matter of factly, "For now. I think we

need to go back to his arrest report and talk to this teacher, Ms. Winston."

The sergeant sighed. "Yep, I guess that's our next stop."

The arrest report was sent to them over the Governet. Lee expanded the report and looked at it while the sergeant drove to Jane's residence. Lee read it aloud for the sergeant, "Dr. Artichoke Benz, born in Angeltown on August nine 2034—"

The sergeant cut in, "Get to his parents' and his arrest."

Dr. Lee scanned through and presented a summary, "His mother and father scored in the top percentile in IQ…they both worked for the Governet…they were suspected responsible for the 2032 crash of the Universal Cloud, and they left civilization into the woods until they were captured in 2046. By the age of eight, Dr. Benz was already hacking and writing his own software. His parents got a light sentence in exchange for Dr. Benz working for the Governet at Caltech."

The sergeant added, "I guess revenge is the motive again."

"Sex, money and revenge, the big three," said Lee.

"Power," added the sergeant.

Lee conceded the point, "And power. But Freud would say, sex, money, and revenge are all about power." Van Heimlich rolled his eyes.

The stores on the way to interview Ms. Winston's residence were shuttered up, except Ray's Pawn Shop on Broadway. It was established in 2028 by a former banker who knew a giant financial crash was coming.

As they passed by Ray's, the sergeant said, "Ray preys on the most desperate, just like he did when he was a banker. It's a living. And he pays no rent. Mainly, it's a front for drugs, but what can you do? Obviously, it's not heavily trafficked, and most of those drugs are legal now, so—"

"So who gives a shit, right?"

"Oh, so you do swear," said Van Heimlich. Dr. Lee ignored him.

Sergeant Van Heimlich and Dr. Lee turned right and drove up to park outside of the alley to Jane's residence on South Spring Street. The windows in the street were either boarded up or left with broken glass strewn on the sidewalks. The sergeant reached into the back seat and grabbed two gas masks, handing one to Dr. Lee. "Put this on, just in case there's a pollution pattern floating in," he warned. They put on their masks before leaving the department's Tesla 5000.

The sergeant pointed toward an alley up ahead. "It's around the corner." He grabbed a multipurpose tablet from the back seat, and as they walked away, the car locked. They went ten feet then turned right down to the end of an alley. On the right there was an oversized, four by ten foot steel-carbon fiber composite door.

The sergeant tapped the address into the display of the tablet. There was sickly sweet, single ping from the device, an alert the sergeant had selected. Then he placed the device's back side flat onto the door. There was a loud click.

"Be careful, sergeant. We don't know what we might be facing here. From the recording, she could be under duress."

"I'm always careful, Doctor."

They stepped inside onto the platform at the top of the ladder, gently letting the door shut behind them. They took off their masks, nodded to each other, and placed them onto the platform. Then they put on their gloves.

They heard a shout. "What, WHAT do you WANT!?"

Dr. Lee spoke under his breath to the sergeant. "Well, that wasn't what I expected."

They walked carefully down the ladder, and the sergeant called out. "Ms. Winston, it's the police. We need to talk to you."

They reached the bottom of the ladder and started down the corridor. They saw Jane, scraggly hair, unwashed, with translucent skin that lacked pigment. She was approaching them slowly, clutching the wall, terrified. "Is it still bright out there?"

Lee and Van Heimlich grabbed Jane. She started screaming, "No, NO! I can't go outside!" The sergeant pressed on her elbow just below the bicep on the outside. Jane instantly relaxed.

Quietly, as if talking to a newborn, the sergeant reassured her, "We just want to talk."

Jane responded calmly, "Would you like some tea?"

The sergeant quickly caught the eye of Dr. Lee and shook his head. Dr. Lee took Jane into the bedroom area and put Jane into the one chair at the desk. The two men stood over her and talked slowly and simply.

The sergeant calmly put his hand on her shoulder, "Jane. You are not in trouble. We are all friends here; we're on the same side." Jane nodded. He continued, "Do you understand, Jane?"

"Yes?" she said.

The sergeant tapped his scanning device, and a picture appeared. The sergeant showed it to Jane, "Do you recognize this man."

Jane looked at the screen, "Yes?"

The sergeant saw right through her need to please him. "Jane, I won't be disappointed if you don't recognize him." He put the device with the picture in front of her once more, "Again, do you know who this man is?"

"No?" Jane answered.

Dr. Lee addressed the sergeant, ignoring Jane. "This question isn't helping. Play her the audio."

The sergeant tapped the hand-held device three times to call up the correct menu. He looked at Jane, "Close your eyes and listen carefully." He placed the device on the table in front of her.

He tapped the corner of the screen.

*Let's talk about your surrender.*

Immediately, Jane shouted. "That's me! I never said that, you stole my voice!" She quickly attempted to stand up.

The sergeant grabbed Jane's shoulder just as quickly and put his forefinger into the indentation where her arm meets her shoulder blade. Again, Jane was calmed and placed her weight back on the chair.

Dr. Lee spoke up, trying to match the sergeant's calming voice. "No, we didn't steal your voice. The person who stole your voice was the man in the photo." He looked to the sergeant.

The sergeant tapped the screen and the photo appeared again. He pointed at the photo. "This is the man who stole your voice. That's why we're here. We want to know how you met this man so we can figure out how and why he would steal your voice."

"I don't know! I never met him." Jane cried in desperation. A look of anger passed quickly over Jane's eyes, followed by a complete breakdown. Her body heaved dry tears.

The sergeant relaxed his grip on Jane's shoulder. "We are going to look around your apartment. Okay?" Jane didn't answer. The sergeant nodded to Dr. Lee to search the apartment. Then the sergeant bent his knees to reach Jane's eye level. "We just need a minute to look around."

"Okay."

Dr. Lee saw the closet-sized bath and shower and saw a hairbrush. He grabbed as much hair from the brush as he could and put it inside an envelope-sized evidence bag and put the bag in a jacket pocket.

He looked at the bed, walked into the kitchen area, noted the dark walls, the long window high up near the ceiling, the packets of food and the water. He took a plastic bag out and snapped it open. Jane jumped nervously in the other room, and the sergeant calmed her again. Dr. Lee put in one ball of water into his bag and sealed it tightly at the adhesive folds.

Lee walked over to Jane. "You get water from the balls in the kitchen area?"

"Yes." She furrowed her brow and became teary-eyed. "Do you have more water?"

"No, I'm sorry. I am sure you will get more soon." He lied.

As they were about to go, Jane stopped them. "Do you have my book?"

"What book is that?" Dr. Lee asked, confused.

"The one about the trapped girl and the bad men who come and take her," her voice fell off.

Dr. Lee didn't know what she meant, but he didn't let on. "No, we haven't found it. Perhaps it's with the man who stole your voice. Should we bring it if we find it?"

Jane whispered, "Yes."

---

"Damn Urban Intelligence; they never tell us anything!" grumbled the rankled Dr. Lee as they reached the car. Then directly to Van Heimlich, "Clearly she's drugged. Why would they drug her is another question."

Slowly, the sergeant turned to the doctor and responded. "So, you figured it out."

Dr. Lee added, "What are we going to do about her, Sergeant?"

"What can we do? It's not our jurisdiction. That shelter is property of the Department of Education. I am sure they will check up on her," said Van Heimlich. *I hope.*

His phone rang, "Yes, yes, Lieutenant, yes sir." Van Heimlich addressed Lee, "We've got to get back to Rampart. L.T.

wants me to take a hike."

                              #

# Chapter 14
# The Bridge

*What is the use of beautiful engineering when the world is a cesspool and the people in it disposable?*
Doctor Artichoke Benz

The SADF Mountain Division drove up to Chantry Flat Road. Fourteen forcemen along with Sergeant Van Heimlich exited their armored vehicle at the gate leaving the Occupied Zone to hike their way to Sturtevant Falls Bridge. They would have sent up a stun drone, but the low ¬canopy of scrub and mountain oak made it impossible for the drones to get close to the road, let alone stun the suspect. Doctor Benz had chosen this location for that very reason.

It was over 110 degrees outside and they were sweating inside their gear: helmet, flak jacket and pants, military boots, all moving with their automatic NanoXD Razor 7 mm rifles pointing forward as they pushed through the brambles. They wore wick-enhanced suits that allowed their skin to breathe and gave them a modicum of evaporative cooling. However, the scrub and low trees made it impossible for the misting drones to get close enough to provide them much relief from the heat.

More than once you heard the painful shouts of a forceman being stabbed by long thorns: *Shit! Damn! Ow! Aye yay yay! Mississippi hell!* They edged swiftly through the brush despite the impediments and the temperature and finally arrived at the bridge by 2 pm. They saw a computer sitting near the edge of the bridge where the cement guard rail had collapsed into the gulley below.

They approached, and the commander signaled two of the

forcemen to go to the right and two to the left of the machine; Doctor Benz was nowhere to be seen. They spread out, looking around for trip wires, IEDs, anything that looked like a trap. They kept looking as they approached the thirteen inch screen.

They crept forward and surrounded the computer in a semi-circle as it sat open at the edge of the bridge. More forcemen joined until the computer was surrounded. They pointed their weapons at it. Sergeant Van Heimlich broke protocol by taking off his helmet. Rivulets of sweat ran down his face.

"Sergeant! You were to leave your helmet on at all times!" shouted Sergeant Powell.

"If you didn't forget, Sergeant, I'm a Sergeant too, and you're here working my case," said Sergeant Van Heimlich.

Powell went back to the task at hand, the computer. "Hold it!" shouted Powell, raising his right hand. He took what looked like a child's toy out of a jacket pocket, a palm drone the size and shape of an American cockroach with a tiny propeller. He put it in the middle of his hand.

The drone took off, and the only sound on the bridge was the faint buzz of the drone's propeller. It approached the computer as the forcemen stood at the ready, the computer in their gunsights. After circling twice, the palm drone landed on the keyboard.

It turned on and a message appeared on the screen. The men tensed up even further. A voice came out of the speakers of the laptop. It was Doctor Benz speaking as the words appeared on the screen:

*The only thing I cared about in this world more than knowledge were my parents. You killed them. All of you. The Governet killed them, and the defense forces killed them. You killed them, and you forced me to work on your brain-washing, propaganda machine. So I leave you a present as I leave this* world.

There was a momentary pause, then a video appeared of Doctor Benz running toward and jumping past and over the top of the computer, over the edge of the bridge, and over the cliff. Everyone on the bridge heard his voice, "Ahhh!" fading into silence.

The men stood shocked. Then computer Rita's voice spoke:
*This computer will destroy itself in 5, 4, 3,*
The armored force-men raced backward.
*2, 1*
The computer fizzled, crackled, sparks flew out scaring the armed military men. They shuffled their feet. Some looked for a place to run, but they were trapped in the brush on the bridge and backed away as far as they could from the device. There was a flash then hissing for about fifteen seconds and a final eruption of smoke. The men froze and pointed their rifles at the remains of the computer until their sergeant broke the silence. "Winn! Front and center!" Private First Class Winn moved forward and stood at attention, facing Sergeant Powell. "Obtain the contraband!"

Winn focused the scope of his rifle at the computer and moved toward it in ever diminishing semi-circles until he could touch the edge of the computer with the muzzle of his gun. He tapped it twice. Nothing happened. He shouldered his weapon, checked to make sure his gloves were on tight and lifted up the computer. The men exhaled in relief. "It's dead, sir," the private explained to his sergeant.

Sergeant Van Heimlich quickly approached Private Winn. "That's evidence in an ongoing investigation." He took the computer from Winn and tried to close the lid in order to put it in an evidence bag. The lid snapped off in his hands. A few of the men laughed to relieve their tension. He glared at the private and put the two parts in the translucent bag of thick plastic to take back to Caltech.

With the computer in hand, the sergeant leaned over the edge of the bridge and looked down. He estimated that it was at least 200 feet to the first ledge then another 100 feet to the bottom of the gorge. There was a jagged rock face, a ledge, then more scrub. He took out his extra eyes, glasses with exchangeable lenses on them for distance vision, and put them on. Van Heimlich looked down into the canyon and saw rocks and broken branches as if a body had bent the trees on the way down. He looked back and forth past the rocks and through the branches and couldn't find a body. *We would have to send out a mapping drone to survey the crevice and crags of the rock face before we could safely send out a search and rescue drone without it crashing, and still we might not find the body.*

He saw a ledge partway down about two feet wide then another drop obscured from above. *He must have fallen off that precipice down another one hundred feet and out of sight.* He muttered under his breath, "Crazy bastard", and walked away from the ledge.

*Damn it, I could have used Lee,* he thought. *What did Benz mean by leaving a present? Did he mean his body? There must be more than that. He must have left us another surprise. We need to get that computer expert in on it. Damn, now we have to walk back down. Benz planned this out, planned it well.*

On the trip back, the troops marched in double time with their guns down and safeties on. It took them twenty minutes to get back to their armored vehicle. They crammed into their military truck and drove toward Rampart. Sergeants Powell and Van Heimlich rode inside the cab while the rest of the men sat on the truck bed with the heat and the misters. "Who is this guy, Doctor Benz?" Sergeant Powell asked Van Heimlich.

"He was a mad scientist." He looked out the window in thought. "Sergeant, drop me off at Caltech." Then he called Lee, "Hey, Doctor. Meet me at CalTech. I have Benz's computer. It might be something…yes, meet you just inside…I'll tell you when I get there." He hung up.

"What's this about Sergeant," Powell probed again.

"I will let you know when *we* know."

They didn't talk until Van Heimlich exited the truck and said goodbye. Another two men got into the front of the air conditioned cab and they drove off toward Rampart.

Van Heimlich trudged the last two hundred yards to the computer sciences department and entered. The building was particularly cold to protect the computers: 10 degrees Celsius. Today, the sergeant didn't mind. Doctor Lee was only ten minutes behind. That gave Van Heimlich enough time to take off his armor, get a drink of water, and catch his breath.

From his seat on the padded bench, Van Heimlich told Lee about the video and then tossed Lee his note pad. On the pad was the message that Doctor Benz had left on the computer. Doctor Lee remained standing and read it to himself.

*The only thing I cared about in this world more than knowledge were my parents. You killed them. All of you. The Governet killed them, and the defense forces killed them. You killed them, and you forced me to work on your brain-washing, propaganda machine. So I leave you a present as I leave this world.*

Lee read it twice. "I could say something about you having contraband paper, but for now, I say, 'well done' Sergeant." The sergeant smiled. "So that's the computer," Lee said, pointing at the bag next to the sergeant on the bench.

"Yep."

Lee continued, "What did Benz mean by 'I leave you a

present?' I get the part about leaving this world, but—"

"Yeah, I was wondering that exact thing. Let's see what Doctor Marlibund has to say about that 'present.' And let's have her look at this computer." Lee nodded, and they entered the reception area.

Lee and Van Heimlich put on booties, lab coats, and hair nets, even though the Sergeant was completely bald and Lee had a number two buzz cut. Doctor Marlibund opened the glass door dressed in the same protective gear.

As they entered the open computer lab, Van Heimlich spoke, "We are sorry to say that your colleague killed himself; he jumped off the bridge up on Chantry Road. The area has a history of suicides."

She slumped into a chair, "I knew he was depressed. I guess I should have seen it coming."

Doctor Lee said, "We can never be certain about suicide, even trained professionals miss it—"

"No, he kept talking about giving it all up, about how now that he finished his work he could 'pass on.' He even gave me his mother's wedding ring, something she had given him when he went to work here. What was it he said, that she told Artie to give it back to her when he returned to his family."

Lee and Van Heimlich quickly looked at each other, both noting the use of 'Artie.' Doctor Lee let that go for now. "It is common for people give away things they value when they plan to commit suicide."

"Why didn't I see it?" she asked.

"We often don't see these things in others. You're a computer genius, like Doctor Benz was. You're not a profiler," said Lee, touting his own credentials.

The sergeant rolled his eyes and went to the heart of the

problem. "Doctor Benz said he would 'leave us a present.' Do you know what he meant?"

She was looking down with teary eyes. "I have no idea. I don't think he would intentionally hurt anyone."

The sergeant got impatient. "What about the way he rigged the educational software to malfunction? Kids were hurt; it could have been worse."

"But it wasn't," she replied, "that was a prank, his way of giving us the piss, if you know what I mean."

"What did he say his plans were?" asked the sergeant.

"He didn't."

"No clue?" asked Lee.

"No."

"We know you are hiding something," said the sergeant, "don't we Doctor Lee?"

"Certainly there's more," Lee said in half agreement.

"No, that's all," she said.

"Then why did you call him Artie and not Doctor Benz if you weren't close to him?" the sergeant asked.

She sighed, hesitated, and then answered. "We became close as colleagues. He liked being called Artie; that's what his mom called him. I prefer it to the formal Doctor Benz. It seemed weird calling this kid *doctor*, no matter how smart he was."

Lee responded. "But you're as smart as him. I looked you up. Two PhDs from Paris and Oslo, a teaching fellowship at MIT—"

"Those are just credentials and jobs. Artie, Doctor Benz, was the only one who had a grasp of what true AI would entail."

"So you respected the man. Enough to help him?" asked the sergeant, "enough to help him get away so he could end it all?"

"No, I asked him not to do it," she let out without meaning to.

The sergeant nodded. "When did you tell him not to do it, Doctor? When was that?"

She shook her head. "I told you where he was as soon as I could track the computer. I was hoping you would be able to stop him," she explained. "He called me at 5 am this morning to say goodbye. I urged him not to…you know…do anything drastic after he told me he left his mother's ring for me here in the office."

"So," said the sergeant, "he never *gave* the ring to you, he left it for you this morning."

"What difference does it make?"

"Okay," the sergeant ended that part of the interview. He put the bag with the computer on the metal table. Then he slid the two parts out of the bag without touching them. "We need you to look at his computer."

Marlibund's eyes widened upon seeing its condition. She put on gloves and looked at the computer bottom. "The screws are fused, melted into the body of the computer. So, it will take some time." Doctor Marlibund grabbed her phone and dialed. "Stanco…yes…I need your assistance…yes…no, no one else can do it…" After a long explanation of how busy Petra Stanco was, Doctor Marlibund finally said, "It's a police matter. Should I send them to your office?" Lee and Van Heimlich passed a glance and grinned. "Petra will be right down, gentleman," she said in a more conciliatory tone. She turned to the two men, "Do you have any other questions?" The men looked at each other, the sergeant glance sideways at her change in tone.

"Yes, how long have you, did you, work with Doctor Benz," asked Lee.

"Twenty-four months, thirteen days and a bit," she said.

Lee continued, "And you never had a thing, a–"

"A relationship, affair as you say," said Marlibund. "Of

course not."

Lee changed subjects. "Why did you come to Angeltown when clearly you could have chosen to work anywhere in the world?"

"The chance to work in the facilities at Caltech, a team dedicated to AI research? It was a unique opportunity," she replied.

"Piz Daint III in the Central European States or K-9 in Japan could have used someone of your talent," said Lee.

"So you did your homework, doctor." The sergeant started fidgeting and looking at the burnt-out computer. "I want to make history, or at least discover if AI were possible." She frowned and shook her head. "Now Artie won't be part of that."

"One more thing—" Lee started only to be interrupted by another scientist, Doctor Petra Stanco, as she entered wearing the same lab outfit Marlibund had on.

Doctor Marlibund greeted her. While ignoring the sergeant, she brought Doctor Stanco over to meet the detective. "Petra, this is Doctor Lee." He decided to use his first name to gain trust. At least that's what his training told him to do.

"Lance," he reached out his hand. "Here's the computer," he pointed at it. Embarrassed he added, "Of course, this is it." He called over his partner, Sergeant Van Heimlich. "Sergeant, could you recount what happened to the computer when you recovered it."

The sergeant jumped to attention. He walked over and gave his hand to Stanco, "Sergeant Van Heimlich. So we went up to the mountain north of Saint Bernard and found the computer, and it melted. That's about it."

"Was there smoke?" Stanco asked as she started to look at the remains of the two parts of the computer and moved the parts around with two long, thin pieces of wood that resembled chopsticks.

"Yes."

"What color was the smoke?"

"White and yellow, I think."

"And were there flames?"

The sergeant fidgeted. "No."

Doctor Stanco brought out a small tablet and quickly typed in some information. "So, you heard a crackling sound and saw sparks then?" she asked the sergeant while continuing to examine the computer.

"Yes," he said, "smoke, crackling, sparks, more smoke, that was it."

Doctor Stanco showed Doctor Marlibund her tablet's screen and commented, "It looks like hydro-sulfuric tri-thermite was used. We don't store any here," she answered before being asked. "HST has such a low flash point and can burn at such high temperatures that it is considered a risk-level five hazardous material."

Doctor Marlibund's eyes widened.

Stanco continued, "But from the looks of this," pointing to the computer, "he used an inhibitor and sprayed it on the circuitry to melt the inside but not melt through the case."

The sergeant asked, "If he sprayed it on the inside, why didn't it just melt down right there?"

"It needed an ignition source, a spark" she answered. "Was the computer on when you got to the bridge?"

The sergeant thought for moment, "No, no it wasn't on."

"There you go," Stanco said. "That explains how it ignited. It must have been a timed ignition from when the computer was turned on."

The sergeant shook his head, "Can you recover anything off this computer, Doctor Stanco?"

She pursed her lips and shook her head. "I highly doubt there is anything left to recover. I can bring it back to the reconstruction lab and look inside. I will, however, confirm my findings regarding how it melted down."

"Thanks a lot. Any help would be great." The sergeant looked at Lee. "I think that's enough, for now." He frowned and nodded to Marlibund. "We are sorry about your loss."

On their way back to Rampart, they agreed that there was not much to investigate. Doctor Benz was dead. Doctor Marlibund, even if they could link her to Benz, didn't do anything they could charge her with by not calling them immediately after hearing from Doctor Benz. And there was no way they could connect her to the computer chaos. She wasn't even officially involved in the learning software, as far as they knew. It was time to move on to the next case.

---

Lieutenant Gomez had created a successful, unofficial, unnamed special unit of four former SADF officers that he used to track down the most elusive criminal suspects in Angeltown. The unit was created in response to the anti-Czarist terrorist rally of May 2053, and they had tracked nearly everyone but two attendees. On this occasion, the Lieutenant needed one man, Martin, to pick up one girl, Chava Chavez.

Gomez called him to his office, "Martin, I have an easy assignment for you, a snatch and return. I'm giving it to you because you're familiar with the area and you're available."

"Sure, I can use the pieces. What does it entail, L.T.?" Gomez showed Martin an enlarged picture of Chava's face from her school track-team photo. "That's all?" asked Martin. "Why's this girl so important?"

"She's from the May 14th rally."

"What took you so long to find her?"

"The Chavez family's residence is not registered with her school or the city." He handed Martin an envelope. "Here are the cross streets and a map of the area. I sent it to your tablet, but I know how you like to have hard copies."

Martin opened the pouch and pulled out the map. "I know the place," he said. "A lot of squatters and people on the run live there. There are a lot of empty apartments and houses around full of vermin, rats too."

"You used to be one of the them," the Lieutenant reminded him.

"Yeah," Martin spun slowly around with his arms outstretched like a spinning helio-drone on display, "and now look at wha' I've made a myself."

Gomez shook his head and turned back to his monitor.

Martin leaned over his desk, something his commander hated. "So L.T., do you want her locked up here for interrogation, or…"

Gomez looked up and frowned. "Bring her back in one piece, if you can…and try not to get carried away this time."

It was a local job, so why not have a little fun, Martin thought. After he put on his personalized vest with a skull and cross bones on the front and black, his leg guards like an old-time hockey goalie, he went down to the bottom floor for one of his favorites vehicles. He seldom wore a helmet; it made it hard to see the enemy while driving.

---

Chava was in the kitchen grilling potatoes for their dinner: onions and garlic in a pan with some mysterious butter, oil substitute, and grandma set the three places at the table. "Okay!" grandma shouted, as if living in a regular-sized house instead of their tiny one. The carrots were already on the table in a bowl, peeled and cooked with yarrow root and a few mustard greens. The only thing they hadn't grown was the mystery oil.

In the past few months, Chava and her dad worked the garden in the back to some success. The soil wasn't great, and water was scarce, but they could grow a couple of things. They saved the brown water and it worked quite well. You didn't even taste it after you picked the vegetables. She missed fruit. The last fruit she had was at school over a year ago, a mealy apple of some kind. Chava trapped a squirrel that was trying to eat the stems of some carrots. It wasn't a lot of meat, but it was something.

Chava remembered the tragedy at the library as the new year came and went, and she was glad to have time to bond with her father. Over a couple of months, they had gathered enough scrap metal, loose chain link fencing, tin, and wood from posts to create a makeshift fence in the back of the house. Chava hurt in muscles she didn't know she had. She also kept up with her self-defense training with her dad despite little use for it.

Dinner was ready and served. Even though Manuel was an atheist and Chava didn't think about religion often, they let Grandma get her comfort by leading the grace as they looked down on their potatoes and carrots.

"O Lord, we thank you for the gifts of your bounty which we enjoy at this table. As you have provided for us in the past, so may you sustain us throughout our lives."

There was a low growling coming from outside, growing louder as grandma recited her prayer. Hard of hearing, and in the trance of her prayers, she did not notice. Chava furrowed her brow and looked at her father who was shaking his head. Grandma kept up with her incantations. "While we enjoy your gifts, may we never forget the needy and those in want."

A smashing sound like a jet plane crashing sucked the air

out of the room. Wood and stucco projectiles flew around as in a tornado, striking the family. Manuel dove to the right to avoid a huge metal spike coming at him through the wall. Grandma's wheelchair fell over and the collapsing wall fell on her along with glass from picture frames and one of two windows in the house. Chava dove to the left into the kitchen area to avoid being crushed.

While she lay on the floor, she looked at poor grandma's head and right arm sticking out of the wreckage of the house. "Go!" her father commanded.

Chava felt an avalanche of grief and anger and escaped out the back of the house the way she had arrived after the massacre at the library.

As Chava got outside, there was another crash against the side of the house. This time, sounds of gears and doors breaking filled the air as the roof was being pulled off by a massive shovel.

Martin drove a small, one man armored carrier with a scoop that had three-feet long prongs for smashing holes in walls and a powerful hydraulic lift to tear open a house. He figured he would capture the girl instead of just crushing her with a wrecking ball. Besides, Martin got in trouble the last time he used the ball, almost killing an Important Citizen with her fugitive man-slave in their love nest. At best the Chavez girl was going to Truancy Prison where she would die a long death, so a quick death didn't seem so bad.

The roof was half-way off. Manuel looked up from the floor and saw the driver of the armored car. As Chava ran past the garden, Manuel grabbed a slim lamp with a heavy base and ran out of what used to be a wall and went after the man. He rammed the lamp base into the window of the vehicle, barely making a scratch. "You mother fucking pinche bastard!" Manuel swore at him and kept hitting the window with the base of the lamp, thinking one time it would break. It didn't.

Martin calmly looked out the window of the vehicle. *The old man's got some spunk.* He put the vehicle in park, and opened the door to the cab just after this crazy man hit the window for what was perhaps the eighth time. That sent Manuel flying backwards onto some rubble. Manuel didn't notice the pain. Martin ignored the man on the ground and went to inspect the debris. He started looking around, but didn't see the girl.

Manuel lunged at the man from behind as he was looking the other way. Martin stepped to the right and Manuel flew past him. Martin looked at him calmly and asked, "Where's your daughter, Mr. Chavez? We need to talk to her."

"Come' mierda!" responded Manuel.

"Was that your mother," Martin asked, pointing at the remains of the house. "Sorry about that. I guess I was a bit enthusiastic."

The father lunged at Martin, who side-stepped him once again and sent him tumbling on the ground. "Look, we only want to talk to your daughter, be reasonable. Where is she? Come on."

Manuel swung the long lamp, extending it outward, and smacked Martin on the right leg. Martin stood tight and barely moved. He quickly moved his leg up and stomped down on the lamp before Manuel could move it to strike again. Like a viper, Martin struck before Manuel could move and had the patriarch's neck in his firm right claw. He tightened his grasp. "I…have lost…my…patience…" Chava's father was dead.

Martin searched through the house, but saw no signs of the girl. He went out the back door and saw tracks in the dirt heading away from the house. After that, there were only weeds. Martin was good at many things, but wilderness tracking wasn't one of them. And the city south of the occupied zone was more overgrown by the day. He had another way to track the girl.

He looked around the destruction and saw plates for the father, the mother and the girl, a few utensils, two beds, one bookcase, and two tiny stand-alone armoires. He saw a decent photo of Chava with an old woman in the rubble near the collapsed bookcase, but when he put it up to the face of the dead woman on the floor, it was not a match.

The armoire to his right was completely crushed with the remains of clothing under the rubble. The one to the left was still intact; it was on the other side of the room from where he entered. "Damn," he said aloud when he realize that it was the father's clothes. *There is nothing in there to help me.*

Martin walked over to the collapsed armoire. He pushed through the debris, lifted up a section of wall with his right hand and dug around with his left. He pushed the pile to the side and saw something small and black. He held it up to inspect it. It was a black sock with purple skulls on it. *It must be the girl's.* He took it out to the cab of the vehicle and went into the driver's side, leaving the door open. He opened the tool chest on the passenger seat and pulled out an eight-inch curved tube with a honeycomb of holes on one end and a bulb at the other.

He placed the device on the seat while holding the sock between his thumb and forefinger of his left hand like it was a new baby or explosives.

Martin then placed the toe of the sock on the front end with the honeycombs and hit a green button to start the machine. He heard the familiar inhaling sounds, the sniffing. The new sniffer drones were not as good as a hound dog, but less messy in the field. He dragged the sock up and around on all the surfaces. *Three passes does it every time, so you can stop the next crime. Stupid rhyme,* he thought, but he never forgot what to do.

He brought out his tablet where the Sniffer data was sent.

He tapped the screen, and it opened the data file.

Female

15-18

No other data available

Martin also made sure to take the photo of the girl with the mystery woman and e-messaged it to the Lieutenant. "That wasn't much, but it wasn't nothing."

Martin frowned. Of course there would be no scent file on Chava Chavez in the data bank; they barely found a photo of her. But with her scent profile, they could track her down by drone. He sent the data to Tracking Central. Gomez would be getting it soon. Yippee, he thought sarcastically. *My 'commander' won't just read about my failure, he'll smell it too.*

Martin got back into his armored battering vehicle and headed toward the station. His tablet started shrieking as he drove. *Damn, Gomez!* The Captain set the alarm on the tablet again so Martin had to respond. It shrieked like wolf caught in a trap. The alarm rang again. *What a noisy god-damn day*, Martin thought as he hit the screen.

Gomez gritted his teeth. "What happened? I thought you were going to knock and apprehend and only use force if you had too."

"Well Sir, I figured they might have weapons and acted prudently," Martin lied.

"No one has guns anymore, and I *know* you can handle a girl, armed or otherwise!"

"There was also the father. He was quite feisty."

Gomez rolled his eyes then calmed a bit. "What's the plan now, Martin?"

"Well, I will track her scent, follow her trail and apprehend her," Martin surmised.

"I would tell you to follow it now, but we should get the

drones up and sniffing first," Gomez stated.

"Okay—"

Gomez hung up.

Martin got back to Rampart III, put the sniffer profile into the Governet and set it for "Search and Locate" and "All Sniffer Drones." *With all the patrol sniffers having this girl's odor profile, we'll have her in custody soon enough.*

#

# Chapter 15
# Chava the Valiant

*Love, success, happiness? The only thing left is survival.*
Chava Chavez

    Chava ran into the uninhabited zone away from the madman who was after her. She couldn't help her dad now. He was dead and would never comfort her again. The adrenaline in her body pushed out her grief. The salty sweat quickly dripped down into her eyes. She leapt over the detritus of Angeltown. Chava ran past a warning sign from the Czar of Education that read:

> You are Entering the Uninhabited Zone
> Violators will be prosecuted
> Czar Law 52

    Chava was a mile away in less than five minutes before hitting her long-distance stride.

---

"*Chava* CHAvez"
The gang of ten-year-old boys surrounded and pushed her.
 "Stupid Jew!"
"No, she's a chalupa, Chava the Chalupa!"
"No, she's a Jewlupa!"
They all joined in, "Jewlupa, Jewlupa, Jewlupa…"
Chava didn't cry. She was used to this treatment by the age

of ten. She maneuvered into the center of the boys, made two fists, targeted the smallest boy and the most hateful, Chandler, standing together. She ran toward them with all her velocity. Chava rammed one on the right shoulder and one on the left. Shocked, they opened up like barroom doors from an old Western. Little Davy collapsed like the old I-10 freeway, and the most hateful, Chandler, stumbled backwards. Then Chava ran up the hill with all her speed.

"Get her!" the boys shouted. Two of them had bikes and started to chase her. After a minute, they gave up. They would never catch her going up the hill, for she was faster than all the boys in elementary school.

---

Chava landed on the remains of Crown Street and turned south. She heard no drones, machines, or vehicles behind her. She ran a serpentine route, hoping that the maniac had not chased her. Chava didn't look back fearing she might freeze and not be able to go on.

She didn't stop until she had run for at least twenty minutes and up the hill past Baldwin Village. The last leg to the top wasn't as tough as she had imagined; she was fueled by fear, anger and adrenaline. She clenched her eyes shut and held back the reservoir of tears.

A week before, the residents on the hill were evacuated and moved to Saint Bernard. They were forced to leave during the recent contraction of Angeltown and had to leave everything but their most precious valuables behind. She remembered hearing all the commotion as the trucks drove near her house and off toward Saint Bernard on the Saint Bernard Freeway.

Chava sensed something following her. She quickened her pace. Now she smelled the odor of animal sweat. She turned quickly to her left and saw a wild dog tracking her. Her senses exploded with input: *German shepherd, big, male, sizing me up.* She glanced over and saw the collar. She exhaled; the dog was once someone's pet.

    She backed up off the road and leaned against a house, nearly tripping over a rock in the overgrown and shriveled garden in the front. Chava picked up the rock; it was twice the size of her left hand. The German shepherd was barking, snapping its jaws and sniffing the air. She feigned throwing the rock, and the dog momentarily jumped back.

    Still holding the rock, she checked the multi-paned window to the left of the door with her right hand to see if it was unlocked. It didn't budge. She peeked at the window. There was a latch. She faked another throw and twisted her body to the right and smashed a windowpane with the rock. While keeping an eye on the dog, she groped for the latch, doing her best to not cut herself. She unlocked the window and lifted it up part way. The shepherd kept growling and snapping which made Chava wonder if it was trained to attack.

    She threw the rock in the direction of the threatening animal so it landed in front of the dog. The German shepherd ran back a dozen feet and jumped out of the way of the rock as it hit the pavement and bounced toward him.

    Chava quickly opened the window the rest of the way, jumped into the living room, and shut the window before the growling beast got back. The dog stuck his nose through the broken pane and snarled.

    Unable to get past the shut window or through the small pane, the dog remained outside growling, and after a half an hour, was silent. Relieved, Chava looked around and found three small bottles of water in a cabinet. She drank one reflexively. She also found a package of shortbread cookies that had yet to be opened, immediately ate four, and then stopped. She had an idea. She found a bowl in a cabinet, walked over to the front door, and felt a tidal wave of exhaustion.

Chava poured half a bottle of water into a bowl and took out a handful of cookies. She went to the door, unlocked the latch, and jumped at the sound of a growling dog on the other side.

She put the water down and a couple of cookies on the floor, placing the rest of the package on the counter. Grabbing a lamp from a table as a weapon, she prepared for the worst. Chava opened the door with her right hand. "Here boy, come on boy!" The shepherd saw the water and moved in on it cautiously while deciding whether to run.

Chava stepped away and put the lamp down on a side table. She picked up the cookies from the counter. The dog kept his eyes on Chava as his tongue lapped up the water. He paused, and then took two big swallows. The cookies were gone. "Good boy, you are a good boy!" She tossed the dog another cookie. The dog jumped back as the shortbread flew in his direction, then sniffed, and swallowed this cookie as well. Then Chava ate a cookie.

She threw the next cookie half-way between them. The dog stepped forward, stopped, looked at Chava to see if it was a trap, took one more step, then swallowed the cookie and moved back. *Good, the dog is familiar with human contact, unlike the feral dogs I have seen in my neighborhood. One more.* She placed a cookie in her hand and the dog froze. He moved closer, sniffed the air, grabbed the cookie gently in his maw then ran to the other side of the room to eat it.

"Okay doggy," Chava said as she ate another cookie and sat down on the carpet against the wall. "Only a few left. If you want one, you know what to do." As she ate, she made loud sounds of enjoyment, "Mmmmm, yummy, yummy, these are good!"

Chava shut her eyes, just to rest them. Seconds later, she was asleep.

When she woke up, it was dark outside but still intolerably hot. She saw the outline of the dog in the room close to the window, and the box of cookies was no longer within reach. "Doggy, did you eat all the cookies?" she asked. As she got up, she continued talking. "I don't blame you; those were good. Did you get enough water?" She found the half-full bottle and poured the rest of it in the bowl on the floor. She saw a silhouette slurping and heard the lapping of a tongue. She made her way in the darkness to the kitchen counter and grabbed the other bottle, took one big gulp, and then slowly sipped the rest to make it last.

"What am I going to call you, doggy?" she said and started to gently cry. Sadness and anger took over. "What did I do, why did they come after us?" She gritted her teeth. "Ah!"

Some people live to hate, and then they die unhappy, her dad used to say. *But at what cost to others' happiness?*

Chava, overcome by fatigue, wobbled over to the couch opposite the broken window and fell into it. When she woke up at sunrise, the doggy was sleeping next to her on the floor. "Doggy! Good boy." For the first time, she touched the dog, pet him on the back. He jumped up and rolled all over Chava, trying to get her to wake. Half on top of her, staring, he hoped for another cookie. "You shouldn't eat so many cookies. They'll make you sick. We need to find you some doggy food." She remembered the stray in the back of her house that she called Fizza, one she fed too much bread to, and how the dog got sick.

---

"Chava," her Grandma Alma said as she pointed to the dog's vomit in the back, "feeding bread to dogs made him sick."

Grabbing a cloth, Chava apologized, "I'm sorry grandma, I shouldn't have, but the dog looked so pathetic."

Alma grabbed her hand and said in surprisingly perfect

English, "It's never wrong to help those in need. It is never wrong to show kindness." Alma squeezed Chava's hand.

---

Still, the doggy was currently not starving. "We need to find some more food." He put his head on Chava's lap. "It's too hot for that!" She gently moved his nose off.

Chava looked at his haunches. "Yea, you're a boy all right." *No tags.* She took off the dog's collar. "You don't need this right now, but we'll keep it just in case," she said, noting the black collar with metal studs on it. The dog looked up again. "Okay, let's go."

Chava stood and he wagged his tail. She gathered herself, grabbed the last bottle of water hand walked toward the door. She took a deep breath and opened it. Manta Drive was empty. There were no signs of human activity. Chava walked further into the subdivision and examined each house. The dog followed and sniffed nearly everything.

After a couple of days, Chava became practiced at scavenging in the recently abandoned homes. She kept calling the shepherd *Doggy*, and without a better name, it stuck. They ate left-behind canned soup and the occasional crackers or cookies stored in cupboards where rats hadn't found them. She collected water from melted ice in freezers and what was left in toilet tanks. No water came from faucets anywhere on the hill.

In one sunken back yard she found a barbecue pit with a spatula, an oven mitt, a four-inch long, sturdy metal fork for stabbing meat and some tongs. She left the tongs and took the rest. She was hoping they could get a bird or a squirrel to eat instead of living off the cold canned soup. Doggy didn't seem to mind, but Chava was sick of it. She would barbecue a squirrel right there and eat it if she could. She desperately needed some meat. Doggy started sniffing between her legs. "Damn it Doggy, leave me alone!"

Chava went back inside and to the bathroom while squeezing her legs together. She wadded up a bunch of toilet paper, stuck it into her pants and covered her groin, hoping that she wouldn't bleed too much or too long. *Damn, why do I have to be a girl!* She sobbed, and then laughed remembering what Theo said, "Girls are way cooler."

With tear-swelled eyes, she looked around the bathroom. She opened all the cabinets and drawers and found nothing for her menstruation. She found two clean wash cloths, some cotton balls, some gauze, and some band aids. *Well, I can't bandage up my vagina, can I?*

Chava heard scratching at the door. "Doggy!" she yelled. Then she changed her tone, "I'm sorry, Doggy. Give me a minute." The scratching continued, and she ignored it. Chava wrapped a washcloth tightly around some cotton balls, pulled down her shorts, and put the improvised pad in place and zipped up. It was a tight fit, which was the point.

Chava gathered more cotton balls, an extra washcloth, and she opened the bathroom door. "Doggy!" she exhorted, and despite being hungry and thirsty, he panted with excitement. "Let's see what they have here, boy," wagging her finger at him, "and no sniffing." *Good luck with that.*

Finding nothing more, they went to the next house and looked around. More soup. She searched the freezer. Trays of water once intended to be ice. "Jackpot!" She set one tray on the ground and Doggy lapped at it. He used to spill a lot of water and lick it off the floor, but now he only missed a few drops the first time. Chava looked for a straw. Nope. She carefully poured the water into a cup and then her mouth. She had learned as well; pouring the water into glasses just wasted it. This wasn't the freshest water, but better than the last house. Four cans of soup.

Two chicken noodle, *everyone had damn chicken noodle*, and two tomato. *Those were the worst*. Doggy wouldn't even eat cold tomato soup.

Chava had to find a backpack or a bag. Tied up bundles of bedsheets were tiresome and often, her belongings fell out from them. *If I had to run, I would lose everything.* She looked down at Doggy gobbling up his can and a half of chicken soup. "Except you Doggy, I wouldn't lose you."

She pulled out a brush she had found from her bundle and sat down. She waved it at Doggy. He looked up, finished his soup, then walked over to her. He set himself perpendicular to Chava, ready for a brushing. She started at the center of the back toward the bottom, back up, and ended on his head. When Doggy really wanted the full treatment, he would roll over and expose his belly and she would brush that too. Today he was okay with just a back and head brushing. He sat in front of her and put his paw up. She grabbed it. "Thank you, Doggy! Thank you very much. Anything else you need?" He just stared at her, panting.

"Let's look around." Chava had gotten used to the styles of houses. The living room was in the front. A kitchen to the right with an open floor plan, a hallway to a bathroom and two bedrooms. There was often a separate shower room. When she found water in the tank of the toilet, it was a good day.

Chava winced slightly at her cramps. Her mother hardly had any cramps, and other girls she knew had to miss school because the pain was too much. It was one of the only excuses the schools still allowed; they didn't want to deal with anything related to sex, even if girls were no longer able to get pregnant due to The Sterilization.

*After the first day, the cramps won't be a big deal.* "Yes!" she yelled aloud. Doggy trotted in to see what the excitement was.

"The toilet tank has water, boy!" She grabbed her clean washcloth, dunked it in, and cleaned herself all over.

She set the lid back on the toilet so that Doggy didn't lap up all the water. *I have to find some plugs or pads. Perhaps there is an abandoned grocery store down the hill in the mall.* She would wait until dark. She checked the closets and only found some loosely fitting sweatpants she could tighten around her, one pair of socks, underwear, big for her but better than nothing (she could bleed into them), some t-shirts, and a sweatshirt. Nothing regular fit; if the pants fit on her muscular legs, they were too loose at the waist and the shirts would be too big on her. She found a small rolling bag with a handle.

She scooped the water into the bowl and used a cup to fill the vessel the rest of the way. And of course, Doggy got a cup of water. Then she shut the door, took off her clothes and washed herself. Chava soaked the other cloth in the bowl. She started washing the areas of her body that were cleanest, then ended with her vagina that would probably bleed for four more days. The rubbing felt good, but incomplete.

Doggy scratch at the door again. *The downside of loyalty.*

---

As Chava washed, she thought about the mixed fourth, fifth grade class she had with Theo, Chava being in a younger grade than he.

"Theo, why don't you tell us where you're from?" said Mrs. Jacobson to eleven-year-old Thelonious Babar.

"I'm from Angel Heights, like almost everyone else here, ma'am." Theo was always polite.

"Well, where are your parents from?"

"My mom is from here, like me, like you," indicating the teacher, "and my dad is from Africa." Theo paused. "But Africa is a big place, and like Asia, there are many different people. He was born in Tunisia, but that country doesn't exist anymore. No, dad is from here too."

Chava sat in the back, admiring how Theo could talk in front of everyone and not be embarrassed.

"Chava," the teacher called, jolting her out of her daydream. "What about your family?"

Chava froze, not knowing what to say.

"Where is your family from?" Mrs. Jacobson insisted.

Meekly, Chava spoke, "Here."

"Were they always from here?"

"As far as I know," Chava looked for the words, "that's where I met them."

The other students laughed at Chava's answer.

"Where did they come from, Miss Chavez?" the teacher asked, clearly getting impatient.

"Here."

Theo jumped in, "What she's trying to say, ma'am, is that we are all from here, and that is what we have in common. We're from here."

The other students' mouths sat agape. But instead of getting a reprimand or sent to the office or expelled, the teacher said, "Yes, we are all from here. Still," she looked at Theo, "we are clearly not all the same."

Chava looked at Theo and smiled.

---

Chava wiped the tears from her eyes. Then she gave Doggy more water and poured the remaining water from the tank over her head and it ran down her body. They she dressed with a pad in place to block the bleeding. After packing up her bag with the barbecue tools, clothes, some water in bottles, two cans of soup and an opener, she headed down the hill toward the old Crenshaw Mall with Doggy at her side. Chava remembered the shopping center from a trip she made with her mom at age eight. She took a deep breath, sighed, and kept moving.

Chava carefully kept to the side of the road while listening closely for drones and other activity and kept an eye on Doggy's reactions as an early warning system. Once in a while, Doggy started at a sound from the brush but then relaxed as the sound faded away. *He really is a good guard dog. I'm glad he's on my side.* She briefly smiled.

At the bottom of the hill was a large intersection at Stocker Street, and Chava took extra caution. She stopped at the crosswalk despite sensing no signs of life. Doggy stopped and sat. Chava noted that he had some training as she scratched his head.

They crossed the street and started walking down Stocker, staying at full alert. They saw a rabbit and some animal that was either a small deer, or a coyote. One growl and bark from Doggy scared them off. Once the shepherd ran off into the brush. Chava hadn't heard a thing. He came back shortly afterward and healed to match Chava's pace. After about thirty minutes, they came across an abandoned grocery store at the front of the mall.

It was a giant. "Come on Doggy," Chava waved her hand and he followed her toward the store. The light waned as the sun set. Chava moved quickly, noticing that most of the shelves were barren.

A sign outside read "looters will be shot on sight." The SADF made monthly sweeps through the area using drones and gas. Any person they found they put in one of the pits or disposed of immediately if they struggled. Wanderers soon learned to avoid the uninhabited zones.

Doggy got excited and started running around the store, clicking his long nails on the linoleum, growling, and barking.

Chava heard the scurrying of rats as they scattered to stay out of Doggy's jaws. She rolled her luggage in and plotted an action plan. On the left was the pharmacy; she rushed over to look for *feminine products*. The shampoo and other cleaning products were mostly gone. But she found some pads and two boxes of Governmed Plugs after rummaging around the shelves, pulling the boxes close to her face so she could read them in the dimming light. She snatched the last boxes.

Chava put a plug in quickly and tossed the used rag on top of a tall shelf out of reach of Doggy. The relief of having it in far outweighed the pinch she felt when inserting it.

She sniffed back tears as she remembered how nice her mother was when Chava got her first period. "It's normal honey. It means you're growing up and getting stronger and smarter." Doggy ran toward her, jumping and trying to get a sniff.

"Doggy, sit!" She pointed her finger at him, and he sat down. "Stay!" He sat still. Chava pointed down an aisle. "Go!"

Doggy ran and slid across the floor, clawing and trying to catch his grasp on the tiles, undulating wildly up and down. *Okay, find some dog food.*

Most of the shelves were barren, but there were a few cans of dog food and more soup. Chava saw no bottled water. She searched and found a row of school supplies and backpacks. She wanted the purple bag, but it would stand out too much. She grabbed the largest camouflage pack, despite her dislike of the colors. She shoved some dog food and soup into the bag and transferred the barbecue tools from the rolling bag into the pack.

There were only a few more minutes of sunlight and seeing became more difficult by the minute. In the hardware aisle, she found small, cheap flashlights on the bottom shelf that came with batteries, but they were low on charge and did not emit much light.

They would have to do. She took out a can of dog food, opened it, and put the food on a paper plate for Doggy. He waited until Chava started drinking her minestrone soup. Then he swallowed his food.

  She wandered around until she found a couch in the back of the store in a small break room near the loading dock. It would be her bed for the night. She grabbed a beach towel for a pillow and one to cover the couch to sleep on in her underwear, being too hot to sleep in her clothes and too uncomfortable with her period to sleep naked.

  Chava woke up at dawn, thirsty and needing to brush her teeth. After feeding Doggy and eating a can of soup, she found a brush and paste and cleaned her teeth. She also found a brush for her own hair. Looking in a mirror, she realized that her hair was too bright and cut it ragged with some school scissors, taking off the purple ends. *Where is the water?* She looked around. She found some bottles of soda, lemon-lime, "Yuck! It's flat." *But it's liquid.* She took a couple of bottles.

  Nothing for Doggy. She kept wandering the store. She stopped and smiled. There was an ice machine behind a food stand that once served hot dogs and pizza. She ran over and opened the front of the ice box. A pool of water lay at the bottom of the ice machine, at least two gallons. She had to find some bottles to carry it. First, she took a cup behind the food counter and filled it with water. "Doggy! Doggy!" she shouted.

  He galloped to Chava. She put the cup down and he lustily licked up the water despite it being warm. Then she drank. *Ugh, hot water.* She sniffed under her arm pits. "Yuck! Doggy, how can you stand my odor? I stink!" He briefly looked up, then kept drinking. "You're a dog, and a male, so you probably like my stench."

  After getting soap, she walked behind the counter and stood over the drain. She created a thin foamy layer of bath wash on her body and touched herself between her legs. As she did, she paused, feeling an incredible loneliness, desire, and loss. *The world is no place for romantic love; I may never experience it.*

She quickly poured the water over herself to wash the sadness away. The water felt cool compared to the air. She took another cup and made sure to rub her whole body clean. She nudged another plug inside before the flow got going. Doggy startled her in the doorway, looking at her with a pigeon in his maw.

Chava jumped. "Ew!" He dropped the bird in front of her. "A gift? Thank you! Hold on." She walked into the back. Sitting on a filing cabinet rested a tennis ball. She picked it up, "Okay boy, here you go!" She threw the ball as far as she could into an empty aisle and quickly went into the back, shutting the door behind her.

She dressed in new clothes, jean shorts and a white shirt. The clothes contrasted with her now misshapen, dark hair. She kept a pair of sweatpants and shirt just in case she needed a change. *What to do with the bird.* Chava brought the bird to the outdoor furnishings area of the store where there was some briquettes of charcoal strewn on the floor. She took a deep breath and thought about her dad. Then she started the plucking. *It's as if dad knew I would use this skill one day.* She collected the coal in a pile and found some matches near the hotdog stand. She lit some paper, then caught the coal on fire. She cooked the bird on top of the pile, turning it will a stick from outside until it was cooked through. The outside was burnt, but the inside was perfect. Of course, Doggy got the innards.

---

Over the next two weeks Chava and Doggy took sunrise excursions down Stocker Drive to find water and food. The area had been shut down several months ago, so there was no water left in iceboxes, just some water left in toilet tanks. There were also cans of soda left behind, but that didn't help Doggy. They would cook up a small animal if they were lucky, and sometimes Doggy would run off and bring Chava a bird that they would share.

The trips out weren't dangerous early in the morning. She never saw anyone and saw few animals. The people were mainly in the downtown areas or the pits after being cleared out by the SADF's monthly patrol.

The trips back were hot and exhausting. Luckily Chava and Doggy had found a way through an old parking lot and along a wash over to the subdivision where they could scrounge for food. By the time they were done the temperature was over 110 degrees, but they had gotten used to the heat. Besides, they were usually done before the hottest part of the day and at least in the store they had cover and a flow of fresh air.

One morning as they were getting ready for another trip, Doggy's ears stood up and he started running around in circles in a panic. Chava looked at him and finally heard the buzzing sound. She knew what was coming, and she had to think fast. She counted in her head: eight, eight buzzing search and stun drones. They were getting closer. Doggy bolted outside and off down the road in a panic. Chava ran behind the counter and emptied cups, plates and napkins from the storage cupboard next to the ice machine and crammed herself in. She pushed the metal door shut. Silence proceeded the buzzing of drones and clatter of armed men on patrol.

Something metallic hit the linoleum floor of the store on the other side of the food counter. She couldn't see the canister from her dark hideout, but she smelled the gas.

Chava coughed and quickly covered her mouth with her shirt. It was the monthly patrol; she had forgotten. She wheezed as the air become toxic, and she muffled her gags. After a minute, she passed out.

---

Suddenly, Chava was dragged out by her arms from the storage cabinet by a huge man in body armor. She flailed her feet, kicking the air as she slid along the floor. She tried to stand, but she could not get a grip with her feet. She screamed, but no sound came out. Her throat was dry and parched. The man let her go and she lay helplessly on the floor, unable to stand. The light behind the forceman blinded her.

#

# Chapter 16
# Trackers

*Hunting means understanding one's prey and predicting its behavior, not empathizing with it.*
Martin

    Downtown Angeltown was a dark abandoned catacomb. Every block had one solar light on the corner, half of which were no longer operative due to excessive solar exposure and damage from pollution clouds. By 2050, Angeltown no longer allocated funds to repair these failing fixtures.

    Ray traded psychoactive nutmeg to a local electrical engineer from the Coso II energy plant to keep electricity flowing to his pawn shop. That night, he organized his inventory of phones, tablets and halo-belts, the most requested items. Many people could no longer afford them even at his *low, pit bottom prices*. He was moving the tablets up and the belts to the bottom shelf of his display case. He heard the door-bell's chime. *It's lunatic time*, he thought.

    Ray looked up at the monitor above the door. Darnell Daft waited outside for Ray to let him in. Darnell was a regular costumer who supplied him with nutmeg and sometimes rare electronics and drones to add to his inventory. Ray buzzed him in. What he hadn't counted on was the Williams brothers crashing in right behind Darnell. They pushed Darnell in front of them as they entered. *Clearly, this was against the man's will,* thought Ray.

    The Williams Brothers looked like heroin-addicted zombies, but they were devilishly fast and agile. They could cut your tongue out before you could say "good morning."

    "Ray!" said Donny, as if they were long lost army buddies.

"We are looking for something special."

Sonny jumped in, "And your boy here, Triple D, says you got it."

"I don't know what you mean, fellas," said Ray as he reached for his shotgun under the counter.

Donny moved forward, quickly pulling out his butterfly knife and putting it against Ray's neck, "Come on Ray, put your hands on the counter before I get all nervous and my knife slips into your throat."

Ray's eyes widened. "Okay." He lifted his hands slowly and placed them palms down on the counter.

Sonny moved forward and tapped Ray once on the face. "That's a good boy."

Ray tripped and fell forward so that his left foot hit a lever under the display counter. "Damn!" said Ray. "You got me all nervous." The brothers gave him a long look.

Just then, Darnell took his chance and ran out the door. Sonny tensed to run after him when Donny spoke up. "Let the kid go. He might be useful in the future. Having a weasel like him working for you might pay off." Donny turned to Ray. "Right?"

Ray nodded nervously. There was an uncomfortable silence.

Sonny finally spoke up, "Donny, tell him what we want." Donny sneered at his brother as if he was about to give him a beat down, then addressed Ray.

"What can I do for the famous and dangerous Williams brothers tonight?" Ray said with a grin on his face.

Donny spoke. "Cut the crap Ray. We need the drone. Triple D said you sell the drones he shoots down from time to time. We want it. It's not your average consumer model, it's one with weaponry and a stun capability. You know what I mean, right Ray?" He looked at the shop owner like he would just as well stab him and take it than negotiate. The problem was, Ray had it locked up with other valuable goods in the back.

Sonny had been looking through the spaces in the sticker covered windows of Ray's corner shop, making sure no SADF were coming.

"Darnell said he recently brought you a drone, a WASP 3000. We want it," Donny said.

"Well, there's no use in denying that I have one, but I was still trying to fix it so its previous owner wouldn't be able to trace it."

"Now that's smart, isn't that smart, Donny?" said Sonny, nearly jumping out of his boots.

"But I got it running," said Ray.

"Did you hear that, Donny? Ray here got it running."

"We'll take it, as is," said Donny. He waved his knife, signaling Sonny to go behind the counter to get the drone.

"Wait!" Ray raised his hand to stop Sonny, and Donny flinched, his knife clipping Ray's neck, leaving a spot of blood.

"Hang on! The floor is booby trapped. If you come back here without me disarming it…I wouldn't want to lose such valuable customers." *What I really wouldn't want is Donny to gut me after the nail filled IED exploded and killed Sonny.*

"Smart man, Ray," said Donny, "and I bet your mother didn't think you would amount to anything."

Ray shook his head in disbelief that these idiots could get the drop on him let alone elude the SADF for so long. After Ray disarmed the IED, Sonny came behind the counter. "Okay, now open the door to the vault, and no funny stuff."

"Damn Darnell," he muttered, knowing Darnell had told them about where he locked up the drone. "That kid is a moron," Ray said out loud. *But he was one hell of a shot with a rifle.* There was a two-foot-thick metal door five-feet behind the counter with a ten-pad combination featuring a shift mechanism for three entry positions. It would take *one million monkeys one million years to crack this lock*. At least that was what the advertising for the door-lock stated.

After a minute, he had opened the safe. He and Sonny went inside, and Ray shut the door to the sound-proof safe to lock out the noise. Sonny looked at him suspiciously. Ray explained, "I have some things in here that could be ruined if exposed to the outside air too long." It was a lie, but he knew Sonny didn't know any better.

Ray showed him the sections of the attack-capable drone. When assembled, it was nearly three feet long, eight inches wide, with a five-foot wingspan, and weighed one hundred pounds, nearly a third of it in the armor piercing machine assault guns. It was made to take down a single target and was most typically used as an assassination drone.

Ray explained some of the features, taking his time to repeat himself. Then he made Sonny repeat the instructions. Afterward, he started the negotiation. "I can't just give this away, Sonny. It's gonna cost you."

Sonny glared at him. "This isn't even the newest model. How do we know it will do the job we have in mind?"

He raised his right hand. "I personally vouch for this drone. If you tell me what the job is, I can even program it for you."

Sonny put his right hand to the knife holstered at his side. "You think I'm stupid?" He spit at Ray. "If this drone works, we can pay you double the rate after the job is over."

"Twenty thousand pieces then," said Ray. Sonny looked at him with disgust. "That's the going rate on the black market, Sonny. Even used, this is a primo drone with lots of capabilities. And it's expandable."

Ray took the parts: the body, the wings, the fins, the propellors and put them on a cart from the walk-in safe. "Open the door, Ray."

Ray opened it and Sonny rolled the drone parts out of the safe.

They went back into the shop and Sonny's brother was nowhere to be seen. Sonny panicked; he couldn't survive without Donny.

He ran past the cart and started running around Ray's tiny and overpacked store as if Donny was hiding among the merchandise. Then he launched himself outside. The first thing he saw was his brother hogtied on the filthy cement on Broadway Street, his face bleeding. Then Sonny saw the bastard that everyone in The Pits had a bounty on.

"Hello, Sonny," said Martin in a gleeful voice that pissed off Sonny even more.

"But how?!" asked Sonny, confused. "We were watching; he couldn't have signaled."

"It was all in the feet," said Martin as he lifted his toes up and down as if pushing a lever.

"That fucker!" said Sonny. He pulled out his knife and circled towards his brother to untie him.

Martin moved swiftly and calmly into Sonny's path, "I can't let you do that Sonny. I have been looking for you. I was so glad to hear that you were stopping into Ray's for a friendly visit."

Sonny spoke, "Well, Ray just called you to your funeral."

Martin looked relaxed, but he was sizing Sonny up. He saw his knife was mostly a stabbing instrument and not well designed for slashing. Sonny was an angry man, even more so after seeing his brother in that state on the street. He was holding the knife in his right hand for an upward thrust. Sonny would go in for a stab to the midsection the first chance he got.

Martin wasn't carrying a weapon. He spread out his gloved hands as if surrendering, opening himself up to be stabbed. Sonny took three fencing-style steps towards Martin.

"Get him!" shouted Donny.

Sonny was less than five feet from Martin when he lunged, his knife coming upward. Martin moved one large step to the left, blocked the wrist holding the knife with his left hand toward the inside of Sonny's body. He punched Sonny in the chin with his right hand, still directing the brother's right arm away from him with his left. Sonny's jaw snapped back, and his body convulsed. With his right hand, Martin twisted the brother's wrist away from him and pushed the knife into Sonny's chest.

"Damn!" said Martin after Sonny collapsed. Martin leaned over him and checked his pulse at the neck. The younger brother was dead within seconds.

All the while, Donny was screaming out, ending with sobbing as his brother died.

"Sorry Donny, I am going to have to take you in," said Martin. Donny thrashed about, cursing. Martin got him on his feet, force marched him to his wagon, and threw him into the cage and locked it.

Martin went to his bag on the passenger seat and took out a small misting device. He sprayed the drug into Donny's cage, and the brother lost consciousness. Then he shut the hatch. "That should do it," said Martin to a sleeping Donny. He grabbed his tablet from the passenger seat and went back into Ray's. Ray was in the process of locking the drone back into the safe when Martin snuck up on him.

"Ray, busy night!" yelled Martin, startling Ray.

Ray shut the safe and pushed his hands forward to tell Martin to keep it down. "Good thing we installed that foot alarm," said Martin. "Otherwise, we don't know what would have happened to you."

Ray, while grateful, was silently hoping Martin would just drive off. "Ray, what are you selling that should interest the

Brothers?" asked Martin as he looked behind the counter. "It was that missing drone that Triple D shot down, wasn't it?"

"Okay Martin, I helped you with this arrest, now, you can look the other way. I am just trying to make a few pieces."

"Sure, but you will have to do something for me," exclaimed Martin as he pulled out his minitablet and the stylus from the side of the device and handed it to Ray. "Write your private number on the pad," directed Martin. "And don't try to give us a fake one. We will check. And if you change your number again, or get a new phone, you will have to tell us. We will be watching you. Get it?"

"Oh man, come on!"

"It's your number or The Pits."

Ray wrote his number.

Then Martin pulled out an iodine spray and misted the stylus. Nothing. "Damn Ray, you really did remove your fingerprints," said Martin. "It just isn't your night, is it?" Martin looked at Ray.

"Look, I burned my hands putting in a fire."

"Sure Ray, sure."

"Martin, really, don't I always help you?"

Martin thought on it, and said, "No, sometimes you don't tell me everything. For now, we'll call it even. Stay in touch Ray. And if you have any funny ideas about that drone, I already called my friends to pick it up…and take Sonny's body from out front."

Finally, Martin drove off with his prisoner sleeping in his cage. *A perfect night.*

After dropping Donny off in the holding tank at Rampart, Martin got some sleep upstairs on the cot in the breakroom. He woke at eight in the morning after a couple hours of sleep, washed his face, and went down to the squad room. He cheerily greeted Lieutenant Garcia. "Good morning L.T., where do I do that paperwork for last night's take down?"

Gomez shook his head. "You don't exist, Martin, you're strictly 'off the books.'" He looked up at his from his desk. "A mysterious witness called from an untraceable phone to say that you saved his life and that the brothers attacked you."

Martin winked at him. "No paperwork, then?" He grinned.

"Martin, how's it going tracking down that Chavez girl?"

"What, no cheer for taking down the Williams brothers?"

"Well, you did kill one of them, didn't you? Half credit." The Lieutenant placed his hands on his desk. "Now what about Miss Chavez? Can't handle the girl? Need help?"

"All right, L.T. I figured she was low priority compared to the last three cases I had: a saboteur, a bomber, and a pair of homicidal brothers."

"And you would be right, Martin. But you've cleared those cases, and I figured you might want to clear your blemished record. Besides, I can't pay you for working out in the gym. You have to do your duty to the SADF."

"Yeah, but I'm off the books." Martin hated it when Gomez talked to him about duty when they once arrested and put in him Pit #1.

Gomez added, "By the way Martin, the Ida Waterholder case, the woman who had killed a school principal and her husband? The one you couldn't find? Her body showed up. It turns out one of the poisons she had been concocting killed her when she mishandled it. She had been rotting in a storage locker for months. So, that's another win for the home team and one that won't count against you."

"Gee, thanks."

Martin sat in a chair and looked over the Lieutenant's desk. "What, nothing to eat?" Gomez rolled his eyes. Martin continued, "The status is that we tracked Chavez as far as Baldwin Village and then lost her scent."

"Did you go out there?"

"Yes, we sent men out there, but she was nowhere in the Village."

The lieutenant sighed. "No, did *you* go out there?"

"I was busy with other cases, if you recall. And the Williams brothers, they did kill two drone inspectors, and who knows who else." He scratched his chin. "Hmm. How did they get into the yard? Well, maybe Donny will tell us, though after I impaled Sonny with his own knife, I doubt it."

"Yes, that *is* impressive. What are you going to do about Chavez? And why can't your infallible sniffer drone detect her? Don't tell me she's applying a masking agent as a counter tracking technique, that she knows you are after her with a sniffer."

"I doubt it, sir."

That made Gomez sit up. Martin never called him 'sir.' He let it go for now. "Did you check on top of Baldwin View and the park on the hill there?"

Martin stood, "I was just going there now, L.T."

"Take one of those new and improved sniffer drones with you. Maybe that will help. And try not to kill this suspect."

Martin grabbed his ready bag that included a multi-purpose General Mechanics pistol that shoots standard 7 mm rounds, rubber pellets, darts (both poison and tranquilizer), and tracking gelatin. He put seven rubber pellets in the one chamber and a tranquilizer dart in the other. His bag also contained steroids, a first aid kit, Nanomed approved anti-poison pills because you never know when a dirtbag will try to poison you, a flashlight, flare and shock canister, poison gas canister. *That should be enough to catch a teenage girl.*

On the way to the garage, he grabbed a new, 6" by 6" square sniffer drone, installed the odor from the suspect into its data bank, and commandeered his favorite three-wheeler from the garage. It's just as advertised, thought Martin, *flexible for pavement and dirt, rubble and road.* He opened the back compartment and put on his flack-jacket, just in case this girl developed some skills. *She's probably dead by now.*

He put the drone and his bag in its compartment in the back with his personalized knife and gun in the right and left pockets of his vest. He pushed a button on the three-wheeler and a portion of the garage door opened just big enough for the vehicle to exit.

Martin drove out and headed up to Baldwin Village, a trip that only took thirty-minutes despite the rubble and an uneven road outside the occupied zone. Martin didn't wear a helmet. He had to keep his eyes open for ASH.

The monthly patrols cleared most of them out, but it was the end of the month, and they are more mobile than you would think. Still, in all his time tracking, he only saw one legitimate ASH. *People somehow find a place to be.* Most often, they moved, died, or got put into The Pits.

At the bottom of the hill, he released the drone, sending it up the road to sniff around. He drove right behind it. He lost it as the road twisted and turned upward. Martin changed the viewer on his three-wheeler dashboard display to track the drone. He saw it turn right and then left onto High Point Drive. Martin followed close behind. He slowed down when the drone stopped.

He passed a house with a window panel broken in, and further down, the drone hovered outside a different residence. He gave the door a quick kick. It flew open and Martin almost fell from his forward momentum. *Idiot. The door wasn't locked.* "Oh well," he said to no one. The drone followed him in and flew around the house.

Martin saw that the cupboard had been rummaged through,

the bathroom had been used recently, the water was gone from the tank. *Someone had been there.* After some time looking around, he looked at the back patio. It was undisturbed. When Martin got in from the back, the drone was resting on the couch. He sat down; the couch sagged under his mass. He picked up the drone to read the display on the top: *SUSPECT DETECTED* and beneath it read, *CONTAMINATION.*

*What the hell does that mean?* He put his finger on CONTAMINATION and swiped left. The screen read, *CANINE. So, there was a dog on the couch sometime in the last ten years, great.* The screen beeped: *MENSTRUATION.* Martin might be aroused if the steroids he took didn't kill his sex drive. But now he had a theory as to why the earlier drones lost her scent: it was being masked by dogs, blood, and excess hormones. *Okay, where would she go,* he thought, assuming they were on her trail.

Martin picked up the drone and looked at the red scale on the front. He pointed the drone's sensors to the couch and the red light showed a reading of 42%. He pointed it away from the couch and it read 38%. He took it outside and it read 35%. *Okay, I'm going to have to do this manually.*

He set the security features on his three-wheeler to *high* meaning alarm, engine shut down, toxic gas and if a thief is really determined to have the ride of his life, an exploding seat ejection. If it didn't blow off his balls, it would incapacitate him and throw him off. Martin's brain was working in fifth gear, *it's much easier to find a dead body with these sniffers.* He started walking around the hill on High Point Drive pointing the drone forward. As he walked away from the first house, the sensor showed 15%. As Martin walked past various houses, he looked inside and saw signs of disturbance. The problem was knowing whether that was people being evacuated, or if it was a new resident. The sensor read 30% as he approached the door of another house. He also got the message *CANINE* but no menstruation. *So, her menstruation started in the other house, probably.*

After wandering in and out of various houses at the top of the hill, Martin knew he had to try something else. He returned to his vehicle and unlocked it. He took out his tablet and opened the link to the *antique online directories* folder. He tapped the button for Old Angeltown and typed in the words: *feminine hygiene.* Then he hit the button for the *nearest locations.* There were five results: two convenience stores, a woman's health clinic, *Miss Honest's Organics* and *Quigley's Super-shopping Emporium.* Martin doubted he would find plugs or pads at the convenience stores and felt pretty certain that if the woman's health clinic were still around, it would have given away all their supplies when the area closed. The organic store would have left with their wares.

*If I were a young, menstruating female, I would want more of a guarantee. Quigley's it is.* He set the coordinates on the drone. He opened the map on his vehicles GPS, clicked on the mall icon, and then clicked on *Quigley's* when given the choice. Martin checked his 7 mm and put it in his flack-jacket, just in case. He checked for his knife. It was still in his inside vest pocket. His headset rang and he tapped it to answer.

"Martin," said Gomez. "Donny wants to talk. But only to you. He says it's about an assassination, and he wants to deal. You need to come back." Martin attached the drone to the vehicle and headed back.

*Damn. She's probably dead anyway.*

#

# Chapter 17
# Chava the Red

*You try to help people with all your force and compassion until there is nothing more you can do.*
Thelonious Babar

Chava floundered like a fish in sand and hit her head on the top of the metal cabinet. "Ow!" *Oh shit! I was dreaming.* Horrified, cramped and suffocated, she opened the door to the metal cabinet and slid out. Chava froze to listen for drones and heard nothing. Then she thought about poor Doggy. *He ran off in such a panic.* She didn't want to call out for him, not yet. Chava would wait until dark to search for him. She bent her head and took in a breath of sadness. *I have to find my Doggy.*

Night brought her a certain amount of cover, but the darkness also made it hard to see wild animals and humans with ill intent. She grabbed a cooking knife from aisle fourteen and her long-handled barbecue fork and got a flashlight with new batteries. She risked walking to Mt. Vernon, back up the hill to where she met Doggy. *Maybe he would return to where he used to live.*

She finally felt comfortable calling his name on the hill, "Doggy, Doggy, here boy, Doggy!" She had been out for nearly two hours, and Chava didn't find him "Damn it!!" She crouched and got her second wind. She had to take the forty-minute walk back after she took two loops around the hill, the inner and the outer circles of houses. She would try again tomorrow.

Chava caught her shoe on a branch and caused the rustling of the shrub's leaves as she moved. Surprised, she was jolted from her trance, put a hand over her heart, took with a deep breath, and sobered. She had to get back to her temporary home.

She didn't like walking in the dark without Doggy. It wasn't safe without him. She entered the store cautiously, making sure no one was about. *Where's Doggy?*

She was exhausted and sat down on a couch in the home furnishings department. *What's the point*, she thought. *Why wash, why brush my teeth, why run and hide, why fight?* Then she thought of her Grandma Chava and decided she would do it for her. *Grandma went through so much loss, having to leave her home, her city, her nation, her people in Israel. If grandma could endure, so can I.*

In the morning, she knew she had to get ready for the next patrol. She found a couple of two-liter bottles of soda that the cola had evaporated from and took them into the appliance section of the store. She rinsed the residue out with a bit of water. There were plenty of vacuums to choose from for the tubing. Apparently, those escaping to Saint Bernard didn't consider vacuums essential. She put the bottles near the vacuum of her choice. Grandma Chava had shown her how to make a gas mask. Grandma had used one when the International Banking Army tried to gas out the Israeli settlers and at times against the encroaching dust and desert.

Chava remember what she needed: duct tape, thick rubber bands, stapler, rubber cement, charcoal and perhaps a belt to keep the mask in place. She wandered around the store and found everything but the rubber bands. *Who knew rubber bands would be in high demand during the end times?* She found some men's white underwear and used the elastic band to attach the mask to her head and cut one band for a spare.

She used one bottle for the filter and one for the mask, crushed charcoal under her shoes for filtration with some rags and cut the hose off the vacuum to connect the two bottles. Chava put all the parts together and tested it by burning a piece of cardboard while breathing in the fumes. It worked after tightening the filter. She put the whole mask in an empty garbage bag in case she needed it later.

If she ran into a patrol or pollution cloud, she'd at least be ready with a gas mask. It had been almost two days since Doggy had run off. She went over to her sleeping couch in the furnishing's department and put her flashlight and knife into her pack. She zipped her bag closed and then saw the barbecue fork on a bedside table. *What the hell.* She picked up the fork. Chava had used it to kill some birds and rats that her and Doggy shared.

Chava turned slowly around and saw Martin standing ten yards away with his 7 mm pointed at her. Martin grinned, narrowed his eyes, and his thick neck bulged. "Chava Chavez: it's time to come in and answer some questions."

Chava dropped her bag, tensed up, and stepped back. "You killed my father, you monster!" Her body shook, her heart pounded in her ears, and her jaw clamped tight.

"Sorry about that, accident." Martin shrugged.

Unable to get to the knife from her bag in time, Chava reflexively waved the two-pronged barbecue fork at him.

Martin laughed. "You think you can stop me with that?"

While every cell fueled her nervous system, she recalled her father's training:

---

Chava pantomimed attacking the vulnerable areas of the

body and called them out as she struck, "The groin; the knee, any of the body's joints; the head and neck area, temples, throat, car…car…"

Manuel pointed to the spot on his neck. "Carotid artery. If cut and bleeding, that artery can cause death, so be careful."

---

She took a deep breath, grit her teeth, and imagined her father's death at the hands of this maniac. *He won't kill me without a fight.*

A blur of a snarling, snapping animal flew with abandon at Martin. Instantly, Chava ran at the killer with all her speed and force. Doggy nearly knocked Martin over with his impact and was clamping down on his right arm, breaking it and forcing him to drop his pistol. "Argh!"

Martin leaned heavily to his left, grunted, and reached for his knife. His right arm was useless, and in his twisted state, he jabbed Doggy with his left hand. Chava jumped at him, aiming the fork at his exposed carotid. Contact.

Off balance, Martin fell from the momentum of Chava's impact, knocked over for the first time since his dad struck him when he was ten. Blood started gushing out from the two incisions in his carotid artery, and Martin started losing consciousness. "Oooh!" *Impossible, I can't die. I caught the Williams brothers, a girl can't defeat…* He passed out.

Blood poured over Chava's left arm as she twisted the fork. She stabbed into the wound yelling, "Die, die, die!!" until her arm could stab no longer. Martin's neck was pulped and the windpipe exposed.

Doggy was bleeding and died before Chava could reach him. She let out a thunderous roar that scattered the birds outside.

She hugged Doggy and cried, rocking back and forth until after ten minutes, he started to stiffen. Chava was enveloped in blood.

She screamed until the fear of being caught overrode her grief. She scavenged Martin's body armor and found his customized knife with his name engraved on the handle. Other than the knife and his bio-locked pistol, he carried nothing.

The blood engulfed her skin and she needed a rinse, but there was no water. However, there were still dozens of bottles of Red Madness Soda. It would have to do.

She wiped the blood off of Martin's knife and the barbecue fork with a torn-up shirt and put them in her bag. Chava paused and looked at Doggy. Then she pulled out his collar from her bag and put it on. She folded the gas mask in the backpack with some other supplies, a few pads just in case, and went to the back where the boxes of soda were.

She took out Martin's knife, opened the box, then put the knife back in her bag. Chava took off her clothes and poured soda over her head. Four one-liter bottles later, she was sticky but no longer bloody. The soda was terrible but better than being covered in blood. She walked over to the dressing room mirrors and looked at herself. Her skin, and even her black hair, were tinted red. That gave Chava an idea.

She dried herself as thoroughly as possible with paper towels and put on a spare pair of shorts and a t-shirt. She took one liter of soda for her hair and put two liters in her bulging hiking pack. Chava grabbed another liter of soda and walked over to the cosmetic section. After she looked around the shelves, she found it. She splashed some soda over her hair to wet it. She opened the package and mixed the honey packet and gel with the red hair dye into her scalp. She used the whole package even though the it read "two applications." Chava scrubbed the dye into her scalp as if scratching a head full of lice. She finished packing and then rinsed off the excess dye.

She looked at Doggy once more and took a deep breath and shut her eyes. Chava needed to move. "Bye Doggy. Thank you for saving my life."

She turned away from the blood and the bodies at the entrance to the store as she walked out. She saw Martin's three-wheeler. She walked around it, threw a rock at it, and poked it with a long branch. Nothing. She checked the side pockets and took the first aid kit and the flashlight. She knew the minitablet would be tracked and she didn't know what to do with the rest of his gear, so she left it.

Chava started down Stocker Street, toward downtown. She needed something she could trade for at *Ray's*; she had an idea. Her shoes were no longer useful for running and barely had any heel for walking. She'd never survive if she didn't get a replacement pair.

She knew she would be moving into the inhabited part of Angeltown where she could encounter the SADF, but she had little choice. Now, she smelled like artificial cherries and looked like a walking watermelon with stop-sign red hair. Doggy's collar was hot around her neck, but she refused to take it off.

She realized that even her parents might not recognize her in her current apparition. *How could I got to school when my mother was dying?* She put it out of her mind and started walking with her heavy pack. She had to stick to the shade when she could and stay away from blind corners.

Martin Luther King Boulevard was broad and open; it was not the best way to go if one wanted to remain concealed. But it was the fastest, most direct route. Theo once told her the Insiders kept the Black man's name on the street to pretend they weren't racist. *Oh Theo, too wise for these cruel times.* She sniffed back her tears and kept moving.

Chava was exposed on long stretches of the boulevard with collapsed buildings on the sides, rutted roads and was hard to access if you weren't on foot. There were also some shrubs growing out of the abandoned lots and buildings that allowed for some shade. The area was, however, accessible by drone, so she kept her ears open for the mechanical vultures.

After an hour, the rising sun blinded her. Her skin became even stickier. *I need to find more water soon.* She came across the collapsed 110 freeway.

She focused on her surroundings and survival and tried to forget. She could still feel the life leave the man who killed her father. The memory was inside her like a parasite. Chava abhorred violence, and she had killed. *It wasn't my choice, none of this was…I took a life.* She ground her teeth and her heart rate increased as she climbed up the side of a dirt embankment to the right of the collapsed bridge overpass. Some rebar and cement blocks of cracked freeway were on the edge of the roadway. She picked up an eight-inch piece of loose rebar. *This might come in handy.*

Once she crossed the 110, she skirted left and took Broadway, heading north. She stopped in a bit of shade from an old office building and drank some *Red Madness* soda. *Disgusting. Why did I ever like the taste?* She placed the bottle back in her bag and trekked toward the occupied zone and Ray's. She looked around, listened, and slowed her breath. Chava was an alert for ASH, drones, SADF, and other dangers that might appear at any moment.

She looked down the road and saw a pollution cloud. *Fuck!* Chava quickly pulled out the gas mask and wrapped herself up for the impact. Up ahead on her left she saw a huge cubical building with a large sign on the outside with cracked letters that read, *hoal.*

She dropped her cumbersome bag to sprint toward the entrance and out of the path of the pollution cloud.

The cloud hit her. It burned her exposed flesh, including her scalp, but she could breathe. She smashed the building's glass door with the rebar in her right hand, her left arm still exhausted from the morning's stabbing. After three strikes, it shattered. She dove inside out of the pollution and rolled up onto her feet.

She quickly wiped the pollution off her skin with rag from her bag to stop the burning. Her mask held, but she would have to refill the filter with more charcoal.

Chava needed to go back for her bag. After thirty minutes, she looked outside. The cloud had passed. One-hundred feet from the entrance, she saw her dusted bag. Chava ran, grabbed it, and brought it inside. *There better be water here.*

Inside, she passed displays of fancy couches and jewelry, dining room sets with cutlery displayed in rows. *Like dad predicted; people were ordered to leave and had no chance to do any looting before evacuation. I hope they didn't get killed like dad said.* She grabbed a couple of the steak knives and put them in her bag; there were no chef's knives or cleavers. Two of the rooms had chandeliers and fancy light fixtures. *No one has a place for such extravagances.*

There were expensive looking rugs and delicate curtains and polished candle sticks, some with candles in them, some without. She took a couple of the candles. There were chairs and couches and dressers and rows upon rows of lamps, beds, and mattresses.

*None of these fancy settings mattered. None of it mattered to life.* The only thing that mattered was that the tanks in the toilets contained water. She threw out the last of her Red Madness soda and filled the two jugs with water. It was stagnant and a relief to have.

Chava only had two containers to carry water. Thus, she was able to dump two liters over her head to rinse off, and then refilled her bottles. She looked in the mirror. Her skin was still tinged red, her hair still crimson. She dried off as best she could with the paper towels in the bathroom. Then she put on a set of sweatpants she had cut into shorts. She touched Doggy's collar and gently sobbed. Her neck sweat, and it made marks on her skin; still she refused to take it off.

Chava refilled her jugs with water to drink. She also wet some paper towels and wiped down her bag.

*What a disappointment. All the fancy dining sets and cutlery and not an ounce to eat.* She swallowed the last can of soup, reflexively tossed the can in the trash, and walked outside. Chava estimated that she had only thirty minutes to Ray's and now the sun's full force was upon her. It was nearly 120 degrees, and the sky was empty. It seemed even the drones refused to travel outside under the midday sun. But now she had shade from taller buildings in the downtown.

Chava went north and encountered the remains of the great I-10 freeway. Theo once told her the I-10 went from one great ocean in the west to another ocean in the east. She frowned and then smiled, knowing he was usually right about these unbelievable facts. On the other side of the rubble was the occupied zone and increased danger of detection. There would be more cover and her new look might throw off trackers. However, her strange look might bring unwanted attention.

Chava moved carefully over the rubble. While the danger of people jumping out and attacking her was almost zero amongst the boulders and the former roadway, the chance of cutting herself on the sharp cement, rebar, and other debris was present with every step. More than once she saw a rat scurry under the rubble away from her. "That's right, run," she said to the rats as they scurried away. Chava knew dinner when she saw it. Not long ago, that thought would have made her wretch.

Chava stepped over concrete, metal girders, and skirted around the holes and piles of debris until she got to the end of the rubble on the north side and looked around. All clear, and thankfully, no fence. *I guess the Insiders thought that the collapsed freeway enough of a barrier. There would not be hordes of people running through this way on foot any time soon.*

Chava noticed things were different on this side of the freeway. There were old-time electrical wires, a water seller, a shop called "Broadway Garden Collective" selling scrawny garden vegetables and of course your usual bail bonds like Empire Bail Bonds and Loan.

The only other stores on the way to Ray's was another bail bonds and a clothier that had a sign that read, "We can Fashion New Garments out of Old Ones." On the sides of the buildings were ads for loans, for the SADF with *that annoying Jane Winston* on it, and of all things, Czar World, which had recently closed.

Chava saw a few people dressed in light-colored rags with head covering to shield themselves from the scorching sun. They scurried in pairs and singles into buildings she assumed had been transformed into living spaces. "Hey!" she yelled out to a man and a woman running into a building near Ray's. They ignored her and ran inside.

She only saw two drones high above since crossing over into the occupied zone. *Perhaps they were clearing out another area of the uninhabited zone or they were too high up for me notice.* Whatever the case, their absence did not comfort her.

As she approached Ray's, Chava decided to act like a broad from one of the Dashiell Hammett novels Theo had given her.

*Here's a chance to really test out my new look and see if Ray recognizes me.* She looked around carefully to make sure no one was behind her. Then, she stepped in front of the camera at Ray's, hit the doorbell, and in a sing-songy voice, she crooned, "Ray-Ray-Ray."

Ray was cleaning his shotgun and was startled to have someone ring the bell at noon. Most of his customers came after six in the evening. He looked up at the monitor and saw a maroon-haired girl. She was wearing a dog collar that he could see when she looked up at the camera. Her skin had a reddish tint.

She spoke in a high-pitched whine of a teenage girl. "Damn it, Ray, I got something for you want; you need to let me in." She reached into her bag and pulled out Martin's knife and held it up to the camera, inscription side out. "Come on Ray, you might want to see this."

Ray squinted, not believing what he saw. But it was worth a look. He closed and loaded the shotgun on the counter, just in case. He touched the buzzer, letting the bizarre looking, red-tinged female in. *Cut-off sweatpants and a pink t-shirt?*

Chava enjoyed the sub-hundred degrees in Ray's. She put her back down and held Martin's knife toward Ray, once again monogrammed side out. "I need some supplies, and I think you can get some pieces for this knife," she said in her annoying affectation.

"Where did you get that?" Ray asked, curious and fearful. He knew Martin would kill him if he found that Ray had obtained his knife.

"I got it off a certain gentleman customer."

"But—"

"I provided a service and he paid in full. So are you interested Ray, or should I talk to my man Martin and tell him how you didn't help me?"

"No!" He raised his hands in protest. *I could make a mint off the knife from an Insider if its authentic.* "That's not necessary. What do you need?"

Chava thought carefully about what to say. She realized that Ray didn't recognize her. "I hear you are a fair trader. I have this knife which is a unique one-of-a-kind item. I want to trade it for some simple supplies, a first-aid kit, some food, some water, some shoes."

Ray had to know before making a trade. He nodded his chin upward and said, "How did you really get the knife? I know Martin wouldn't have handed it to you. Are you a master thief?"

Chava let out a laugh as she planned her response. "Ray, I am not a master thief. I traded Martin with what I have. My most valuable…assets." She fumbled as she rubbed her hands past her hips. *What the hell am I doing?*

Ray took a second to catch on. Then he stated bluntly, "Hmm. I thought Martin had lost interest in sex because of all the steroids he takes."

"I found the right buttons," she said. "And he was extreeemely grateful." Then Chava quickly changed the subject to avoid being caught in the lie. "So, a trade. Give me some water, and…" she reached for some packages on the counter, "some rabbit jerky, you got any fried crickets?"

Ray squinted at her. "Sure, I can trade you a couple of ounces of roasted crickets."

"Okay she said, and these shoes." She plopped the size six all-terrain shoes on the counter, made locally as the tag said.

Ray stopped her. "I was saving those for someone, but…I don't think she's coming for them. Sad thing, the SADF has her, so I heard. And her father was killed." He frowned. *I really liked Manny.* "Okay, all that for one knife? I don't know."

Chava didn't realize how valuable the knife was, or she might have asked for more in trade. "All this for a famous, one-of-a-kind knife," she said, barely holding in her emotions of grief and anger.

"Okay, but only one packet of the rabbit Jerky. I'm making a killing off that stuff, so to speak. All the junkies love it," Ray explained, then looked up at Chava. "Sorry miss."

Chava waved it off. She put the shoes immediately on her feet and slid her old ones to the side. She put the food and five water balls in her bag. She also grabbed a back-up first-aid kit and put it in. She had to take out a liter of water to make it all fit.

"Hold on a moment." Ray brought out a scanning device that detected trace amounts of sweat and DNA. He took the knife and slowly moved the handle under the digital device. Then Ray looked at the read out: *DNA, 40-year-old male, sweat contains high levels of steroids and other performance enhancing drugs.* He also found female DNA from Chava and a strange reading from the blade: canine. *Huh? It's Martin's alright.* Ray tapped the device and it stopped reading. "If you get any other verified Martin memorabilia, let me know," he said to Chava.

She nodded to Ray.

"And don't do anything criminal, or at least get caught. Martin's not a man to mess with, from my experience. Oh, and if you were thinking about squatting around here, they're shutting down everything to the east." Ray gestured with his thumb behind him. "I don't know how long I have left," Ray mused.

"Thanks Ray, you're a peach." Chava pick up her bag, and as she exited, she started to sing the tune to *Bad Reputation* under her breath: *I don't give a damn about my bad reputation...*

Ray turned to look, but Chava was already out the door. *Was that...No it can't be*, thought Ray.

# Chapter 18
# Split

*My life thus far has amounted to nothing.*
Jane Caitlin Winston

Jane once looked younger than her years. Now she was prematurely aging with a puffy face and a malnourished fleshiness. She began hearing things in the night; a voice haunted her after she fell asleep.

*Jane, Jane, Jane...*

Every time she turned on the light, the voice stopped.

*Jane, why Jane, why...*

Again, the voice stopped as she illuminated the room. The voice echoed off the walls. At first it occurred once a month, then once a week. Jane would jolt up and shout at the voice. "Stop it, stop it!" Now she heard the voice every night.

Jane started having nightmares that her mom was still alive, that when she went to hug her, she would bleed from her belly, her womb. *Why did you kill them?*

For the last couple of months, Jane rarely slept more than three hours a night.

After several sleep-deprived weeks, Jane became immensely thirsty and ran out of water days before she would get more. She had to have more water. Jane drank the water from the shower, but it didn't quench her thirst.

*Get out, get out, get out...* the voice of Jane's sleep compelled her.

She woke up one morning screaming. "Leave me alone!"

Jane ran to the drop point for water. Still none. "There is never enough *water*!" She stopped, and in only her sleeping gown, ran and smashed her hand against the door; it unlocked. The light was blinding. The door clicked behind her. *Ray's, must get to Ray's for water.*

---

Chava exited Ray's and turned right. At the end of the block she turned right again, wondering where she could find cover. She saw a woman screaming and running toward her, "I need water, I need water!" Jane looked up and noticed a strange woman with red hair and a large pack. "I must stay on task! I must not waste time. I need water!" Jane hurtled forward.

Chava put up her hands and stopped Jane from crashing into her. Jane flinched and looked at Chava, "What are you doing!"

Chava calmly looked down at Jane's feet, pointed and said, "You're bleeding." Jane looked down and saw that both her feet were leaking blood.

Horrified, she turned away from Chava and ran. "You witch, witch! What have you done to me?" She hurried back toward home.

"Wait!" Chava chased after her. Jane limped, hobbled by glass-cut feet. Chava caught up to her and grabbed her arm.

Jane pulled herself away. "Leave me alone, you devil!" Jane froze in a daze. Moments later, she looked around wildly for who was screaming.

"Let me help."

"No, I don't need help, I am Jane Caitlin Winston!"

*Oh shit, what happened to her?* Jane jerked and looked Chava in the eye. Jane's eyes had dark rings around them, and her pupils were dilated. Her teeth were yellow and chipped. Her dark hair was turning prematurely white, was uncombed with bald patches, but one could see she was once pretty. Jane's transformation was so complete that Chava would not have recognized her as the girl from the SADF ads or the dancer from Czar World if she hadn't blurted out her own name.

"Jane, where are you going, do you live around here?"

Jane looked scornfully at her, "How dare you!" Jane hobbled off. Chava followed her. Jane labored for ten minutes to travel the two blocks to her door, losing blood with each step. Chava saw a big metal door with a handle but no place to put a key or type in a code. Jane nearly collapsed as she twisted her frame to put her right hand on the door to unlock it. She entered as quickly as she could on two bleeding feet filled with glass shards.

Chava grabbed the door before it shut, pulled it open, and slipped through. Jane stumbled down the ladder, nearly falling. Chava stopped on top of the platform to let her eyes adjust to the darkness. She looked down and saw Jane who was struggling to stay upright. The door shut behind Chava with a loud click.

*I might regret this.* Chava carefully climbed down with her heavy bag and rushed to Jane. She coaxed Jane to sit against the wall and opened her pack. She brought out a jug of water and rinsed Jane's feet. Jane screamed, partly in physical pain, and more bitterly, in emotional anguish. Chava pulled out a ball of water and gave it to Jane.

"I want *my* water!"

Chava looked puzzled. "It's good water, from Ray's."

She snatched the ball from Chava after hearing it was from Ray's and swallowed it. Chava was trying to stop the bleeding with strips from cut-up sweatpants sopping up the blood. She picked out as much of the glass from Jane's feet as possible.

Jane started crying. "That was *not* my water! I need *my* water!" She started to shake and tilted downward. Chava bandaged Jane's feet as well as she could using all the gauze from one of her first aid kits. *She must have a bed.* Chava ran down the hall, looked into the right and saw the kitchenette. Then at the end of the hall she saw the large room with a bed and desk with a computer.

Chava rushed back and got Jane to her feet. She led her down the dark hall and placed her on the bed with a pillow under Jane's feet to elevate them.

Chava was shocked. "Jane, wha…" She stopped herself. Silence. Finally, Chava said, "Jane, we have to get out of here. This will soon be part of the uninhabited zone. This area is now redundant. It is being cut off. And we need to get some water and food in you."

Jane whined like a whipped dog.

The computer on Jane's desk started beeping. Chava stood, keeping an eye on Jane as she inched toward the desk. Chava looked at the computer screen. Jane stood up and swayed to keep her balance. The screen read, "Jane told them about the rally."

*What, who the hell is that on the computer?* Then Chava realized what it meant. She gritted her teeth and tensed her body. "What!"

Jane's voice came out of the speakers. "The rally is on the fourteenth at the library."

Jane recoiled at hearing her stolen voice.

Chava turned and screeched at Jane. "You bitch!" She yanked Jane by the hair and flung her across the room. She recoiled at the clump off Jane's hair that came off in her hands, dropping it like a hot coal.

Jane collapsed and lay motionless. Chava calmed herself.

She was caught between sympathy and rage. *The rally is on the fourteenth at the library,* the computer rang out.

Jane looked up at Chava and cackled. "You're the devil, a Jewish devil. They told me you'd come for me. I must tell them you're here." Jane struggled to her knees.

Chava moved toward her, grabbed Jane's head in both hands, and examined her pupils. "They drugged you."

"Ha, I am of sound mind, and body."

Chava stepped back. Jane held onto the desk, pushed herself to her feet, and laughed. Jane waddled toward Chava.

"You're just jealous that no one wants a little girl like you, an evil Jewish Devil! My lover comes to me every night to be with me. Who do you have… little girl, little, little girl?" Jane touched Chava's red hair.

Chava grabbed Jane's arm, spun her around and tossed her like a sock monkey. Jane scraped her cut feet on the floor, reopening her wounds. She toppled over and hit her head on the edge of the desk as she fell onto the floor. Jane grunted as the air shot out of her lungs, and she lost consciousness.

Chava bent to look down at Jane, the empathy squeezed out of her. She reveled in her hatred. "There is no evil, no devil, only people who work to destroy others and their happiness. I almost pitied you." She took a deep breath. "You killed Thelonious, and now it's time for you to finish killing yourself. You've earned this prison." Chava stood up slowly.

---

*Jane is five years old, running through a field of poppies and daisies. Jane smiles: those are her favorites! She is wearing her prettiest white Easter dress with the crinoline petticoat, skipping through the fields with her long curly, dark hair flowing. The sun shines brightly behind her, giving her a halo. Jane sees a man wearing a white shirt and white pants in front of her standing with the flowers up to his knees. She runs up and grabs the man's hand in her tiny hand. He is pale with dark hair, but we don't see his face.*

*They walk away. "Daddy, will I become an angel some day?" "You already are, Jane," the man says. "Then why can't I fly?" "Not all angels fly, sweetheart." "Oh," she says, disappointed. They keep walking and see a lemon-colored train station up ahead in the middle of the endless field of flowers that hide the ground. They walk a while more and then suddenly they are upon the station. The copper tracks sparkle in the sun. A train approaches from their left. It is an old, black steam train that goes faster and faster as it nears the station. Everything is silent as the train passes and disappears with its white smoke trailing behind.*

*"Daddy? What are you going to do now that you are gone?" "Nothing is ever gone Jane, but everything changes," he answers. "Daddy, I don't understand." "Neither do I, Jane," he said. They stand there silently as another train passes like the first. "Why don't the trains stop, Daddy?" He shrugs.*

---

Chava clenched her fists and scowled at Jane. "I guess if I were merciful, I would kill you right here. But you haven't earned my mercy." Chava walked away, up the ladder, and tried the door. It was locked. Chava was stuck inside. She stomped back to the semi-conscious Jane.

---

*"Daddy, where are all the people," asks Jane. "I don't know." "Why not, why don't you know daddy!" She starts pounding on his leg with her tiny fists. Her crinoline dress is now blinding. He stands motionless and voiceless as she pleads with him.*

"Wake up, you bitch! You killed them, but you won't kill me, you won't have the satisfaction." Chava slapped her and shook her. A faint groan emanated from Jane. She thought for a moment and remembered seeing Jane press her hand on the door to get in. In vain, Chava asked, "Is that it, do you use your hand to get out?" Chava groaned and strained to drag Jane to the ladder. Chava tried pulling her up the steep rungs to the platform. She could not lift Jane who now weighed 140 pounds. *I need some rope.* She started running around Jane's apartment, searching. She grabbed a bed sheet to use as a sling to drag Jane up the ladder.

As Chava turned, she heard a beep from the computer. Chava leapt over to the table and looked at the screen:

# Get out NOW!

Chava did a double take. *Who the hell are you?* Her heart rate rose, and she hyperventilated. Then these words appeared:

# They're coming

Chava jumped, grabbed her bag and put it down next to Jane. "You need to open that door…now!" Jane didn't move. Chava wrapped Jane in the bed sheet like swaddling a baby. She attempted to drag her up the ladder, head and feet first. Jane's weight was too much for the exhausted Chava. Jane slid down to the bottom of the ladder after each attempt.

Chava unzipped one of the side pockets on the backpack and pulled out a steak knife. She sucked in air through gritted teeth and muttered under her breath. "I'm not going to die with you."

Chava remembered the times she cut the heads off pigeons after her father taught her how to saw into the bird's neck. She grabbed Jane's right wrist and moved it into position. She thrust down with the knife, and blood gushed onto Chava's face, onto the ladder that led outside and onto the floor. She was in a panic, ignoring the fluid as she thrust again into Jane's wrist. More rushed upward and onto the ceiling and entered Chava's nose and mouth as Jane's body convulsed. Another thrust brought a cracking sound as the vital fluid splashed into Chava's eyes. She wiped it away with her shirt as Jane's life flowed out.

The knife stuck in Jane's wrist socket, and Chava twisted the blade, generating more ripping sounds. *Give me that hand!* After some sawing from the killing blade, only tendons kept the hand attached to the arm. Chava placed the knife back in her pack, grabbed Jane's hand with both arms, put her legs against Jane's body and pulled. The wrist came free like a leg from a turkey carcass.

Chava stood and paused for a moment to look down at the body. "Sorry Jane." She grabbed the hand, put on her pack and climbed the ladder to street level. She placed the hand onto the steel door and the lock clicked open. Chava opened the door, dropped the palm onto the platform, and exited out to the alley. She threw her bloody t-shirt onto the ground and put on another from her pack.

---

The regular patrols of Angeltown's uninhabited zones were on schedule until a discovery at Crenshaw Mall that shocked the security world. Lieutenant Gomez received a call that he part expected, part dreaded, and part shocked him. Martin, star of "The Middle Eastern Hunt", expert tracker and over all invincible man, was dead.

"You sure it's him?" Gomez asked.

"Lieutenant, I'm sure, the DNA, the blood, it all matches."

Still, Gomez kept thinking Martin was playing a trick on him. After he thought on it a moment, Gomez started yelling at his Sergeant, "How the hell did this happen?"

The sergeant wasn't fazed. "It looks like a dog mauled him, but Martin was able to get in a good blow and kill the mutt. Perhaps it was rabid. If we hadn't found Martin's favorite three-wheeler out front, we might not have known it was him. His face is all chewed up by rats and other—"

"I get the picture. I guess they chewed on the dog too?"

"Yep," the sergeant said. "There's lots of blood and flesh around."

Gomez kept quiet. "Okay," said Gomez, still in disbelief. "Secure the area and I will send a crime scene unit out there to investigate. And don't go making any assumptions, Sergeant. Martin had many enemies who will be celebrating his death, many who might have killed him or hired someone." He thought for a moment. "Don't move the body until after I get out there."

Crime scene came, and they found the body too chewed up to determine the exact cause of death at the scene. Perhaps some lab analysis would do the trick. The dog appeared to have been stabbed in the chest and died.

Many assumed a gang ambushed him, using an attack dog to weaken Martin so they could all get in blows to bring him down. There was no other explanation for them. Gomez closed Martin's secret file, but he left the murder case open.

He ordered Lee and Van Heimlich to talk to Martin's enemies. He didn't expect much, but those guys had a knack of getting people to talk. Then he left the station to visit the crime scene.

---

The metal door opened to Jane's residence at midnight, the usual time for the collection of samples. Agent Petrov entered wearing a cherry-colored three-piece suit, white gloves and a gas mask with night vision goggles. She carried a steel medical kit that contained needles, serum and vials to store blood. Standing on the platform, she saw Jane's body splayed at the bottom of the ladder. She flinched at the sight of Jane's detached right hand at her feet.

Petrov disengaged the door's locking mechanism, stepped outside, took off her mask and made a call. "Clear the room…Yes, ventilate the Spring Street residence…And send the Investigation and Decontamination Unit." Petrov looked down the alley and waved at the two agents to come over. "Secure the alley, don't let anyone, or anything near. Shoot down all snooper drones."

"Yes ma'am!" the two agents said in unison.

The officer recorded a note on her phone, "Night visits to Miss Winston's, once routine, had become a recurring nightmare. Jane Winston was ruined by addiction to the serum, and her blood had a viral load that was off the charts. Winston's constitution couldn't process the drug and virus combination. It had been killing her for months." Petrov stopped recording. She then opened an app and spoke into the mouthpiece, "Spring Street, lights on." Halon lights illuminated the apartment.

Her phone beeped three short bursts. It was her boss, the Woman in Pink. "Yes ma'am, Jane Winston is dead."

"Take the usual blood sample. I will be sending Flex to look around," said the Woman. She hung up.

*Damn, I hate that man. Her little lap dog, wolf hound with a rat face*, thought Petrov.

Agent Sasha Petrov wondered again why her parents ever

left Russia, but being double agents would have gotten them killed back before the last collapse. Now there weren't armies or nations, just the corporate states fighting against the unrest right under the surface. And in that room behind that steel door lay the creeping unrest.

Certain that the submission gas had been sucked out of the residence, Agent Petrov went in and examined the hand. Then she examined the door. She grabbed the hand, careful not to get any blood on her gloves, and pressed it against the door. *Click! Palm lock.*

She jumped at the presence of someone behind her. "Get that blood sample from the victim. I will examine the hand," said Flex, the man in the purple suit and white tie.

"What the—?" Petrov started to ask how he got there so quickly.

"Drone drop," said Flex. "Now get to work."

Petrov climbed down the ladder as Flex looked at the hand. He held it up to examine it. *Not exactly sawed off, but not chopped either.* His eyes detected metal traces, simple cutlery steel, European, Spanish, *Isabella Collection*. Then he noted the tearing of the flesh. He brought out an evidence bag and put the hand in.

He stepped outside and made a call to the Woman in Pink, "Yes commander, yes…It's Jane Winston all right…Blood loss, it looks like…Ironic, yes. I hope Nanomed doesn't cancel our contract over this…Right." He hung up.

After getting the vial of blood, Petrov examined the scene. From Jane's right, handless arm was blood splatter on the floor and the lower stairs. She looked up and saw blood on the ceiling high above and on the walls. "The killer must have gotten blood all over himself," yelled Petrov to Flex. Then she walked down the hall.

Flex examined the body as Agent Petrov searched the

residence. He agreed with Petrov's conclusions. "Yes, this was messy and bloody."

After a few minutes, she came back and reported, "There's nothing here of interest except perhaps her computer."

"Pack up the computer," said Flex, holding out an evidence bag to her. She rebuffed him by showing Flex a bag with the computer in it. Petrov paused a moment, then said to Flex as she looked down on the body. "Too bad, she was once a child star, and quite pretty."

He responded. "Don't worry, it was only a teacher."

---

Several hours later, outside the confines of the dark prison on Spring Street, Chava Chavez, enraged and heart-broken, pushed onward. Fueled by grief and anger, she rushed to get out of downtown Angeltown. She listened for drones and the State Autodefense Forces and heard nothing. The area was deathly silent except for her own heartbeat. She looked up past the collapsed buildings, past the Saint Monica to Saint Bernard Tram and Roadway to the mountains and kept walking.

\* \* \*

Joseph Callahan is an instructor of adult education at a community college, earned an MFA and has a written extensively on politics and nearly 200 film reviews on Wordpress and Hubpages.

www.ingramcontent.com/pod-product-compliance
Lightning Source LLC
LaVergne TN
LVHW011946060526
838201LV00061B/4224